THE HEART
OF LEADERSHIP

THE HEART
OF LEADERSHIP

*Inspiration and Practical Guidance
for Transforming
Your Health Care Organization*

M. Barbara Balik
Jack A. Gilbert

HEALTH FORUM, INC.
An American Hospital Association Company
Chicago

AHA and American Hospital Association are service marks of the American Hospital Association used under license by Health Forum, Inc.

Printed in the United States of America—09/10

Cover design by Cheri Kusek

ISBN: 978-1-55648-374-5   Item Number: 108105

Library of Congress Cataloging-in-Publication Data

The heart of leadership : inspiration and practical guidance for transforming your health care organization / [edited by] M. Barbara Balik, Jack A. Gilbert.
    p. cm.
   Includes index.
   ISBN 978-1-55648-374-5 (alk. paper)
  1. Health care reform—United States. 2. Leadership—United States. 3. Health services administrators—United States—Interviews. I. Balik, M. Barbara. II. Gilbert, Jack A.
   RA395.A3H4395 2010
   362.1′0425—dc22   2010015220

With deepest gratitude:

To Dan—for abiding love, amazing humor, a slightly off-balance view of the world, unwavering support, and a belief in what is possible;

To my family—for endless support, abundant love, great memories, and the gift of story;

To my colleagues—my role models for leaders who make a difference every day. They are exemplars of leaders with a soul.
—*Barbara Balik*

In loving memory of my parents,
Henry and Millie Goldberg
—*Jack Gilbert*

Contents

About the Authors

Dr. Barbara Balik is the principal of Common Fire Healthcare Consulting and a senior faculty member at the Institute for Healthcare Improvement. She previously was hospital chief executive officer in an integrated health system, a patient care executive/chief nursing officer, an executive leader of quality and safety within a large health care system, and a maternal-child health nurse. Her areas of expertise are leadership for quality and safety, patient- and family-centered care, effective health care systems design, and policy/systems development to promote cross-continuum care and reduce avoidable rehospitalizations.

She most recently co-authored the chapter on leadership for safety in the *Essential Guide for Patient Safety Officers,* published by Joint Commission Resources in 2008.

Barbara holds a doctorate from the University of St. Thomas, St. Paul, Minnesota, where her dissertation explored clinical and executive leadership attempting to improve care in a newly integrated health care system. She is a member of the National Patient Safety Board of Governors, Sigma Theta Tau nursing honor society, and the board of the American Society of Health System Pharmacists Foundation.

Dr. Jack Gilbert is director of the Master of Healthcare Innovation program and clinical associate professor in the College of Nursing and Health Innovation at Arizona State University. He is also the president of New Page Consulting, Inc., and a noted expert in organizational and personal integrity, leadership, and large-scale change.

His book *Strengthening Ethical Wisdom: Tools for Transforming Your Health Care Organization* was published by AHA Press in 2007 and is a recommended title by the American College of Healthcare Executives (ACHE) 2009 James A. Hamilton Book of the Year Award Committee. His book *Gilbert's Fables* was published by Sleeping Lion Press in 2009. He is also the author of

Productivity Management: A Step by Step Guide for Health Care Professionals, published in 1990 by American Hospital Publishing, Inc., and awarded Book of the Year by the Healthcare Information and Management Systems Society.

Jack holds his doctorate from The George Washington University in Washington, DC, where his dissertation focused on the role of ethics in decision making. He is a Fellow of ACHE and in 2008 received the College's Service Award.

Preface

More than a decade ago *To Err Is Human,*[1] with its call to reduce deaths from preventable medical error, ignited a renewed focus on and vigor for safety and quality improvement, accompanied by a wide range of proven processes and evidence-based practices with the potential to reach that goal. What has happened since that landmark Institute of Medicine report? Nationally, the number of people who die annually from medical error is estimated to be as high as or higher than previously thought.[2] Furthermore, the gap between identifying a life-saving, evidence-based practice and its full implementation is a staggering seventeen years.[3] How can so little have changed when the tools, processes, and knowledge to improve safety and quality of care are far more widely known than a decade ago? And why do some health care organizations stand out positively in safety, quality performance, engagement, and financial health?

We say it is not about the tools, processes, and knowledge that are available to all. Our response is that it is about the focus and implementation shaped by a certain kind of leadership that produces and sustains dramatic improvement in safety, quality, financial condition, and organizational vitality. This book seeks to understand and describe what is distinct in this leadership by interviewing ten transformational leaders, then presenting in their own words their background, experience, and what is at the heart of their leadership.

This book is an appreciative enquiry, meaning that its focus is on the positive aspects of their leadership. None of the leaders we interviewed will say he or she is perfect—far from it. They continue to challenge themselves as leaders. Nor do those who work with them, while admiring them, say they are perfect. But these transformational leaders do have a compelling story to tell.

The process used to create this book was as follows. We used a snowball approach to find candidates for interviewing: We polled our contacts and their contacts and so on for names of transformational leaders in health care, defined as leaders who have produced documented, sustainable, positive results when most of their peers in similar circumstances have not. Within two weeks we had identified seventeen candidates, most of whom had been recommended by at least two different sources. We pared these down to ten leaders representing a variety of work environments— multi-hospital systems, community health systems, academic teaching centers, and a safety net organization—and we choose two leaders who lead change in health care nationally through their influence. Five are women and five are men. Four are nurses, three are physicians, and three come from an administrative or business background. Each leader who participated in this inquiry is the subject of one of chapters 2 through 11 of this book. The following is a brief introduction to each leader.

Maureen Bisognano is now president and chief executive officer of the Institute for Healthcare Improvement in Boston. When we interviewed her, she was the Institute's executive vice president and chief operating officer. The Institute plays a leading role in improving patient safety and quality of care not from a position of authority but rather by working through influence. She is a nurse.

Patty Gabow is chief executive officer and medical director of Denver (Colorado) Health and Hospital Authority. Denver Health is a safety net organization that provides care to 25 percent of all Denver residents and one of every three children. She is a physician and nephrologist by training.

Larry Goodman is president and chief executive officer of Rush University Medical Center in Chicago. Rush is an academic medical center that includes a 671-bed hospital in downtown Chicago. He is a physician and practices as an infectious disease specialist.

Gary Kaplan is chairman and chief executive officer of Virginia Mason Health System in the Puget Sound region of Washington, including a 336-bed acute care hospital. He is a physician and practices as an internist.

Mike Murphy is president and chief executive officer of Sharp HealthCare in San Diego. Sharp is a multi-hospital system with almost 14,000 employees and 2,600 affiliated physicians. He is an accountant by training.

Phil Newbold is president and chief executive officer of Memorial Hospital and Health System in South Bend, Indiana. Memorial owns the MEDPOINT express® urgent care centers located in Walmart stores. His background is in hospital administration.

Tim Porter-O'Grady is senior partner at Tim Porter-O'Grady Associates, based in Atlanta. He is a consultant, a university professor, and an author. Tim is best known for bringing the shared governance model to health care, a model that has had a transformational impact on the nursing profession and on cross-disciplinary collaboration. He is a nurse.

Sister Mary Jean Ryan is chair and chief executive officer of SSM Health Care, based in St. Louis, Missouri. SSM is a 23,000-employee health care system with locations in Wisconsin, Illinois, Missouri, and Oklahoma. She is a nurse.

Julie Schmidt is now chief transformation officer of HealthEast Care System, based in St. Paul, Minnesota. When we interviewed her, she was chief executive officer of Woodwinds Health Campus in Woodbury, Minnesota, part of the HealthEast Care System. Woodwinds is an eighty-six-bed healing environment with extensive outpatient services. She is a nurse.

Donna Sollenberger is chief executive officer of the University of Texas Medical Branch (UTMB) Health System in Galveston, Texas, a network of hospitals and clinics. She was previously chief executive officer of the Baylor Clinic and Hospital and executive vice president of Baylor College of Medicine; prior to that Donna was president and chief executive officer of the University of Wisconsin Hospitals and Clinics. Her background is in hospital administration.

We explored their leadership with each person individually in a three-step process. The process began with a two-hour recorded and transcribed interview exploring many aspects of their background and their leadership. We followed up with a second, shorter interview a few weeks later to extend our understanding of what we had heard. In addition, we conducted interviews with others who have worked with the leader, usually including a member of their board, for their perspective. Each interview is organized by the following headings:

Growing Up

Influences—People and Situations

Pathway to Health Care

Pathway to Leadership

What's Important to Me as a Leader

A Good Day

A Bad Day

When the interview process was complete, we took a step back to look for themes that had emerged and would be useful to their peers, to aspiring health care leaders, and to boards and their hiring practices.

The book is presented in the following order:

- Themes for leadership presented in a model developed from a synthesis of the interviews

- Individual profiles, including interspersed quotes from those with whom the leaders work, and laced with reflection points from the authors

- Guidance for growing leaders, including a personal diagnostic tool

- Guidance for boards in strengthening their practices for hiring chief executive officers (including interview questions)

- A short reading list for your consideration

You may approach the content of this book in any of three ways: Read the themes and guidance, and then dive deeper into the source of the themes and guidance by reading the profiles; read the profiles first to immediately understand the foundation of the book, and then read the themes and guidance that stemmed from the profiles; or jump around the book content as you wish!

Finally, we recommend strongly that you use the book as a basis for self-reflection and enrichment. These leaders are lifelong learners who have a great deal to offer us from their experiences and insights. We believe the book is also a great resource for reading groups, mentoring relationships, and leadership development.

Barbara Balik
Jack Gilbert

References

1. Institute of Medicine, *To Err Is Human: Building a Safer Health System* (Washington, DC: National Academies Press, 1999).
2. Hearst Newspapers, "Dead by Mistake," 1999 [www.chron.com/deadby mistake/]. Accessed March 8, 2010.
3. M.B. Melnyk and E. Fineout-Overhold, *Evidence-Based Practice in Nursing and Healthcare: A Guide to Best Practice* (Philadelphia: Lippincott Williams & Wilkins, 2004).

Acknowledgments

Learning from the practice wisdom of others is a privilege. We have had the gift of talented people willing to share their wisdom with us in achieving this book. Without their generosity this work would not have occurred.

We first acknowledge our great appreciation of the talented leaders who shared their leadership journey and perspectives so generously: Donna Sollenberger, Gary Kaplan, Maureen Bisognano, Mike Murphy, Patty Gabow, Larry Goodman, Phil Newbold, Sister Mary Jean Ryan, Julie Schmidt, and Tim Porter-O'Grady. They embraced our request to tell their personal leadership story as a contribution to improving health care for those who entrust us with their care.

We learned equally deep lessons about leadership from those who work with these leaders. Their diverse roles—direct caregivers, board chairs, middle managers, physician leaders, administrative executives—provided additional insights of leadership that illuminated our perspectives. Their insights and voices enhanced this work far beyond our highest expectations.

Others influenced our thinking about this work in numerous conversations and through their own practice wisdom—Jim Conway, senior fellow, Institute for Healthcare Improvement; Kathy Malloch, clinical professor, Arizona State University; and Richard Hill, our editor at Health Forum and the editorial director of AHA Press.

THE HEART
OF LEADERSHIP

1

Themes and a Model
for Leading and Sustaining
Transformational Change

In seeking to understand transformational health care leadership, we were interested to see whether common themes would emerge in the basic values of the ten leaders profiled in this book, and the kind of work environments they foster, even though these leaders are very different in their personal background, organizational environment, personality, and manner. We found surprisingly strong, common themes, and we present these themes in this chapter. Figure 1-1 shows the themes in the form of a model.

We discovered a thread that weaves together the personal passion for patient care (their own and that of others in the organization) and the organization's vision and goals. Not every one of these leaders is a great speaker. But they all speak from the heart and communicate what is important to the organization in words that listeners can hear and connect with. In so doing they touch the hearts and minds of others at all levels in every role. This attribute is pervasive and resonates beyond any single theme.

At the center of the model are four shared personal characteristics—what makes them tick as they perform their role as leader. The next circle shows the organizational characteristics they foster—how their personal characteristics express themselves in organizational action. And at the head of the model are the major outcomes in performance their organizations produce. In our view, it all adds up to what we can best express as a "single brain" organization whose aim is that every person, every process, every system, and every action is focused on the

1-1.   A Model for Leading and Sustaining Transformational Change in Health Care

Transformational Results through a Single-Brain Organization
Safety and Clinical Quality
Patient and Family Experience
Commitment of Staff and Providers
Financial Vitality

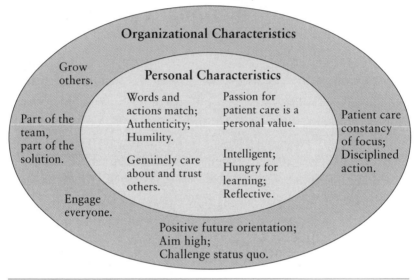

vision and mission and is reflective of the values of the organization. None of these leaders says he or she is "there." On the contrary, they say there is always more to do and that is what they are working on.

Personal Characteristics

Four personal characteristics are found in these transformational leaders:

- Their words and actions match; they are authentic; they demonstrate humility.
- Their passion for patient care is a personal value.
- They are intelligent, hungry for learning, reflective.
- They genuinely care about and trust others.

The most important point we want to make about these personal characteristics is that they are not what these leaders *do* (a role they play); it is *who they are*. These characteristics pervade their lives and their leadership in every context and every conversation, to whomever they are speaking—the board, a housekeeping aide, a physician, the community—and these characteristics are as natural to them as breathing.

Words and Action Match; Authenticity; Humility

"I'm here because of you"—e-mailed from the CEO to all staff after a meeting at the White House.

She is impeccably true to her words—she is a servant leader.

He has innate integrity that makes people want to do the right thing.

I trust him with any decision because he will always do the right thing for patients, the business, employees—and he will not accept otherwise.

We noticed two reactions immediately when we approached the leaders who appear in this book to ask them to participate. First, their assistants were uniformly enthusiastic and pleased that the leader had been singled out. Second, the leaders themselves expressed surprise and gratitude at being asked to participate. We realized early on that they chose to participate for many reasons, but one of them was not for self-promotion.

Their employees talk about them as being "real," "genuine," "not arrogant," "easy to talk to." Simply put, what you see is what you get. And what you get is a focus on doing the right thing, communications you can count on to be consistent with their actions, transparency, no hidden agendas, and natural ease in giving credit to others for success and in assuming responsibility themselves for failure.

Nine of these leaders never set out in their careers to be a CEO. They are CEOs in many cases because they were asked to assume the role by their board even though they had not applied for the position. For them, being a CEO is not a reward or a title. It is an opportunity to continue to make a difference in the lives of their patients, employees, and the communities they serve. And even though they did not set out to be a CEO, they are suited to the role.

They have not used their position as CEO as leverage for personal ambition. With one exception, they have worked at their current organization for many years. They show the value of a substantial tenure to producing and sustaining great results—not tenure for its own sake, but tenure in service of performance and contribution.

Some sample behaviors include spending time on activities they say are important for the mission; being a humble learner; being comfortable with not knowing the answer; developing new skills to improve outcomes; saying they made a mistake and what they learned from it; respectfully listening to all.

Here are examples of this characteristic taken from their profiles:

> *I think it is crucial to have integrity, to be real to your organization, and to be visible and accessible. When it's hard, being okay saying it's hard. Being open and honest with the organization about where we are and where we're doing well and congratulating them. Telling them we've got to do better when we've got to do better. Try to help them understand decisions when they might not make sense to many in the organization. Acknowledge when we are wrong because we screw up and we do make bad decisions sometimes, and acknowledge when we should have done something differently.*
>
> *I talk a lot about integrity. To me it means being fair with people at all times. Treating people with respect, regardless of who they are or who you are. Being a part of the community, knowing that we have a responsibility to it. That it is more than just about you. It takes courage to be a leader. For me, courage as a leader means doing the right things in an honest way, including the hard ones along with the easy ones. It is also part of courage to acknowledge and learn from when you mess up. And to do all of this with openness and visibility.* (Mike Murphy)
>
> *In my junior year of nursing school, I decided to work as a student nurse in the operating room that summer. I remember there*

was a particular surgeon who was horrible to work for—very demanding and very rude and crude. I was scrubbing in a case with him one day. He was angry and threw a scalpel—he wasn't angry at me but threw a scalpel. After the case, I was shaking but I went to him and said "I'm never going to scrub in with you again because of the way you acted." Then I walked away. He requested me on his cases from that day on and never did anything like that again. When I look back now, that was a big deal to have the courage to do that. His behavior wasn't the right thing to do. It clearly was not right. (Julie Schmidt)

Well, I'm pretty much known for always saying what I think. I am very straightforward. In many ways that takes some kind of courage in our society. There is a difference between being direct and having no civility. My COO always says I have perfected the ability to have whipped cream on battery acid. I think I can say some very tough things in a way that is not hostile. That's served me well. (Patty Gabow)

Any credit that I get is only because of the work that people in SSM have done. When I give outside presentations, I use employee stories to illustrate to the audience that change actually can happen. I am very, very proud of the people of SSM Health Care. They are absolutely remarkable. (Sister Mary Jean Ryan)

Passion for Patient Care Is a Personal Value

He is unwavering about the mission; he has a constancy of purpose.

[With her] we are totally clear on our own values and align with others with the same values.

He defines the vision with great clarity but not the answers. He integrates the vision into everything he does.

He is our spiritual leader.

For these CEOs a focus on patient safety, quality of care, and community health is not a strategy or an important organizational emphasis. It is why they are in health care and it is what drives them every day, pure and simple, irrespective of whether they come from a clinical background or not. It is their North Star and the context by which they organize their thinking.

Patient safety and patient care are so important to them that they do not delegate accountability for it. They also avoid the cost-quality trade-offs that sometimes dominate executive leaders' conversations. Their confidence in the focus on safety and quality is clear—always.

Some sample behaviors include time spent reviewing all serious patient harm events and overseeing performance improvement, storytelling to illustrate the link between the mission and an individual's role, asking others why they are in health care and thereby nurturing the passion that brought them to it, and learning anything they can to improve care.

Here are examples:

I think I've always had a fairly clear True North, what really matters to me. In my mind there is a hierarchy: patient, organization, department, individual—all important and in that order. That hierarchy is now reflected in our strategic plan. That True North has helped guide me, given me resilience in terms of dealing with tough issues. At the end of the day, we have to do what's best for patients—they are at the top. (Gary Kaplan)

I prepared to go to medical school without knowing much about what it meant to be a doctor. I purposely took the bare minimum pre-med courses that were required. When I started to actually take care of patients, I absolutely loved it. I liked every clinical rotation in medical school. I liked talking to patients of all types. I liked hearing about what was going on. I liked the challenge of trying to figure out what was wrong. To be able to combine two things I am passionate about, taking care of patients and teaching, has been ideal. Part of the reason I love to practice medicine is because it is challenging, intellectually stimulating, and very personal. There are few things more important to people than their health or the health of their loved ones. You put on a white coat, you walk in a room, and you meet a stranger who is often willing to tell you just about everything from surreptitious drug use to marital infidelities, and then they'll take their clothes off and you'll examine them. It's an incredibly intimate relationship with a patient and it's a tremendously trusting relationship. It is a huge honor to be able to take care of people. It really is. (Larry Goodman)

I'm the oldest of nine kids. In my early twenties I was in nursing school when my brother got Hodgkin's disease. My mother and I took care of him for two years. He died just after his twenty-first birthday. The first-born of the grandchildren had a DPT[1] reaction and died within twenty-four hours, which was really a tragic error. Three years later my father died of colon cancer when he was fifty-three. Everybody in our family had roles to play; everybody had a contribution to make. That gave the family a very strong sense of teamness—coming together when there was a personal crisis in the family meant that everyone had their part. For instance, my youngest sister, age nine, would do my brother's foot rubs every day. I think these early experiences in caring for my own family members in the way that they wanted to be cared for and then in dealing with the personal consequences of medical error really shaped my future. Not immediately, but years downstream. (Maureen Bisognano)

Intelligent; Hungry for Learning; Reflective

She continues to expand her personal management tool kit and inspires me to do the same.

He is a tremendous learner and listener.

She has a great capacity to integrate information; a student of leadership.

He role models that just because you are the CEO you don't stop learning.

We frequently heard from others such comments about these leaders as "so smart," "the smartest person I have known," "a quick study," "can grasp complex issues and quickly make sense of them." These may, in fact, be the smartest kids on the block. Whatever their innate intelligence and smarts, they are complemented by a hunger for learning. Some set up book clubs, some are described as voracious readers; they read articles and books to learn; they go outside the organization to learn; and they listen to their leadership team, their employees, and other stakeholders and engage them in dialogue in order to learn.

---

[1]Diphtheria, pertussis, and tetanus vaccine.

They match this intelligence and desire for learning with the ability to be reflective—to take the learning and to consider how what they have learned can improve themselves, their colleagues, the life of patients, and the welfare of the communities they serve. Reflection on learning is a major source of organizational improvement.

Some sample behaviors include a questioning mind—asking "Why?" or "How could we do this differently?" They take time to learn about the barriers to better care, asking others outside the organization for support and new ideas.

Here are examples:

When I experience something or I read something, I always ask the question What can I learn from this? How can I apply this to what I'm doing or to what we're trying to do? How can I take that experience that someone's talked about at a meeting and be able to apply that to what I'm doing so it will be meaningful? So I am constantly interested in what I can learn from something. I'm sure I drive people crazy, but people will tell me something and I will say: Well, what can we learn from that? Not because I'm trying to be a smart aleck but because I am curious. It's important enough for you to say it, so what can we learn from that? I do that all the time. Patient letters come in and I'll say Gosh, what can we learn from this that we could share with the staff to help them understand something we need to do better? Or what can we learn from that organization that was able to turn itself around financially or improved its satisfaction? I don't take something on face value. I drive home thinking I wonder what I could learn from that or I wonder how we could apply that? (Donna Sollenberger)

My philosophy is that leaders need to learn every day. I assess that by looking at how often leaders ask questions versus how often they give answers. Leadership is learning. It's being open to the gifts of the people who work in your organization. The more that we as leaders open ourselves to what's really happening on the front line, we are closing that gap between the front office and the front line. It gives leaders courage and ideas. It is an honest inquiry, creating a culture that says we value every-

body's assets in this organization and together we can solve these issues faster than any one person can by themselves. (Maureen Bisognano)

Genuinely Care about and Trust Others

There's a "thereness" when she's with others. She will swivel her chair, move in, and doesn't look at her computer while listening.

He has the employees' best interests at heart, meeting with them on their shift, answering their e-mails in a thoughtful way.

He has a desire to be with and around people to hear what is important to them, what they need.

When discussing what we would write about this characteristic we were reminded of the difference between an activity and the way in which an activity is performed. We thought of executive rounding. Some CEOs and senior leaders will tell you they round, but the way they round is to breeze through the units or departments so as to be seen and to be heard. Not the CEOs in this book. When they round or otherwise engage with employees in one-on-ones, small groups, meetings, town hall meetings, casual conversations, or by e-mail, they do it in a genuine spirit of engagement, because they deeply care about others and what they have to say. More than that, they trust others, believing that they want to do the right thing and make a positive impact during their work day. They are not naive. They know that not everyone will rise to the challenge or be a good fit for the organization. When a mismatch occurs between the individual and the organization, they are firm and respectful in dealing with it. Nor are they are cynical or negative. They encourage the better angels of others. They live in hierarchies, but they do not allow themselves to be above others.

Some sample behaviors include behaving consistently and respectfully with everyone, exhibiting no difference in behavior depending on role; asking others for their advice and tapping into what they know from their role; and listening with singular, full attention.

Here are examples:

The expectations of leaders here is to put everyone else first, including our employees, who we then expect to put their patients first. We round with our leaders, asking "Are there any barriers that I can remove for you so that you can do your work better?" It's all about putting everyone else first. That's the expectation of leading around here, very little about egos. It attracts a particular kind of leader. (Julie Schmidt)

I want everyone who works here to believe that Rush is success-ful because of others. They are important. I'm sure it doesn't always feel that way to people, but it's very important to talk about it, to let people know. That's why at the many employee meetings I attend it's important that people realize that they are taken seriously. It's not that hard for me to push back on somebody's concern with five facts of my own. But it is much more honest, really more respectful, to say "Here is the fun-damental issue we are all dealing with," "Here is what we are trying to do," "Here's how it hasn't worked for some groups," "Here's what we are thinking about doing now," "And if you have got some other ideas, it is important that we take them into account." I always get concerned when people say that the way they do this CEO job is to say "I'm mission driven. I'm value driven." Well, I think everybody is. I'd like to think everybody is trying to do the right thing and do their best. I assume right off the bat that I don't have the corner on being value driven. There's no reason why I suddenly have a different set of values than anybody else who works in this place. To say that I have some value-driven approach is not respectful of them. I do think they care a lot and I do think that caring is going to make the institution a lot better. (Larry Goodman)

I believe that leading an institution is an intimate relationship. It's really caring about the well-being of the institution and the people that are here; wanting the best for the institution and hav-ing goals that are noble. When I said it's an intimate relationship, I don't see this as a job. It is a relationship between me and this organization that has gone on for more than three decades. I think it is hard for me to draw a line between the enterprise and me in many ways. My son always used to say "Denver Health is another kid. You think of it as another kid, Mom." I have two children, a daughter and a son, and I guess a third—Denver Health. I love Denver Health because it does the right thing. I feel that some of health care in America has been taken over by greed, that money has become more important than mission. In some health care institutions, the mission statement has nothing to do with actual behavior. We always say Denver Health isn't for everybody, but the people it's for, it's for life. It's an extraordinary institution, and the people who work here are extraordinary. And it's easy to love. (Patty Gabow)

Organizational Characteristics

Five organizational success factors are fostered by these transformational leaders, as shown in the outer circle of figure 1-1:

- Patient care constancy of focus; disciplined action
- Positive future orientation; aim high; challenge the status quo
- Engage everyone
- Part of the team; part of the solution
- Grow others

Who these leaders are shapes how their organizations create exceptional results. If we looked at an organization's structure, it would not look much different from any others. They all have leadership teams, chains of command, committees and meetings, and staff functions. But the areas the organizations emphasize and the action of the CEOs to create this emphasis are distinct and fuel their effectiveness and success.

Patient Care Constancy of Focus; Disciplined Action

She is not distracted by the crisis of the day; she doesn't jump around or vacillate.

She has a no-nonsense approach to problem solving, adheres to her principles, and doesn't have a political appeasement approach.

Our strategic plan is alive and well: What is best for the patient? What will make a perfect experience for the patient?

Clinical quality is her overriding mission and drives business goals.

It's not our improvement method, it's our management system.

Their personal passion and commitment to patient care fuels and sustains their organization's focus on the same. They communicate this by the way they approach decisions and what they talk about with others, leaving not a shred of doubt that patient care trumps everything else as a priority. They are responsible about the financial health of the organization—that is evident from the results they have produced—but finances, processes, management systems, strategies, goals, personnel decisions, day-to-day action, and so on are viewed through the screen of patient safety, patient care, and community health.

They combine their sensitivity to the needs of patients and staff with well-ordered and disciplined, accountability-driven approaches to decision making, leaving their leadership team and employees in no doubt about the leader's expectations of them.

Here are examples:

The first thing the board asked me and the senior team was "Who is your customer?" Just like everybody in health care, we said "Oh, the patient." And they said "Take a closer look." The fact was our systems and processes were designed for us—physicians, nurses, managers, and staff. What are waiting rooms but big spaces for patients to hurry up, be on time, and wait for us? We design it into our facilities. We design it into our workflow. It's total arrogance. So we got really, really clear what it means to be patient driven. I used to be so proud to say we are a physician-driven organization. I'd be embarrassed to say that today. We are patient driven. (Gary Kaplan)

We have a huge mission at the Institute for Healthcare Improvement to change health care worldwide. Don [Berwick] and I decided on a strategic approach that we would not grow. We would stay small, and we would operate through leverage and through our culture. We studied other organizations that grew very quickly. We saw that growth, not change, became the objective. Where revenue or growth became the aspiration, organizations started to become beholden to themselves and they lost sight of the mission. Growth becomes the conversation, the number one strategy. It takes over from "How are we doing with the mission?" (Maureen Bisognano)

Once you have a path, and that path has been determined not just by you alone but it's a path the organization wants to take, I think you have to be persistent about it. I don't think that they can go off in fourteen different directions. Obviously there will always be those things that distract you, but you'll always have to come back to what's the center of this. The center of all that we do has to be the patient. If you are veering away from that, I would suggest that maybe you don't belong in health care. Because if you don't have that as the core of what you do, then I don't know why you would work here. I worry about finances, capital, and so on. But none of it matters if we can't provide safe care. (Sister Mary Jean Ryan)

The number one thing that I most notice at the senior level of health care organizations is that they often forget the business they are in. Or they never really knew. In order to really under-stand this field of health care you have to be reflective enough to understand that the work that we do is different from the business that we do. So many people in the C-suite are so subsumed by the business that they either never figure out what we do or they lost track of what we do or they simply gave up what we do. What we do is we provide health care to the community. When you lose your core, you lose everything." (Tim Porter-O'Grady)

The Connection with Personal Characteristics

This organizational focus is fueled by the leaders' passion for patient care. It is a personal value. Leaders who maintain constancy of focus on patient care and are disciplined in their action accomplish at least three outcomes: They put their personal stamp on the organization, they focus the organizational priorities around care, and they mobilize the passion for care that pervades every part of the organization.

Positive Future Orientation; Aim High; Challenge the Status Quo

We can always be better. She's always asking "What's the next best?"

Restless discontent; he is always looking for bigger impact; "How can we better serve our community and fulfill our vision and mission?"

She thinks above and outside the moment. She frames a more powerful view that offers more daylight.

She sees leadership as a responsibility, not as a reward for time served.

These leaders live comfortably in the gap between current reality and the organization's vision. And they are able to live in the future and in the present with equal power.

They are happy to celebrate success, but they are always conscious that there is more to do. So they are never satisfied. This dissatisfaction energizes rather than distresses them. They do not act from blame. On the contrary, they convey a positive spirit to the organization, and they look to the future with appreciation for present challenges and those to come with an underlying optimism and commitment. They are undaunted.

Here are examples:

> *All of the uncertainties we are facing are a blessing. There are so many things we could not have predicted, like 9/11, the rise of China and India, the housing and stock market collapse, health care reform. Leadership is not about trying to predict the future as much as it is about making sure the organization and its people have enough capacity, leadership, and agility to make the best of any situation, expected or not. Innovation is one of those capacities that will get you beyond a challenging situation. Part of the job of a leader is to learn and to be a good teacher.*
>
> *Another part of the job of a leader is to create a culture that supports and engages others with new ideas, allows room for experimentation, helps others understand the expectations and rewards, and recognizes that culture. Leaders must themselves step out and be willing to be uncomfortable with risk, never*

doing it by themselves, learning along with others what does and does not work, and making sure that organizational courage is rewarded. (Phil Newbold)

I think leaders get caught up in what I call "problem du jour." They never really get to the things that need to be done, that take time. When I started at the University of Wisconsin Hospitals and Clinics, every other month the leadership team had a two-day retreat to address a significant issue that we needed to define. For example, we needed to revamp the whole quality structure. We had a vision to be the safest hospital in America, and what I wanted, and we needed, was to rethink how we did quality. With my teams, what I generally do when they get into what I would call status quo thinking, saying "Maybe we don't need to do that, or maybe this isn't as serious as we think, or maybe we should just leave well enough alone," is that I push them to think more about what the possibilities are. Maybe we are good, but we need to be great. I try to push conventional thinking, not for the sake of change for change's sake but for the sake of making us better. To get better results and to do what we do in a much more meaningful way. (Donna Sollenberger)

Those who take the first step to challenge the status quo are more likely to be viewed as an anomaly. A way to deal with being an anomaly is to stay connected to the current state as a way for people to not be so fearful of change. If you come up with new ideas too quickly it will feel like a hammer rather than allowing it to grow and evolve. You have to have a perfectly clear vision and then allow it to evolve.

A hospital with integrative therapies was odd, so I needed to stay very close to the MDs. Using influence we developed an environment for creative ideas rather than for a dictatorship. We talked to the community, who wanted both traditional and integrative therapies. We wanted to bring credibility to the process. We knew it was the right thing and revolutionary so we talked a year before we opened, educating physicians and creating education for holistic nursing. We created the Strategic Steering Team for Integrative Services to accomplish four things: (1) a visible focus, (2) involvement by other credible leaders in the community, (3) a focus on how and not if, and (4) generate support for the process and outcomes. (Julie Schmidt)

Leadership confidence is required to create a major change. It basically required us to say "Look, the status quo is unacceptable. People are dying in American hospitals, including ours. We're making mistakes every day. The economics are not working. Do you have a better idea? If not, we're going to explore and find out whether there is something in this for us." One of the keys to this journey, the first step, was to change the minds of the senior leadership. Don't start with the middle. They're critical to the journey, but if you don't have the senior leaders' minds changed it's just going to be a huge frustration. I was changing my mind, too. (Gary Kaplan)

The Connection with Personal Characteristics

This organizational focus is fueled by the leaders' passion for learning and their personal ability to step back from the fray and reflect on what lies ahead and how they will approach it. It is also fueled by the primacy of care as a personal value. Whether the organization is dealing with success or failure, obstacles or progress, stressful or good times, patient care remains their North Star and that of their organization.

Engage Everyone

He believes in the wisdom of employees and asks them to be the architects of change.

There are [people] you'll run into a brick wall for. She's one of those people.

She has the ability to make people belong and matter and want to work hard for themselves and the institution.

For these leaders everyone is a significant part of the whole. By engaging everyone they are optimizing organizational performance. They engage through their clarity about organizational priorities and especially the primacy of patient care (as opposed to other cases where primacy of the bottom line dampens the passion for care in the organization). They engage by being transparent about the organization's condition, goals, successes, and failures. They engage by expecting everyone to step up and embrace their own accountability by doing their part in realizing the vision and meeting goals. In these organizations the sense is that people *are* accountable, not *held* accountable.

Here are examples:

Our work with teams, combined with shared governance, has gone a long way toward flattening the organization. What I want to know is: Do the people who do the work know that the work that they are doing has a purpose, and do they know why they are doing it? Why are you in health care? Why do you do what you do? Tell me why you're at this facility. I think we're at the point now where we no longer invite *but rather* expect *engagement from employees. When you come to this organization we expect you to have ideas. We expect you to have good thoughts, to be able to recognize when things are not working. Those are the expectations, because if we can't do that and if we have people who for whatever reason aren't getting what we're all about, even though they've been coached and worked with, they have to leave the organization. Anyone who stands up for the right thing for patients, who says "No, that's not safe and I won't do it" is a leader just as much as anyone with a title.* (Sister Mary Jean Ryan)

I'm not concerned when others question me for spending so much time talking to employees and doing employee lunches where I can only meet with fifteen to twenty employees once a month in small groups. Or when they question why I do second- and third-shift town hall meetings when I get 200 or 300 attendees during the day but only 10 or 20 at night. Some ask me "Why are you going in at three in the morning for that? What are you doing that for?" I think it's a good thing to do. But it's not a prescription for everybody else. I just think it's respectful of the people who are working at night, and I think the ones who don't even go like to know that the CEO is there sometimes.

What I find is that students and employees are incredibly forgiving. It's the most amazing thing. They're so incredibly nice as they explain to you something isn't working well; you hear it and you think "My goodness, these students are paying tuition" or "This employee shouldn't have to put up with that." But they are so pleasant and respectful in the way they are trying to express the problem and grateful that anybody's trying to help turn it around. People are very open if they feel like they're going to be heard. I have received a huge amount of positive feedback on this, and if, at times, I am less certain about whether having these sessions for a small group is a good idea, every single time I've done it I leave those sessions thinking that it is only ten or fifteen people, but I'm glad I did it. (Larry Goodman)

One of the things we did at the start with our Getting It Right initiative was that I held focus groups with all the employees, starting with the housekeepers. We did it by groups because I didn't think that, if surgeons and housekeepers were together, the housekeepers would ever say anything. We gave them questions to answer in the meeting, and those questions were not the usual focus group questions like "How is your pay?" or "How are your benefits?" The questions were "What do you see happening to patients that you don't think is right?" "Do you know who to tell if you see something not right happening?" "What keeps you from working efficiently?" "What part of your job should someone else be doing?" "What part of someone else's job should you be doing?" I decided to do it for two reasons. One, I wanted to get input regarding our transformation journey, and two, I wanted to create a willingness for transformation. And it served both purposes. (Patty Gabow)

The Connection with Personal Characteristics

It is the leaders' genuine care and trust of others that fuels this environment of engagement. They want everyone in the organization to feel successful. And they understand that if everyone in the organization is successful, whatever their role, then the organization will prosper; they recognize that the effectiveness of every individual and the effectiveness of the organization are inextricably linked.

Part of the Team, Part of the Solution

The toughest decisions are never made hastily or alone; he ensures that others are heard.

He seeks advice from others, and you can see your thoughts reflected in the outcome. He believes you get the best thinking when you get the positives and negatives of a decision.

*She translates what it means for everyone; everyone has a stake, and
"Here's what you can do."*

*She recognizes when the team needs to do the work—she trusts in
the team to find the answer.*

These leaders do not see themselves as *the* decision maker,
nor will they make a decision alone for the sake of appearing
decisive or because they think it is their job as CEO. On the
contrary, they see their job in decision making as enabling the
best possible decision or solution. Even when they have a strong
point of view, they resist the temptation to decide, appreciating
that a full discussion that entertains different points of view
will validate their personal bias or yield a better solution.

Their use of teams is not situational but part of their philosophy of leadership. They look to teamwork throughout the
organization as a fundamental vehicle to get work done well.
And they see themselves as team members. They know they
have a unique role but not as the brains of the operation. The
whole organization is the brain, and they are part of it.

Here are examples:

*I always believe that everything I talk about is talked about in
terms of teams because I think the team really changes my thinking; they can help you come up with a better solution. I've had
the team meeting where I was thinking I knew where I wanted
to go, start talking, and have people challenge me or say Well
I'm thinking about it differently. And we end up actually not
going where I originally had thought we should go. I sometimes
have an idea, but I'm always open to others' ideas because I
really believe that's when you get the best thinking and the best
outcome. You have members of your team there because they're
experts in these areas, and they can bring that expertise to the
topic you are discussing.* (Donna Sollenberger)

*Teams all the way through are what win, including winning at
work, meaning good performance and being able to have high
quality and good results in services and outcomes. It has always
been important to me to bring teamwork to what I do. Plus, it's
a lot of fun. It is important that we get to celebrate team success*

in large organizations like winning teams in any other field. All improvement comes by way of a project because it gets people to work together focused on a common goal. Having different skill sets enhances team performance. When I am interviewing [candidates] I look for someone different, someone who has a broad background coupled with a deep expertise we are looking for. (Phil Newbold)

I am just a part of the leadership team. It takes a collaborative effort to run an organization this large and this complex. I see my role as helping everyone get the job done. Staying focused on what matters—our people and the purposeful work they do every day taking care of patients. My job is to help them get the resources, the technology, the equipment, and the systems to allow them to do really, really well.

I rely on a great leadership team. Most of us have been together since 1996. We work well together. I would say the vast majority of the great ideas that have moved Sharp HealthCare forward have not been my ideas. They have been other people's ideas that we collectively figured out how to prioritize and how to implement. (Mike Murphy)

The Connection with Personal Characteristics

The leaders' trust in others and their humility are essential to their belief in teams as a powerful vehicle for planning and decision making, as is their commitment to learning. If they were filled with pride they would be more likely to think themselves better decision makers than anyone else. And if they did not trust others, why would they vest others with an influence over any decision?

Grow Others

She finds out what is good in people, exposes it, grows it, and helps you master it in pursuit of the group goal.

She hired me with no hospital operations experience. She said she was looking for leadership skills and that operations could be taught.

He puts time, effort, and resources into grooming supervisors and above, making sure we are all on the same page.

These leaders make others better. They show this in many ways: by having a strong presence in every employee orientation; by creating training and development structures that provide for employees to grow in ways personally and professionally, beyond their job requirements; and by unpredictable personnel choices that reflect the leader's identification of a potential hidden to all, including the candidate. They get deep satisfaction when their people succeed. And they are mindful that personal success will usually translate into greater organizational success.

Here are examples:

I think being a mentor is essential to good leadership. And you can never be a good mentor if you try to get them where you want them to be, instead of get them to be better where they are and to be more strongly who they are. So I spend time in mentoring, asking: Who are you? What does that mean to you? How does that translate into what you're going to do as a leader? Contrary to a lot of folks, I don't think leadership is a predisposition or a gift. I think there are people who are born with the potential to be leaders and that potential can naturally lead them. They could be Al Capones and still be leaders. Being born with the potential for leadership doesn't really mean that much. (Tim Porter-O'Grady)

Somebody said to me "I've been here twenty years, but I go home every night and I know that I've learned something new every day." And I said "You're the perfect kind of employee." (Sister Mary Jean Ryan)

I am a very optimistic person. I tend to always see the good side or the better side of people and situations. There are some things that I steer clear of because they are not a fit for my skill set and talents. I think you make your career and your life on your strengths, not by trying to shore up a couple of weaknesses you might have. I think the only time you really spend a lot of time on weaknesses is when they are either very toxic or career limiting in some way, things that are really going to hurt you. But other than that, rely on the strengths, because where you make your life and your biggest contributions are with your God-given talents or greatest interests. (Phil Newbold)

When I'm mentoring people, I say that the most important thing is to figure out who they are inside. I think we're all influenced by what we think we should do. But who are you really inside? What really drives you? What's going to really make your career so fulfilling you are bursting, because it's just so who you are and you're able to be the most fulfilled? It may not be something your parents want you to do or something you think you should do. It's who you are, really. Then line up with an organization that shares your personal values. (Julie Schmidt)

The Connection with Personal Characteristics

Development of others is fueled by the caring and trust the leaders have in others. They look to build on strengths rather than focus on weaknesses. And their integrity demands that they support individual growth as much as they expect employees to support organizational growth.

A Single-Brain Organization

Taking these organizational characteristics as a whole, they add up to what we are calling a single-brain organization, one in which:

- Every person's contribution is needed for optimal performance.
- Different parts work together for a common goal.
- Every part needs to be nurtured for the health of the whole.
- Diminishment of the value of one function, one level, or one person diminishes performance of the whole.
- The wisdom of every person combined far outweighs the wisdom of one person or group, including the executive team.

These elements, combined with the organizational characteristics, which are fueled by the personal characteristics of the leaders we interviewed, paint a picture of possible paths to transformational results.

What Follows

In chapters 2 through 11, the leaders provide us with their personal story, their narrative of their life and work, through the profiles. We chose to let their words, their voice—and the words of those who work with them—tell their story. The profiles offer insight into the leaders' personal journey, their unique perspectives, and style. As you will learn through the profiles, they are unique and reflect the individual style and personality of each person, further reinforcing our discovery that there is no one style or personality that illustrates a transformational leader. The profiles give an intimate insight into their unique perspectives that illuminate choices leaders can make in their own journey to transformation.

Each leader faced, and continues to face, unique challenges in their path to transformation. Many encountered challenging financial and organizational problems (Patty Gabow, Gary Kaplan, Larry Goodman, Mike Murphy); others dealt with an organization that was strong, had a reason to be proud of what they had done, and were at risk of resting on their laurels (Donna Sollenberger, Sister Mary Jean Ryan, Phil Newbold); still others had the opportunity to lead change from positions of influence, not authority (Maureen Bisognano, Tim Porter-O'Grady). And one led a hospital from concept to successful reality (Julie Schmidt).

We asked the individuals to tell us about their personal lives—growing up, who and what influenced them, how they got into health care, their pathway to leadership, what is important to them as leaders, and what defines a good day and a bad day—as a means of offering a holistic picture of who they are as people, not as a role or position. Chapters 2 through 11 present a distillation of these conversations under each of those topic areas.

Within each profile you will also find more information about the leader's organization, the voices of others (what those who have worked for and with the leader have to say about him or her as a leader), and reflection points (opportunities for the reader or a reading group to stand back from the profile and to reflect on the implications for their own leadership in what they are reading).

Chapter 12 provides guidance for growing leaders in the words of the profiled leaders under the following topics:

- Know yourself
- Know why you are in health care
- Career planning
- Be effective in your job
- Know what will be asked of health care leaders in the future

Chapter 13 provides guidance to boards for the selection and development of exceptional leaders for their own organizations using the model presented in chapter 1 as the framework for the discussion.

Finally, the Selected Readings section lists books that the profiled leaders have found valuable in their own development as leaders.

2

Seeing Possibilities, Not Obstacles: Donna Sollenberger

Donna Sollenberger is executive vice president (EVP) and chief executive officer of the University of Texas Medical Branch Health System in Galveston, Texas, a network of hospitals and clinics. She was previously EVP and chief executive officer (CEO) of the Baylor Clinic and Hospital and EVP of Baylor College of Medicine. Before that she was president and CEO of the University of Wisconsin Hospitals and Clinics (UWHC). Her background is in hospital administration.

Wherever Donna has worked she has made a memorable impact on performance and on those who have worked with her. She is an example of the portability of great leadership.

Growing Up

From the age of three I lived a block from a farm at the very edge of Springfield, Illinois. I lived in that community until I was forty-one. While I was going to school I lived there. My kids were born there. I married my husband there.

Influences—People and Situations

Growing up in the Midwest was great for me. There is a work ethic to the Midwest that is defined by farming. If you have to work seven days a week, you work seven days a week. You get up early; you may need to stay late. That work ethic was prevalent, and even though we weren't farmers, that value was important. I think it is part of the perspective I bring to work; just do what needs to be done at the time.

Background Information

Executive vice president and CEO,
University of Texas Medical Branch, Galveston
www.utmb.edu

Former president and CEO,
University of Wisconsin Hospitals and Clinics, Madison
www.UWhealth.org

Organizational Mission

University of Wisconsin Hospitals and Clinics is dedicated to fulfilling its fourfold mission:

- *Provide safe, high-quality health care*
- *Educate the next generation of health professionals*
- *Conduct research to discover new methods of treatment and prevention*
- *Provide education and outreach services to the community*

System Information

- Begun in 1924 as Wisconsin General Hospital and established as a four-year medical degree program in 1925 at the university. The health system is now a 471-bed hospital and clinic organization with 960 physicians and 7,500 employees in Madison, Wisconsin.

Donna joined UWHC as president and CEO in 1999 and left to accept another position in 2007.

Selected Results for UWHC

	2000 Percentile	2007 Percentile
• Patient satisfaction: adult inpatient		
Overall rating: all hospitals		
455–599 beds	39th	97th
Overall rating: academic		
medical centers	71st	99th
Nurses	57th	95th

	2000	2007
• Financial		
Total margin	1.2%	6.2%

- 2009: Magnet designation awarded
- Results from University HealthSystem Consortium (UHC) benchmarking study of safety, mortality, clinical effectiveness, and equity of major teaching hospitals since 2005
  - —2005: Lowest risk-adjusted mortality of all of the hospitals in the survey
  - —2007, 2008: Participant in the quality and accountability study by UHC that recognized UWHC as the number one organization in 2005; one of nation's top ten (2006–2007) and top five (2008) best-performing institutions
- 2008: Recognized by the Premier Healthcare Alliance as a winner of the Premier Award for Quality (AFQ). The health system was one of twenty-seven winners out of 3,800 eligible hospitals. The AFQ recognizes leading health care organizations that efficiently provide outstanding patient care and consistently set the standard in clinical excellence nationwide. Quality was measured by the incidence of three adverse outcomes: mortality, morbidity, and complications.

Baylor Clinic and Hospital
- In 2007, Donna accepted a senior position at Baylor Clinic and Hospital to lead the building of a green field hospital. However, because changes in the financial markets made building the hospital untenable, Donna and her team recommended suspension of the project even though it meant the loss of all their jobs. She is now EVP and CEO of the University of Texas Medical Branch in Galveston, which is still recovering from the devastating effects of Hurricane Ike in 2008.

Individual Recognitions for Donna Sollenberger
- 2007—Recognized as one of the Top 25 Women in Healthcare by *Modern Healthcare*
- 2006—Best of Madison Business Award for Children's Hospital Leadership
- 2005—University of Illinois Alumnae Achievement Award

My dad was a huge influence in my life. He really opened a lot of doors for me, even as a child. I remember I wanted to play Khoury League [George Khoury Association of Baseball Leagues], which was sponsored by the city, and he was informed that it was for boys only. He found out it was paid for with tax money and told them that he paid taxes and he wanted me to play. They ended up forming girls' teams and my dad was a coach. It was important to him that we girls learned to throw correctly. He really believed in treating people like they could do anything they wanted.

Both my parents emphasized that I could do whatever I wanted. That was important when I was growing up because there were a lot of stereotypes of what women could do, even when I went to college. My dad didn't ever see boundaries for me, and that was important because in my work I don't really see boundaries; I see possibilities. I don't see obstacles; I see challenges, or problems that need to be solved.

They also have ingrained in me a real love of education and stressed its importance. I was the first person in my family to graduate from college. My dad went to two years of college after World War II, but he never finished. My parents felt that education was critical to helping shape you. I think you would characterize us as low middle class, but we always had books, we always went to the library, and we always ate together even though my dad was a grocery store manager with weird hours. We had good conversations around the dinner table.

At Southern Illinois University School of Medicine, the big influence on my career was Dr. Roland Folse, the chair of Surgery. What I learned from him was to see the big picture. If he said that once, he said it a million times: "You know, Donna, you need to look at the big picture." I think it really forced me to always step back before I opened my mouth and assess, really, what is the big picture? What is the big idea here that we need to be thinking about, so that we started thinking about how to change things in a systemic way, not just the pieces of a broken system? The other thing he taught me was that every individual had a unique quality about them that contributed to the success of the organization. In my career if people complain to me about someone else, I try to help them understand the good qualities of that individual and help them see that as long as someone is doing their job, getting us to where we need to be and not leaving twenty-five bodies behind, it's okay. Everybody approaches work differently, and we need to be more accepting of that.

Effective mediation of conflict among senior team members is a hallmark of successful executives. *When team members bring you complaints about others, how do you handle the complaints? How do you help others sort through their complaints about team members? Do you stress the positive qualities of others as Donna does?*

The things I learned from Dr. Charles (Mickey) LeMaistre, president and CEO of the University of Texas M.D. Anderson Cancer Center, were fundamental. One is that the patient always comes first. Period, end of statement. Everything I do in the hospital and clinics, and everything I tell our staff to do is: Think of the patient first. The mantra at UW was: "Ask yourself what is in the best interests of this patient, and you will never make the wrong decision." At Anderson, if we were planning, I would present something and Dr. LeMaistre would say "How will this benefit patients? How will patients react to this?" The first few times I said "I don't know." Then I realized that I hadn't done my homework. So we created a patient advisory council and started involving patients in discussions about things we were trying to change.

Two other things I learned from Mickey are you must know the staff. He knew everybody and about their lives. I remember saying to him one day: "How can you possibly know all this?" And he said "How can you possibly not?" He said if you want to lead people, especially in tough times, they have to know you and they have to know you're genuinely interested in them so you can create trust. You have to be fair and consistent. That was one of the most incredible lessons I learned even growing up from my mom: to treat everybody well, to understand that "everyone is as good as you are, Donna." When I got to UW, I made sure I did rounds on all shifts, that people knew me, that I talked to them, even when I was busy, that I took time to get to know them and what their concerns were. I created avenues for employees to communicate with me. I also tried to create avenues for the whole team to be approachable and accessible. That was another reason we were successful at UW. I learned those lessons early and have Dr. LeMaistre to thank for that.

Donna learned to develop relationships and trust with staff as essential to a leader's work. *What does it mean to you as a leader to know people in your organization? Do you know them? Do you respect them as peers no matter what position each of you holds?*

Pathway to Health Care

I completed college at Sangamon State University, which is now part of the University of Illinois. Then I started work as an English teacher. The school district encouraged us to take a master's program, which they paid for, so I got a master's degree in literature.

Later I moved from teaching to work for the Department of Conservation. My candidate, the incumbent, lost in the primary. Since my position was a political job, I knew I had eight months to find another one. That's when I got into health care, in 1976.

A friend at Southern Illinois University School of Medicine told me that they needed a surgery administrator. I said "What does a surgery administrator do?" She said "I'm not really sure but I'm sure you'd be qualified." So I sent in my application and

I was eventually hired for that position by the chief of Surgery. I had responsibility for research, academic, and clinics administration for the Department of Surgery. I did that for fifteen years, with one, two-year interruption when I went to work at a community college after my daughter was born.

Pathway to Leadership

I am the oldest of three children. I had a brother four years younger and a sister seven years younger. I think I learned my leadership skills with them. They would say I honed my leadership skills on them. They would also say I was bossy.

Dad also believed that you shouldn't let things get you down. He really taught all of us kids that anything was possible. I can remember taking plane and solid geometry; it just wasn't clicking and I was probably in tears at the kitchen table. Dad's response was: Pull yourself up by your bootstraps, just dig in and it'll come to you. Over time, these kinds of conversations made me start thinking about solving problems maybe differently than a lot of people, because if I am trying to visualize solving a problem, I do not see it as a sequential, linear process. It's really a problem in the center, and to view the solution, you can go all the way around so it becomes very circular. It really is 360 degrees that you can look at the problem and at some point you'll find the way in.

He never let us feel that there was something we couldn't solve. I translate that to my work where I see opportunities where others may get discouraged. I usually don't take "we can't do that" for an answer, because I really do think anything is possible, not just who you are going to be but with the work that you are doing. That is something that I really expect of the people that work with me, and it is my job to help them learn how to do that.

My boss at Southern Illinois University School of Medicine, Dr. Folse, the chief of Surgery, asked me at one point if I would be the head of marketing. I said "I don't know anything about marketing" (you're going to hear this theme in my career), and he said "You can learn." I was silly enough to think I could learn it, so I took the job.

There are many challenges to be faced in health care, and their scope and depth can be overwhelming. *Would others think you naive to believe anything is possible, as Donna does, or would that point of view strengthen your power and performance as a leader?*

In 1991, I decided I wanted to see if I could do this surgery administration thing on a bigger stage, so I applied for a job at M.D. Anderson Cancer Center as the administrator for surgery and anesthesiology—a big job. I also got a 25 percent appointment in the hospital at M.D. Anderson to run the clinics and thought that would be a wonderful opportunity for me to learn more about hospital work. Two years later the head of the hospital quit. The CEO, Dr. Charles LeMaistre, said to me: "The current head of the hospital is leaving in two weeks. I know you're not qualified for the job, but I've met with the chairs and they would like you to do it in the interim while we search for someone who is qualified." I thought, wow, this is a great opportunity! In six months or so I can fix some things that are driving me crazy, run the clinics, and learn something about a hospital. A few months later Dr. LeMaistre called me to his office and said: "We've run this search. We haven't found anybody we want and everybody agrees that you're doing a great job, so will you just stay and do it permanently?" That is how I got into hospital administration. But I have seen every challenge as an opportunity and was not afraid to do anything; I was willing to learn. I have seen every opportunity as having great potential.

In 1996, the chief of Surgery at Anderson that I'd worked with went to City of Hope to be the CEO. He called and recruited me to be the chief operating officer at City of Hope.

I felt I had the opportunity to learn a lot there and also think about how to integrate research and clinical care.

Almost three years later, I got a call from a recruiter that the University of Wisconsin Hospitals and Clinics was looking for a president and CEO. I thought this is finally an opportunity to be the leader and to start addressing the things that drive me crazy. So I pursued it and got it. We embarked on what became, I think, a huge transformation for that organization.

What's Important to Me as a Leader

The Power of a Vision That Resonates

At UW I learned the power of creating a vision that resonates with people and unleashes their potential because UW Hospitals and Clinics was ready to be great. It had really good leadership in terms of positioning it well in the marketplace, good business leadership, but not the leadership to help everybody pull in the same direction, everybody doing their part.

A big job of a leader is being able to unleash other people's potential. And to do that you have to create a good vision, but it has to be simply stated. I did lots of rounds and town hall meetings. The mantra early on was "The patient must be first." They have to be at the absolute center of everything we do. Every decision has to be around patients. And everybody's important in getting that job done. One person or 12 people on a leadership team working together might have great ideas, but it's the 7,500 other people that worked at UWHC that made the climb to excellence happen.

If I am successful it is because our organization is all thinking the same way and all working toward the same goals.

The power of many, not of a few, is evident in Donna's approach to leadership. *What is one thing you can do immediately to unleash others' potential? What is one thing you can do immediately to unleash your own potential?*

Voices of Others

She has the ability to make people belong and matter and want to work hard for themselves and the institution.—SG

Clinical quality is her overriding mission, and she is also highly driven by business results.—JR

The patient matters most to her.—MW

She does things for the right reasons and for the right ends.—DE

She has this amazing, charming, unfluttered way of dealing with issues so you want to be aligned with her and be counted on.—DJ

She has a leadership presence and command—not in a directive way, but in a way that engages those around her.—DC

Breaking through the Status Quo

I think leaders get caught up in what I call "problem du jour." They never really get to the things that need to be done, that take time. When I started at the University of Wisconsin Hospitals and Clinics, every other month the leadership team had a two-day retreat to address a significant issue that we needed to define. For example, we needed to revamp the whole quality structure. We had a vision to be the safest hospital in America, and what I wanted, and we needed, was to rethink how we did quality. With my teams what I generally do when they get into what I would call status quo thinking—saying "Maybe we don't need to do that, or maybe this isn't as serious as we think, or maybe we should just leave well enough alone"—is that I push them to think more about what the possibilities are. Maybe we are good, but we need to be great. I try to push conventional thinking, not change for the sake of change but for the sake of making us better. To get better results and to do what we do in a much more meaningful way.

I used Jim Collins' book *Good to Great* [HarperBusiness, 2001]. I read all the time and I will use articles or books that help to capture what I think about an approach to something. They may not be from health care and may not be exactly the same thing that we need to do. But I use them to jump-start thinking in a different way.

Voices of Others

When she came to UW we were suddenly being acknowledged and appreciated; we felt connected and valued.—SG

She took quality of care personally, walking the walk and talking the talk; how can we say these things are not important!—JR

One day the valet parking was backed up, so she started parking cars. It was an inspiration to staff to get done what needs to be done when it needs to be done.—DE

Developing the Potential in People

I love to find people who I can help unleash and release their potential. I see people who need a place to start to grow. They have the right values, they put patients first, and they are well trained. There is a passion about them and how they want to make a difference in other people's lives and in their field. You know this extraordinary person can do the job as long as you spend the time to help them and provide the direction they need to be successful. I look to create the next set of leaders.

Voices of Others

She made me feel proud to be a UW nurse. She enabled my career and recognized I could do other things beyond bedside care.—SG

She has great empathy for all levels of employees, and she took great time and energy to be visible and accessible to all. She knew their names and the names of their family members.—JR

She makes it her job to make sure we are growing, challenged, and meeting our personal goals.—MW

Donna has a way of seeing future abilities in people and then developing that potential. She has made a huge difference in my life, making my education and career progress possible while providing me emotional support along the way.—SO

She promoted me to COO when I was fairly young; what Donna engendered was mentorship and nurturing my ability to be successful.—DE

Her first concern is making those around her successful.—DC

She finds out what is good in people, exposes it, grows it, and helps you master it in pursuit of the group goal.—MW

Collaboration and the Importance of Teams

Sometimes I know where I want to go and try to bring others along. But I will also say there were times when I thought I knew where I wanted to go, then we would start a conversation and I realized there was another way. I always believe that everything I talk about is talked about in terms of teams because I think the team really changes my thinking; they can help you come up with a better solution. I've had the team meeting where I was thinking I knew where I wanted to go, start talking, and have people challenge me or say Well, I'm thinking about it differently. And we end up actually not going where I originally had thought we should go. I sometimes have an idea, but I'm always open to others' ideas because I really believe that's when you get the best thinking and the best outcome. You have members of your team there because they're experts in these areas, and they can bring that expertise to the topic you are discussing.

Using the wisdom of the team while still carrying a specific point of view is emphasized here. *How open are you to the ideas of others? Whom will you ask to test whether your view of your openness is shared by those with whom you work?*

Other times, when we were trying to redo the whole quality structure, I didn't have a clue where I thought we should go. [The health system] was a unique organization. I'd read a lot about quality and I had our University HealthSystems Consortium information on what others were doing in quality, but

I didn't really have a preconceived notion where I thought we should go. It was a totally collaborative process. It ended up taking us six full days of discussion, but I think the benefit of taking the time to have those discussions, to focus on something that's really important, is that you take time out to move the organization along. As we did this we had ground rules. We did the meetings off-site, not expensive places or fancy places; they were just in town, but no pagers, no cell phones were allowed in the meeting. Everybody had to stay focused on this topic for the whole day so we couldn't get distracted. I think our team members would say that those sessions were one of the most beneficial parts of being able to achieve the transformation. We not only had a vision of what we wanted and where we wanted to go, but we spent the time talking about what we needed to do to get there, in answering these important questions.

I really think as a team. I don't believe any one person in this organization is more important than another. We all have a job to do and need to work together to do it. My view is: Yes, I'm the leader and ultimately I'm responsible, but I certainly don't have all the answers, and I'm not going to make all the decisions. I let people disagree with me, and I think some leaders don't like that. Somehow that challenges their authority. I don't view preventing disagreement as authority.

To get things done, involve the people who do the work. I learned a huge lesson at M.D. Anderson from a food service worker. She had wanted to see me, and because she was persistent I scheduled her for a half hour. We had gone through a reduction in force because we had had some difficulties with our budget. She wanted to tell me about how stressful her job had become because she was now doing two jobs on the tray line. When I asked her what she would do, she actually had a solution to her stressful situation. What I learned from her is that leaders don't have all the answers. We may be able to create a vision. We may be able to create an idea of where we want to go. We may be able to even create the strategy, but the practical, tactical things of what need to get done, you have to involve the people who are doing them. They have to be part of the process. Understand that you don't have all the answers, do not jump to conclusions, ask the right questions, and facilitate trying to find out by asking why we are having that issue or what the problem might be.

Senior leaders are frequently rewarded for making quick assessments and taking fast action while diminishing the diagnostic phase in which the problem is deeply understood. *What price do you and the organization pay when you jump to conclusions or jump in with "the answer"? How can you ensure that you and your colleagues collectively understand the situation better before moving to action?*

When I got to the University of Wisconsin Hospitals and Clinics, our patient satisfaction was at the thirty-seventh percentile of academic hospitals, and cleanliness of the patient room was at the ninth percentile; there were comments that we weren't cleaning people's room. Rather than assume what happened, I called the director of environmental services and asked: What do you think is happening here? Why would patients say that? He responded: "We're cleaning the rooms. I have no idea what's going on." So I asked him to get an answer because there was a disconnect with our patients. He asked people at a housekeeping staff meeting about it. An environmental services worker who cleaned rooms told him: "I can tell you why patients think that. When I go onto the unit I check with the head nurse to find when a patient is going to be out of the room for a test or surgery or whatever else. Then we go in and clean that room when the patient isn't there so that we don't intrude or bother them. So maybe because they don't see us they don't think we ever clean the rooms." And this worker also had a solution, which was to supply cleaning staff with cards like they have in hotels saying: "Elena cleaned your room today. If there is anything else you need, please call this number" and to leave the card on the over-the-bed tray. It was simple, so we tried it. Two years later, Press Ganey reported them as the top performing environmental services department of all hospitals in the country, and the hospital as a whole was performing at the 95th percentile. I have learned not to accept the common assumption (in this case that we weren't cleaning the room) but rather to give people an opportunity to try to figure it out, not to put them on the defensive. I mean, she was right and she solved the problem. Maybe that's part of the research piece in me from my old English training, to really look into something carefully and to not make assumptions.

I have become more and more convinced that a fundamental underpinning of any leadership wherever you are is to appreciate the people. Not just "You're doing a good job, Joe," but that you genuinely appreciate what they do. You try to understand what they do. You involve them in making decisions that affect them. People crave knowing how their job contributes to the organization's success.

Voices of Others

She knows what it is to be a leader: that you have to lead all the people.—SG

Her senior team was a close-knit group who had received clear and rigorous expectations.—JR

She sees leadership as a responsibility, not as a reward for time served.—MW

She is not driven by ego or personal ambition.—MW

She recruited great people who worked together in great teams.—DE

She understands that her aspirations can only be met through other people.—DE

She is always willing to share the credit with others.—DE

Push to Achieve Your Vision

We pioneered a lot of the work in quality and safety at UWHC. This was after we had been named by UHC the top quality hospital in their grouping. People said "Well, why would we want to work on quality now when we're the top?" It was because we had flaws in our process and in the way that we handled quality issues. We wanted to improve that. The other reason was that the gross score was something like 69 out of 100. I pointed out in any other place that was poor to failing, so we have a long way to go.

We worked hard to organize the effort in a way that created avenues for participation and input from everyone in the organization. We educated the board to understand their role in quality and the importance of their support. We made improving a blameless process. One of the big issues was: How can we get the nurses, pharmacists, and environmental services workers, everybody, to agree with this if the physicians didn't participate? We felt we would never get there if the physicians didn't participate in a way that created a higher-quality outcome or better satisfaction. We talked about how I would work with the dean of the medical school to get his support, this was important, and this was something that was an achievable goal. We met all sorts of challenges: How do we communicate what we are going to do? How do we create accountabilities? How do we measure that we are being successful at this?

I was in the cafeteria grabbing some lunch one day, and one of the surgeons came up to me after I said we wanted to be the safest hospital in America; he told me basically that was the stupidest thing he ever heard. I mean, why would we want to do that? My response was: Well, it's a big goal, and it's a lofty goal. But I guess I would ask you if there is one time we make a mistake, is it okay if it's on you or your family member or a friend? [Is it] ever okay to make a mistake on a person?

At that time, UHC was looking to benchmark to other hospitals. I felt that was critical to knowing how we were doing. But our attorney told me we can't do that. Well, my dad's favorite saying was "Can't never did anything," and I told them to figure out how to do it because we need to do it. He said "Are you serious?" And I said "I am dead serious. You need to figure out how you can be comfortable in setting parameters for us to do this." So we became the alpha site, the only hospital in UHC that participated. After we did it, some others became beta sites. It is now a widely used patient safety reporting tool for UHC hospital[s]. It was all about how you push an organization to begin to do things differently so you can achieve your vision.

Donna illustrates vision, mission, and values in action—especially in addressing tough issues. *How much is your organization's vision, mission, and values present in your thinking, your conversations, and your decisions? If your vision, mission, and values are not driving action, what is? What is on the agenda in your meetings? How often do you mention patients and the mission in your daily encounters with others?*

Voices of Others

She is goal and project oriented; she has a logical, progressive underpinning to tackling problems.—SG

She connects with everyone at every level with warmth. She really cares what they have to say.—SO

She adheres to her principles and doesn't have a political appeasement approach.—SG

All I saw was a principled person staying the course. She never wavered. And she garnered a lot of respect for that.—SG

She has an innate drive for excellence.—DE

Being a Learner

When I experience something or I read something I always ask the question What can I learn from this? How can I apply this to what I'm doing or to what we're trying to do? How can I take an experience that someone's talked about at a meeting and be able to apply that to what I'm doing so it will be meaningful? I am constantly interested in what I can learn from something. I'm sure I drive people crazy, but people will tell me something and I will say: Well, what can we learn from that? Not because I'm trying to be a smart aleck but because I am curious. It's important enough for you to say it, so what can we learn from that? I do that all the time. Patient letters come in and I'll say Gosh, what can we learn from this that we could share with the staff to help them understand something we need to do better? Or what can we learn from that organization that was able to turn itself around financially or improved its satisfaction? I don't take something on face value. I drive home thinking I wonder what I could learn from that or I wonder how we could apply that?

I didn't spend a lot of time outside my organizations because I always felt I had so much work to do at home, meaning my own organization, although I was aware of what was happening at the state level and nationally. I read about it; I would read books and I would read articles. I scoured those, but I didn't really spend time going to the meetings because sometimes, frankly, it felt I wasn't really learning much.

But I got thinking that I should get more involved, and I was encouraged to do so. I became involved with work at the American Hospital Association, and the experience was great. I met people who had a big picture for health care. What I realized and learned from them is that I didn't spend enough time getting the big, more global, picture for health care and health care policy and how it impacted what we were doing in my organization. That was one of the things I learned from being exposed to a national organizational environment.

I also think having people that are your peers that you can learn from is helpful as well; having sounding boards that you feel safe with. We had a wonderful leadership team at UWHC, but there were two individuals in particular who I felt really comfortable bouncing ideas off of; they would give me their honest thoughts or honest opinions. They really helped me think about and shape our ultimate strategy.

Leaders who consistently learn bring benefits to their organization and its results. *Where do you go to learn beyond an occasional conference? Is learning a daily activity for you? Do you see the value to your leadership in making it so?*

Voices of Others

She continues to expand her personal management tool kit and inspires me to do the same.—MW

Great teacher and a good role model, she works very hard to acquire the knowledge she needs.—DC

Swimming in the Gray, Swimming in the Matrix

When I came to Baylor and before I recruited my leadership team for the planned new hospital, I started to draw out an organizational chart for approval so I could begin recruiting. Suddenly, I noticed that I am drawing the typical COO, VP of this, and then I thought: I don't have to do this! I need to think about this differently! That's why I came here in the first place. So there were three hospital leaders and a leader for ambulatory, and I made them all the same title: VP of Operations. They just had different responsibilities, because I wanted people to start thinking about interchangeability and that as you grow something, the job you have today may not be the job you have tomorrow.

I started thinking about How do I do that? One thing I was thinking about was a flat organization that didn't distinguish one title as being more elevated than another. So it made sense that everybody was at a VP level. Then I started thinking if I am going to ask people to live in this structure, I am going to need people who are going to be flexible and comfortable with change. Frankly, I think most of life is gray and most of what we do is gray; there's never an ideal 100 percent right answer. There are things that are wrong and things that are right, but there is a lot of gray in life, and people need to be flexible. I called it being able to swim in the gray, to swim in the matrix, and to realize that their position might morph and change. So I asked candidates a lot of questions about how they felt about that. There are people who are wed to titles or really need to understand exactly what they are responsible for. I think it's great, and I have detailed position descriptions, heaven only knows, but I also think it is important for people to understand that circumstances change and their jobs may change. That is what I was trying to convey through the organizational chart. I was looking for flexibility, adaptability, creativity, not being afraid to venture into the unknown, and also valuing people.

Donna looks for flexibility, adaptability, creativity, lack of fear to venture into the unknown, and a sense of valuing people in selecting leaders. *Are these criteria you look for? If not, why?*

Swimming in the matrix means you're not someone who is hierarchical. People might say to me Oh, I can't report to the head of nursing and the head of the service line. Well, that's kind of how life is now. It's being able to manage multiple reporting relationships or manage multiple complexities when everything isn't that clear. Organizational life is not generally hierarchical and is not generally black and white, and in my opinion in the future people aren't just going to have a single boss they report to.

Voices of Others

She is understanding of larger goals and can still relate to someone in an entry-level position.—DE

She is able to validate confounding variables with seamless ease.—MW

She demonstrated business acumen, personal accountability, and accessibility.—JR

She is sheer brilliance in a humble presentation.—MW

She knows that improving the bottom line feels good.—SG

She doesn't talk about people in a negative way; she looks for their innate good and never demeans anyone.—DE

Sorting through the Noise

I gather information and look for common themes in all the noise. When people start talking to me about problems, I can start to see a bigger topic and major themes emerge. I have learned that listening is a huge part of the leader's job; to hear what people need to say and sift out the true issues that will become major focuses for change.

Voices of Others

She is able to link business, operations, and vision into a whole and make it come to pass.—DE

She embodies what a CEO should be: [a] real person, a professional leader, a hard worker, always willing to share the credit, dealing with those who are not performing, focused and patient when necessary.—SO

She develops shared goals and clear action steps, communicates them fully, and focuses on them.—SO

She is not distracted by the crisis of the day but focuses on what she needs to be doing and communicating; she doesn't jump around or vacillate.—DE

Creating Sustainable Change

The hardest decisions I ever made were to leave M.D. Anderson and to leave UWHC. I was very attached to people at both places. But I think another mark of a leader is the ability to transform something and create sustainable change. I always say that if I got hit by a bus tomorrow, I would want two or three weeks to pass before someone would say: "We haven't seen Donna around lately. I wonder what happened to her?" When I talk to the people at Wisconsin, which I still do, the one thing that they comment on is that the change was sustained. We changed the organization. It wasn't just the leader. Maybe that and because I'm constantly wanting to learn new things and try out things, is why I am willing to leave.

I think it would be selfish on my part—and I think a lot of people do this—to go to a place for two or three or four years. They don't make a lasting change in the organization and then they leave it. I think successful organizations do have constancy of leadership. At UWHC my predecessor had been there twenty-five years. I was there for eight. And there is a point of view that after ten or twelve years a leader should move on because you've done about all you're going to be able to do in changing the organization, and maybe it's time to get some new blood in. I do think that some leaders stay too long and they get complacent.

I've never wanted to be complacent, and that's why I always like something new and exciting, so I was ready to try this at Baylor, but it was hard to leave people at UWHC; it's still hard to leave people behind. I think there's some satisfaction in knowing the organization has intrinsically changed once you've empowered people.

I think that you can make changes and you can move on if you really change the organization. If you haven't, shame on you.

Deep cultural and organizational change requires five to seven years of sustained behaviors to embed new ways of functioning. *Is it ethical for a leader to voluntarily leave an organization when the positive changes they have made are not yet sustainable?*

Voices of Others

She has experience and a great track record.—DC

She has been successful in a variety of organizations and situations and has created sustainable success.—DC

She is a national treasure and needs to be known.—SG

She was here long enough that we got hard-wired by her leadership.—SG

She was a living example of our values.—SO

A Good Day

A good day is when I've been able to get our team together and talk about a problem that needs to be solved and we come up with a plan. A good day for me is taking the strategic plan, working with a group, and coming up with what the annual operating plan [is] going to be to meet the strategic plan. A good day is having time or making time to get out and talk to employees and asking them what they like best and least about their job and, if you could change one thing what would it be? Going into patient rooms and saying: "How are you doing? Is there anything we can do to make the experience better?" Talking to physicians who have great new ideas of something we could introduce into the hospital and then sending them off to work with someone on our team to develop a business plan.

A Bad Day

A bad day is only dealing with routine operations. I get bored easily if I have to do things that are repetitive. I lose attentiveness if I get too bogged down in details or organizational politics. I actually look to have detailed thinkers around me. A bad day is if I don't get to talk to employees or I don't get to see patients.

Voices of Others

SG   Susan Dillon Gold, *nurse clinician, HIV Clinic, University of Wisconsin Hospitals and Clinics*

JR   James Roberts, *senior vice president and general counsel, Shands HealthCare at the University of Florida*

MW   Melanie Wong, *director, Business Development and Clinical Planning, Baylor College of Medicine*

DE   David Entwistle, *CEO, University of Utah Hospitals and Clinics*

SO   Stephanie Orzechowski, *director, Oncology Services, University of Wisconsin Hospitals and Clinics*

DJ   Dan B. Jones, MD, *Sid W. Richardson Professor; Distinguished Service Professor; Margaret Root Brown Chair; director, Cullen Eye Institute, Department of Ophthalmology, Baylor College of Medicine*

DC   David Callender, MD, *president, University of Texas Medical Branch*

3

True North
("Who Is at the Top?"):
Gary Kaplan

Gary Kaplan joined Virginia Mason Medical Center (VMMC) in 1978 as an internal medicine intern and in 2000 became the seventh chairman and CEO in the organization's eighty-year history. He became CEO in a time of significant financial distress that required dramatic changes in governance and operational functioning.

As the first health care organization to adapt principles of the Toyota Production System as a means to transform health care, Gary and his colleagues have accomplished significant improvement in quality, safety, and experience of care. They actively teach others in health care how to transform their organizations.

Growing Up

I grew up in the Detroit area, the oldest of three children. My parents, who are both still living and in their eighties, were great models of hard work. My mother was a school teacher and the first college graduate in her family. My father dropped out of college a semester before graduating with an engineering degree because he wanted to go into a business that he and my uncle started. They bought a small hardware store in Wayne, Michigan, and grew the business to the third largest True Value Hardware store in the United States. I started working there at age five and continued to work there through my senior year in medical school.

Background Information

Chairman and CEO,
Virginia Mason Medical Center, Seattle, Washington
www.VirginiaMason.org

Organizational Vision

To be the Quality Leader and transform health care; to become the Quality Leader, we must first change the way health care is delivered. Our aspiration is not to be the biggest, but to be the best. We will differentiate ourselves on the basis of quality.

Virginia Mason Medical Center Information

- Virginia Mason (VMMC) has 5,000 staff and 440 physicians serving 807,000 patient visits and 17,000 inpatient visits.
- In 2004, a medical error caused the tragic death of a VMMC patient. This event and the subsequent decision to be fully transparent was a defining moment for the organization. Within weeks of the error, the board and leadership agreed that VMMC would have only one organizational goal: *Ensure the Safety of our Patients through the Elimination of Avoidable Death and Injury.*
- Caring for patients safely means zero defects in the care provided and is the foundation for VMMC's vision of becoming the Quality Leader. Virginia Mason holds the view that the best clinical outcomes cannot be achieved without establishing the safest possible environment in which to deliver care. Safety was not one among many competing goals; it was to be the focus of the work.

Selected Results for Virginia Mason

- The computerized provider order entry system reduced medication ordering errors to near zero and has sustained that performance since July 2005.
- Ventilator-associated pneumonia (VAP)—2002: 34 cases. 2004: The organization identified VAP prevention as one of its safety initiatives and implemented the ventilator bundle (a set of specific steps proven to reduce the incidence of VAP):

4 cases; bundle compliance: remains at or near 100 percent.
2008–09 VAP: zero to three cases per year; central line bundle compliance to reduce central line infections: increased
from 46 percent to 95 percent in 2007; sustained performance at or above that level; medical emergency team calls
to reduce cardiac arrests: from an average of ten per month
to eighty-five per month while codes outside cardiac care
unit dropped to zero for five months; congestive heart failure
bundle compliance: 93 percent since December 2008; 100
percent June–September 2009; stroke bundle compliance for
rapid treatment of strokes increased from 34 percent to 100
percent compliance for four consecutive months; surgical site
infections have fallen below 1 percent.

- Culture of safety: Staff response rate for the 2009 survey—
  81.1 percent, an increase of 42.5 percent from 2008. Nine
  of twelve categories showed improved results, including the
  category "Overall Grade for Patient Safety": increased from
  78 percent in 2008 to 80 percent very good or excellent. The
  largest jump occurred in "Management Support for Patient
  Safety": 15 percent improvement (78 percent in 2009 versus
  63 percent in 2008).

- Staff engagement/satisfaction: Staff response rate for the 2009
  survey—73 percent, an increase of 14 percent from 2007.
  Ranking within the national Press Ganey health care database moved from fifty-third in 2007 to seventieth in 2009.
  The category showing the biggest increase between 2007 and
  2009 is "Satisfaction with Leadership and Systems." Virginia
  Mason achieved strong increases in staff satisfaction with
  leadership communications—one of the continued focus areas
  for improvement. The results showed significant increases
  from 2007 to 2009 in the percentage of staff who agreed or
  strongly agreed that leaders really listen to staff (+22.9 percent), can be trusted to be straightforward and honest (+12.8
  percent), respond promptly to most problems (+12.9 percent),
  and do a good job of communicating major developments
  (+10.2 percent).

- Patient engagement: 2006 to 2009 clinic patient/outpatient satisfaction ratings increased by 35 percent. During the period 2006–2009, inpatient satisfaction improved by 50 percent.

Individual Recognitions for Gary Kaplan
- Recognition at the 2009 National Patient Safety Foundation Congress, where Lucian Leape noted: "one of the exemplars of front line patient safety work is VM. They have a culture of safety which is a culture of truth-telling; they traveled as a team from Seattle to Washington, DC, to learn together—the CEO, four board members, four MDs, and five RNs."
- 2009: American Jewish Committee Human Relations Award.
- 2009: John M. Eisenberg Patient Safety and Quality Award, National Quality Forum and The Joint Commission.
- 2009: Harry J. Harwick Lifetime Achievement Award, Medical Group Management Association and American College of Medical Practice Executives.
- 2008: Recognized as one of the 50 Most Powerful Physician Executives by *Modern Physician*.
- 2007: Recognized as one of the Top 100 Most Powerful People in Healthcare by *Modern Healthcare*.

It was a very formative experience for me over those twenty years. I started working in nuts and bolts and I ended up running the paint department and garden supplies. I met thousands of customers and got to know them and their families; I learned a lot about interpersonal relations. I loved talking to people.

Influences—People and Situations

Being part of the hardware business was great because I got to watch my dad and to spend time with him. The business was all about personal relationships. That was what sustained this small business in very competitive times.

I'm an extrovert but I'm very reflective. I think that comes from my father, who is a highly intelligent, idea-seeking, relationship-driven person, a person who believes anything is possible. He told me: "There's no reason you have to go into this business. My role is to help support you in whatever you decide to do with your life. But you've got to figure out what your strengths and weaknesses are and where your passions are."

Gary and other leaders profiled in this book identified people who encouraged them to be anything they wanted to be, the key being to figure out what that was. *What are your passions, and how do they match the work you do? Why did you choose to do the work you do today? What work, if there were no constraints, would you choose that matches your passions? Is it the same work you do and role you play today? If not, what actions can you take to move closer to expressing your passions?*

After completing my undergraduate work, I stayed in Ann Arbor, Michigan, for another five years, including medical school, before moving to Virginia Mason for my internship in internal medicine. Ann Arbor was a great place to go to school. It was a very liberal, forward-thinking community which shaped my politics and world view quite a bit. I made lifelong friendships there. No less than four couples from there moved to Seattle, where we have all lived and raised our families over the past thirty years.

My wife, Wendy, and I have been married thirty-six years. We met in high school when I was a junior and she was a sophomore, so we defied a lot of odds by sustaining and growing our relationship over many years.

We were in the middle of this Virginia Mason Production System journey [based on the Toyota Production System] in November 2004 and a patient, Mary McClinton, came to us for a tertiary procedure—something we do every day. And we failed her. She died here of a preventable medical error. Mary's death was the darkest day in my career and the darkest day in our history. But what we needed to do was very clear to us. We went public immediately when we found out what happened. We were featured in the local, regional, national, and international media and it was not flattering. We subsequently found out that the same mistake had been made in another hospital in the same community two years earlier and had been swept under the rug, reinforcing our decision to go public. It was one of a few defining moments on this journey which really spurred us on to work even harder and faster.

This year (2009) we celebrated our annual Mary McClinton Patient Safety Award for the fourth year with Mary's family. The award recognizes the performance of a safety team at Virginia Mason. This year was the first that Gerald McClinton, her son, was ready to speak to the great work going on here in his mother's memory. I cannot talk about myself, my journey, and the organization's work without acknowledging the memory of Mary.

The personal impact on these leaders when a patient is harmed or dies in their care is massive. It can also be transformative as a force for good. *Can you identify a defining moment in your leadership work? What path did that defining moment take you on that perhaps was unexpected and positive? Do you share that experience with others?*

Pathway to Health Care

A customer at the hardware store was a family physician who became a good family friend. He took me with him to the hospital to make rounds when I was fourteen. He was an old-time general practitioner and a very good doctor. He did a lot of minor surgery, and I became really taken and enamored with the relationship aspect of patient care: how he knew his patients and they knew him. I got to watch him do a tonsillectomy, which can be a fairly bloody procedure, and found myself waking up on the floor of the operating room—this was a fourteen-year-old kid in the OR! There was a time many years later when I was seriously considering becoming a surgeon, but in that first encounter in the OR, I passed out almost without any warning! He and I stayed in touch and he became something of a mentor.

I knew I wanted to be a doctor when I went to college at the University of Michigan. I was a psychology major in undergraduate school. I spent the year in between college and medical school working as a psychiatric case worker on an adolescent girls' inpatient unit with severely disturbed adolescents. When I went to medical school I was fairly certain I was going to be a psychiatrist. But one month into medical school I realized I loved gross anatomy. By the end of my first year I decided that I didn't want to be a psychiatrist, and my focus shifted to internal medicine.

I built a very loyal, interesting, and challenging internal medicine practice, and it continues to be important to me. It is part of my anchor, part of who I am. And as the seventh CEO at Virginia Mason I am maintaining the tradition that every one of us has been a practicing clinician.

Pathway to Leadership

First of all, I had this business interest and background in leadership from working in my father's store. I saw how he ran things, how he led the business.

I was heavily recruited as an internist to join the downtown general medical section. I was optimistic I would be offered the position. When I wasn't hired I was devastated, because for at least a year I had come to count on it. I thought Well, what am I going to do now? I'll just have to go back to square one. But I was given the opportunity to cut my teeth on leadership soon after. It was one of those formative experiences when just when you feel most disappointed you're redirected, and in a much better way. What happened was that after I didn't get the internist position I wanted, Roger Lindeman, who was my predecessor as CEO, a dear friend, and a mentor, said: I think we have better and bigger things in store for you. Within a year of finishing my residency I was asked to lead the regional clinic development of Virginia Mason. As it turns out, I would not be sitting here today if I had been slotted on the career track of being an internist at the downtown general medicine section.

Gary's career exemplifies the fact that the path to leadership is rarely straight and seldom goes as planned. When Gary did not get the position he expected, he faced a "now what?" moment in his career. His path was very different as a result. *What does Gary's example tell you about the value of career plans? In your own leadership path, are you focused on the position you want or the work you want?*

That first regional clinic was quite successful within a year. The organization wanted to expand. Our leadership decided to take the model that was working and take the leader who was leading it (me) and asked me to lead the development of a second clinic. I, along with a great team, planned it, identified the right clinicians to staff it, and created some standard practices around how these regional clinics would work and interface with the mother ship. Over time this work led to the development of a clinic system that at its peak had sixteen or seventeen clinics. I personally recruited and hired 150 physicians to staff these regional clinics.

In the early '90s we had to close and consolidate several of the primary care practices we built or acquired. That was a growth experience. It was almost like giving up the children to whom you gave birth. That was a really emotional, trying, and formative time in terms of learning what it means to be clear, learning what it means to be tough, and learning what it means to put the organization before the individual.

I became vice chairman of the medical center and co-chair of the operations committee. I still was chief of satellites, but now I was wearing another, much broader, hat. I had day-to-day responsibility for overseeing operational decision making for the whole institution—capital budgeting allocations, operational budgeting. These responsibilities were a very important learning for me.

In 2000, I was asked to run for chairman and CEO. At the time it was an elected position for which I had to campaign—an archaic way to run a three-quarters of a billion dollar company with 5,000 people and maybe 10,000 mouths to feed. It was at a tough time in our history. My challenge was: How do I position myself as the change agent I have always been while also being very much part of the leadership team of the past? During the campaign I talked about a platform for change. I talked about wanting a vision. It was very challenging to be respectful to the past but also be clear that change was needed. I was uniquely capable of speaking to the past and building on the traditions and understanding where we came from. I won and became the seventh CEO in February of 2000.

I wouldn't say I always wanted to be CEO. But one of my mentors told me "You have something; if you play your cards right and if things work well, you could be leading this organization someday." Now, that was a new idea to me. But the seed was planted and it germinated over twenty years.

What's Important to Me as a Leader

True North ("Who Is at the Top?")

The first thing the board asked me and the senior team was "Who is your customer?" Just like everybody in health care, we said "Oh, the patient." And they said "Take a closer look." The fact was, our systems and processes were designed for us—physicians, nurses, managers, and staff. What are waiting rooms but big spaces for patients to hurry up, be on time, and wait for us? We design it into our facilities. We design it into our workflow. It's total arrogance. So we got really, really clear what it means to be patient driven. I used to be so proud to say we are a physician-driven organization. I'd be embarrassed to say that today. We are patient driven.

I think I've always had a fairly clear True North, what really matters to me. In my mind there is a hierarchy: patient, organization, department, individual—all important and in that order. That hierarchy is now reflected in our strategic plan. That True North has helped guide me, given me resilience in terms of dealing with tough issues. At the end of the day, we have to do what's best for patients—they are at the top.

Clarity of vision and direction is a consistent theme from these leaders. Where the patient fits in health care work—really fits, not just in words or slogans—is an essential part of that clarity. *What actions do you regularly take to demonstrate and make clear to others your own commitment to patient care as your True North? How would others know about your commitment to patient care as a personal value?*

The bar has been raised for everybody—the individual staff member, the sections, the departments, the organization, and particularly the patient. The patient and clinician are more valued than ever before. I believe that keeping the patient at the top of the hierarchy means we also have to create a great place for a physician to practice, as opposed to putting the physician at the top like we used to. You can ask any one of our 5,000 people here—anybody—"Who's at the top?" and they will tell you it is the patient. That clarity empowers the role of the individual in providing great care.

Voices of Others

He is unwavering about the mission; he has a constancy of purpose.—SP

He beats the same vision drum—he is steadfast.—CB

With the death of Mrs. McClinton, Gary set the example. He told us "We will walk straight into this"; "We will make meaning out of it and honor her"; "This will make us stronger."—KP

He defines the vision with great clarity but not the answers—he integrates the vision into everything he does.—VF

Leadership courage and perseverance—how you choose to communicate when bad things happen or when it may be unpopular—our True North leads the way.—LC

It's True North and sticking to it—putting the patients at the top, not physicians.—BC

The perseverance and the optimism makes people want to move forward.—SP

He knows the details from a base of knowing the reality—he loves patient care.—SM

His key behaviors are clarity of vision and purpose—to serve something bigger than self and the steps to get there; to optimize the success of others—inspiring, seeing things I didn't see.—DS

Homegrown

Looking through the window of our past, we see promise of our future.—From a sign at VMMC

One of the key things about my career and my leadership is I'm homegrown. I went from internal medicine intern to health system CEO, and that's a long journey.

I don't think being homegrown is a critical success factor for all leaders by any means. For me it has been both a challenge and an asset. I knew the culture, the very rich heritage of this organization, and I knew the people intimately, particularly the physicians but also the nurses and other key people. I know what it means to live in this organization, work in it, grow in it. I believe in the leadership thinkers who say you sometimes have to step out of the culture from which you came and get up on the balcony; spend time with others outside to separate from the intensity and passion of the work. Doing that is critically important. Deliberately getting out of the culture at times has really helped me as a leader.

Being homegrown can give you managerial courage if you have clarity of purpose, your True North, have decision rules, and you are able to get on the balcony. If I didn't do that, we wouldn't have been able to change governance or accomplish the other transformational changes we've done. A leader can come from the outside, but they will need to spend lots of time building credibility—and the organization may lose something in that time.

But what's most important, most necessary, is a passion for the vision with a commensurate passion for the organization.

Getting on the Balcony

I'm very involved in the world of health care outside of Virginia Mason. My experiences predispose me to looking outside as well as inside for answers, for relationships, for positive reinforcement and validation, which I think are all important to developing as a leader.

In recent years, particularly as CEO, I have come to realize that the more I was immersed in the culture the harder it would be to lead the change that was required. So I looked for confidants, mentors, relationships. The Rockport Institute, a group I helped to start with Jack Silversin and Mary Jane Kornacki, is an example of an outside peer group that provides frequent support. That and the relationships that I have been able to develop outside of here have helped me get a perspective and get me out of the mind-set of being trapped in the intensity of the moment, in the culture, and all the things that I as a leader can get so wrapped up in.

Voices of Others

He seeks advice from others—"tell me your thinking about this"— and you can see your thoughts reflected in the outcome. He asks people who are not directly involved, uses outside resources. He believes you get the best thinking when you get the positives and negatives of a decision.—SP

He has a steel-trap memory, and he uses it to connect to people. He likes people and it shows; he is interested in what others are doing, listens well, and is approachable. But he doesn't expect to know everything, so he gets help from others.—SM

It's a learning organization—everyone reads, shares articles and books. I was reading Atul Gawande on vacation!—JL

Learning is embodied by Gary. The CEO doesn't need to stop learning, so he leads by example. He does what he asks others to do.—BC

Conventional wisdom encourages hiring leaders from outside the organization. The intent is to bring in "new blood" that will aid in achieving transformation because those inside the organization are too confined by the culture. *What examples of stepping outside the organization to learn more about your own culture would avoid confinement in the current culture? What would you want in an organization that aspires to be committed to learning? What regular practices do you and your colleagues use to get on the balcony? How do you model your own commitment to learning?*

Learning to Become a Quality Leader

We said we aspire to be the Quality Leader. We want to be looked at as the best anywhere. Not just Seattle or the Northwest or the U.S. but in the world. We had the vision, improved our governance, and created physician and leadership compacts. But *how* were we going to become the Quality Leader?

We discovered, through our colleagues at Boeing, the Toyota Production System and how helpful it had been to the Boeing assembly process. We decided to see the Toyota system firsthand. I wanted to make sure the board was on board, so we took the chair of the board finance committee on our first trip to Japan and so began to educate the board as well.

Leadership confidence is required to create a major change. It basically required us to say: "Look, the status quo is unacceptable. People are dying in American hospitals, including ours. We're making mistakes every day. The economics are not working. Do you have a better idea? If not, we're going to explore and find out whether there is something in this for us." One of the keys to this journey, the first step, was to change the minds of the senior leadership. Don't start with the middle. They're critical to the journey, but if you don't have the senior leaders' minds changed it's just going to be a huge frustration. I was changing my mind, too.

In 2002, we went to Japan for the first time. The week before we left, the *Seattle Times* put out a front-page story, "Doctors to Lead Boondoggle to Japan." Many of our people, staff and physicians, said "Well, now we know he's lost it, gone off the deep end." We spent two weeks there and we were transformed. We worked at a Hitachi air conditioning plant where we actually redesigned air conditioner assembly on the line. Several things happened, including a total leveling of the hierarchy. It was a totally foreign environment in which we couldn't speak English. We learned that you don't have to know anything about Freon or building air conditioners to redesign the processes so that they're better. How humbling is that, that you actually don't need to know anything about health care to redesign a lot of the processes in health care?

We had deep conversation in that milieu during our trip about how this applied to us and what were our barriers. Toyota was like a state-of-the-art symphony. We asked ourselves what health care would be like if it could be 10 percent as good as Toyota is in creating synergies, flow, just-in-time, and zero-defect production. The "we're different because we deal with life and death in health care" mentality is our arrogance. We say "We don't build automobiles." But if a family of four dies in an accident going down the freeway or a plane falls out of the sky, that's life or death, too. The fact is that in health care we make things. We're in a very special kind of industry, but we make things. We make office visits, surgical procedures, inpatient stays, lab tests, bills. When you make things, and you realize you make things, you begin to think of things as aggregations of processes. We began to realize that if we were serious about quality, a zero-defect product was possible, which in and of itself changed our thinking.

We were transformed. We came home saying: We can create zero-defect care. We can learn methods and tools that we can apply to everything. We said this will be our management system. It's not our quality improvement method. It's not how we do some projects. It's going to be how we're going to run our company.

Today it's a way of life. It's about vision. It's about compact. It's about a way of thinking. And it's about tools. When we said it's the management system, some of the first to resist were in finance. "Well, you know, we're finance, we don't have to do this." Wrong. Then it was the information technology people. "You know, we're programmers and computer whizzes, we don't have to do this." Wrong. Then it was critical care doctors. "This is fine for primary care, but we take care of really sick people." Wrong. What deploying it as a management system did was give us huge leverage so that we could actually train everybody in a common language, a common method.

Voices of Others

The Virginia Mason Production System gave me hope about being a doctor.—JL

We have a consistent management method that is holding a paradox—go slow to go fast; work with teams, which seems slow at first; standard work leads to creativity; trust to take risks. We can always get better. We get the facts from where the work is. We respect those who do the work. The gaps in our metrics from where we want to be energizes, not demoralizes, people—we ask "why?" We don't talk about money much—it is about the ROI—the return on investment for patients.—DS

The Virginia Mason Production System has committed leadership to a different role—to challenge the traditional assumptions regarding leaders, to change the mental model to move from scarcity of resources to value added to the patient, and to keep the diligence that everything comes back to that.—LC

He makes a few decisions that enable and encourage a lot of other actions. His work is highly liberating. He has a direction and stands by it even if there is discomfort. That consistency over time leads staff to believe that direction.—BC

He is courageous in holding other executives accountable—and he is willing to be held accountable, also.—AJ

Change Sponsorship ("We Change or We Die")

One of my biggest jobs in this organization has been that of change sponsor: to effectively sponsor and lead change. You really have to understand different motivations, career anchors, ways of thinking, and then flex your skills to work in those domains. I spend a lot of time working, practicing, and thinking about that. I'm also willing to take risks. I stood up in front of the physician group in October 2000 and said "We change or we die." It became clear we needed to modify our trajectory. We needed to figure out how we built on the great successes of the past but lead in a new direction.

Being a change sponsor means leading change and creating an environment conducive to change, helping move the organization forward in an adaptive, evolutionary, strategic way. As change sponsor, my job is to ensure that our people feel the urgency, that we have a shared vision, and that the vision is articulated and understood.

What is sustained is a focus on transformational change. The Virginia Mason Production System is a way of life that has tools in it. It is a critical competency within Virginia Mason Medical Center—it is our management system, and we train everyone. It is part of our change management—vision, compact, and method—all a construct for transformational change.

I have to walk the talk by articulating the vision, being on the shop floor, leading the work, knowing the tools, understanding what others do—not by delegating it but by doing it. That's what we are requiring of our leaders, and I've got to do that as well, to lead by example.

Change sponsorship as described here is different from traditional change management. A change sponsor places focus on transformational change based on vision, engaging everyone and providing skills to work differently—not delegating but seeing this as leaders' work, and leading by example. *Reflect on a large change for which you were responsible. Were the expected outcomes achieved? Were they sustained? What do those closest to the work involved in the change say about it? Do they say you welcomed disagreements and used them to get to better outcomes? What more can you do to demonstrate that the changes you seek begin with you?*

Voices of Others

He's very hands-on—he notices something you did to benefit patients, and he uses it in talks or to recognize people. It's a good way for a leader to stay in touch.—SM

In the past leaders would say "No diverts from the ED." Now, we don't have targets but we are challenged towards ideal. Now, diverts mean "patients don't have access to us." He doesn't provide the solution—he puts that back on the people who know the work.—VF

He's a great communicator—it's about what you say and how you listen. He's adept at processing information that fosters open dialogue. He listens well. He sets the tone.—LC

He welcomes others into the discussion, including those who disagree. He believes the disagreement will add to better decisions, not [present] an obstacle to be overcome.—SP

He demonstrates integrity every day. When the economy went bad and there were challenging questions in a leadership meeting, he listened respectfully and answered honestly.—CB

Complex problems are simplified so I can take action.—VF

He's open to questions and is accessible. I don't have to edit what I take to him. He stays out of the way and trusts me to do my job well. He coaches and knows the details but doesn't manage the details. He's not distant—to be informed you have to be close to the work.—LC

He has huge integrity. You always know he has your back.—JL

Living in Two Worlds and Cultural Learning

I think it is a false dichotomy, being a clinician, a member of the tribe, and part of the professional culture versus being leadership, management, the dark side, the suit. Early in my career I began to live in two worlds—one being that of leadership/management/business and the other being the professional culture of practicing clinical medicine. That false dichotomy plays to a we/they mentality, to physicians as victims of all the changes that are happening.

I believe that health care administrators are mission driven. There are a lot easier ways to make a good living by building a career in administration or business outside of health care. But because they want to be in a caring, helping profession, health care administrators chose to go into health care. I don't think many physicians get that, and so you're either one of us or one of them. I think we've torn down a lot of those barriers here. I think you need to have everybody bring something to the table. I also believe that administrators have much to offer in the clinical domain and that physicians have much to offer on the business and change management side of health care. Often, places that talk about that partnership really speak in terms of separate accountability. We believe that working together is not the Noah's Ark two-by-two program but joint accountability.

Voices of Others

Executive leaders are actively involved in improvement—it's not an option; I'm general counsel and I am leading a transition in care improvement.—LC

I am VP of Communications and Public Policy, and I was observing in the cath. lab yesterday as part of improvement work.—KP

Realigning the Deal

We also knew if we were going to change, that we had to realign the deal, the expectations, and that's when we got engaged in the physician compact work.

The old deal between physicians and health care organizations, although never written down, was alive and well at Virginia Mason and still is in most health care organizations: entitlement, protection, and autonomy. "I'm a physician. I'm entitled to patients because I joined a group. I've got a reputation. I'm protected from the environment by business managers, and I can do whatever I want whenever I want to because I'm a doctor. The buck stops with me. Only I know what's best for my patients." It didn't sync with the needed organizational change, evidence-based medicine, focusing on value, teamwork and collaboration, and patient safety. That's when we knew we needed a new compact.

As important as the words on the page was the process. More than a year of deep conversation led by a committee of frontline physicians brought a new compact. What are the expectations a physician should have from the organization, and what are the expectations the organization should have of the physicians? No sooner did we have a physician compact than our leaders said "We want a compact, too." So we have a leadership compact. We went through a comparable process. We talked about the expectations of the organization of its leaders and the expectation of the leaders, anybody from the CEO to frontline working supervisor, of the organization.

The type of changes reflected in the compacts did not come from traditional structured meetings but from a willingness to listen and learn from each other, to get to the heart of what is really important to all involved. Sustained dialogue on complex issues is a characteristic of many of the leaders profiled in this book, coupled with an ability to not compromise to fix a problem but to craft something completely new. *Have you been involved in conversations that lead to remarkably different outcomes than you had predicted? What helped most to create the environment for those conversations to happen?*

Voice of Others

Consistent behavior tells what the culture is about. You change the culture by saying what's important. There is a difference between having a compact and having key people using it.—JL

Joy in Developing Others

My greatest joy is mentoring these people who didn't even know they had this leadership spark, seeing skills in others they may not see. It's part of me showing up as a leader, paying attention, and being relationship based. I look for integrity and for interpreter skills of a sort so they can interpret for others what is going on. Interpretation is a key skill for leaders: the ability to articulate the vision and anything important so people can understand. If it is not communicated in a way people can understand, they won't see how it relates to them.

It is also about a person's warmth and ambition. It is putting opportunities out there for them and making a commitment to their passion for leadership. It's a no-brainer to support them through tough issues—they take on very challenging issues, but they're so good.

Leaders highlighted in this book frequently speak about spending time identifying current and future leaders—seeing something in them that they might not yet see in themselves and making it safe for them to try, learn, and fail. They genuinely care and learn about others, then spend time growing the capabilities of others through assigning new responsibilities in nontraditional areas, offering activities that are a stretch, or expanding current responsibilities to try on new ways of being a leader. *Have you experienced this type of growing experience provided by another leader? Are you engaged in providing that kind of experience for someone in your organization?*

Voices of Others

I was surprised—I hadn't thought of myself as a leader. It is who he is; he identifies people and helps them develop; he builds teams. He asked me: "If we need a leader in an area other than your specialty, would you take it on?" He's a mentor that helps you be who you are.—DS

When someone asks him for advice, he says "I think intuitively you know what to do." He wants you to think for yourself.—SM

I didn't seek out this role; Gary asked me. He helps others develop their careers and brings out the best. He's a coach matching work needs with a skill set.—AJ

He helps people develop what they can be, what they ought to be.—VF

I'm a leader by accident. He nudges. He is subtle, not condescending.—JL

"I'm here because of you"; that was his message to all staff after he was invited to the White House to talk about health care policy.—KP

He has humility. He is interested in what motivates people, very relationship based. He recently received a humanitarian award, and he invited four team members to join him; he said the award was to Virginia Mason, also; he shares the credit.—KP

A Good Day

A good day is an opportunity to get out where care is given—meeting with staff, learning about their concerns, sharing ideas, and observing what is going on. It's an opportunity to connect with others, to speak to the vision and get the perception that it's resonating with others. It's having frank conversations where challenges are openly discussed, where there is candor. It's when I can help another team reach their full potential, connect others to our story, and generate passion for our mission in our organization, regionally and nationally.

A Bad Day

A bad day is too many meetings with little accomplished, moving slowly, or avoiding issues in our work. It is conversations that are "all about me" and not about the patient or the mission.

Voices of Others

SM   Sue Morris, RN, *clinic nurse working with Gary*

DS   Donna Smith, MD, *medical director, Virginal Mason Hospital*

KP   Kathleen Paul, *vice president, Communications and Public Policy*

LC   Lynne Chafetz, *senior vice president, general legal council*

SP   Sarah Patterson, *executive vice president and chief operating officer*

CB   Connie Barnes, RN, *director, Acute Care Services*

AJ   Andrew Jacobs, MD, *chief medical officer*

VF   Val Ferris, RN, *administrative director, Kaizen Promotion Office*

JL   Joyce Lammert, MD, *chief, Department of Medicine*

BC   Bob Caplan, MD, *medical director, Quality*

4

Leadership as Learning: Maureen Bisognano

Maureen Bisognano, a registered nurse, joined the Institute for Healthcare Improvement (IHI) as executive vice president and chief operating officer in 1995. The organization was less than five years old and embarking on the ambitious aim to change health care based on improvement. Today, this still-small organization reaches millions globally as a testament to its commitment to improving health care worldwide. Maureen was named president and chief executive officer of the Institute for Healthcare Improvement in July 2010 after Donald Berwick was appointed administrator of the Centers for Medicare & Medicaid Services.

Maureen promotes a focus on strategic nongrowth—to reach many by leveraging IHI resources and not through the organization's own growth. Currently, more than 55 countries, 25,000 organizations, and millions of individuals are working with the 110 IHI staff members in some way.

Growing Up

I'm the oldest of nine kids, and maybe there're some leadership skills that come from that; needing to help my parents with the kids in a big Irish family. We are still very close. My mother was a nurse, and my father was a manager at IBM. It was very wonderful growing up, with lots of fun, lots of laughing, lots of conversation.

In my early twenties I was in nursing school when my brother got Hodgkin's disease. My mother and I took care of him for two

Background Information

President and Chief Executive Officer, Institute for Healthcare Improvement, Cambridge, Massachusetts
www.ihi.org

Organizational Vision and Mission

Who we are: IHI is a reliable source of energy, knowledge, and support for a never-ending campaign to improve health care worldwide. The Institute helps accelerate change in health care by cultivating promising concepts for improving patient care and turning those ideas into action.

What we will accomplish: We aim to improve the lives of patients, the health of communities, and the joy of the health care workforce by focusing on an ambitious set of goals adapted from the Institute of Medicine's six improvement aims for the health care system: Safety, Effectiveness, Patient-Centeredness, Timeliness, Efficiency, and Equity. We call this the "No Needless List":

- *No needless deaths*
- *No needless pain or suffering*
- *No helplessness in those served or serving*
- *No unwanted waiting*
- *No waste*
- *No one left out*

Institute for Healthcare Improvement Information

- Based in Cambridge, Massachusetts, IHI was founded in 1991 to assist health care organizations to achieve better outcomes. It was preceded in 1986 by the National Demonstration Project on Quality Outcomes in Healthcare.
- Stages of IHI's development from 1986 to 2009:
  —Awareness: Building the will for change and the conviction that improvement is possible
  —Education: Building the capacity for change through knowledge exchange and training

—Collaborative improvement: Working together to spread best practices and yield breakthrough results

—Redesign: Moving beyond best practice to innovative designs based on novel concepts

—Movement: Unifying the industry around the common cause of improving health care for all

—Full scale: Changing mainstream practice standards by ensuring widespread deployment

- The Open School launched in 2008—"an interprofessional educational community giving you the skills to be a change agent in health care" for health professions students. The intent is to provide content that students may not learn in their health professions program.

Selected Results for IHI

- Open School, launched in 2008, by September 2009:
  —10,000 students, 1,600 faculty and deans newly registered on IHI.org
  —Chapters in 36 states, 19 countries, and 161 campuses
- The 100,000 Lives and 5 Million Lives campaigns contributed to significant improvement nationally and measured its progress against four explicit aims:
  1. Avoid 5 million instances of harm in participating hospitals over two years.
     - An estimated 207,000 unnecessary deaths were avoided.
  2. Enroll more than 4,000 hospitals in the initiative.
     - 4,054 hospitals were enrolled, representing more than 80 percent of hospital beds in the United States.
  3. Strengthen the campaign's national infrastructure for change and transform it into a national asset.
     - In the absence of a formal, national health care system, IHI has been able to develop a network of national partners, nodes, mentor hospitals, and more than 4,000 U.S. hospitals.

----

4. Raise the profile of the problem of variability in the quality of U.S. health care—and hospitals' proactive response
to it—with a larger, public audience.
  • The 5 Million Lives Campaign garnered more than
    55 million media hits and published twelve studies in
    peer-reviewed publications.

Individual Recognitions for Maureen Bisognano
  • 2008: Elected to the Institute of Medicine
  • 2005: Appointed to the Commonwealth Fund's Commission
    on a High Performance Health System

---

years. He died just after his twenty-first birthday. The firstborn
of the grandchildren had a DPT reaction and died within twenty-
four hours, which was really a tragic error. Three years later my
father died of colon cancer when he was fifty-three. Everybody
in our family had roles to play; everybody had a contribution to
make. That gave the family a very strong sense of teamness—
coming together when there was a personal crisis in the family
meant that everyone had their part. For instance, my youngest
sister, age nine, would do my brother's foot rubs every day.

Influences—People and Situations

I think these early experiences in caring for my own family
members in the way that they wanted to be cared for and then in
dealing with the personal consequences of medical error really
shaped my future. Not immediately, but years downstream.

My father comes to mind first. He's the first person I think
about who influenced me. My mother drew me to nursing, but
my father pushed a lot; he just had infinite faith in his kids.

I was working as assistant director of nursing when we
brought in a management company—a very value-laden company. They hired me to be the vice president of nursing, and
then the chief operating officer at that hospital, and later to be
the CEO of another hospital in Massachusetts. There I found
not so much a single mentor but a system for nurturance of

leaders that was really effective. The CEO of the system had every one of our pictures on his wall—he knew us personally.

They knew about each of us. If somebody wasn't good at public speaking then at the next event, wouldn't you know, you would show up on the agenda to give a lecture! There was mentoring and support to create success. They were constantly challenging you. They created a set of experiences in addition to the educational sessions that gave you confidence, exposure, skills, and a new way of viewing things, so that the vast majority of us succeeded.

Four times a year we would meet together for a deep learning session. It might be the latest issues in financial management, and certainly it was about quality. They set up a whole quality division, and all of us were focused on our quality metrics before the rest of the industry. I remember we had a session on ethics lasting several days. It was a conversation that started with "Are you ethical?" and everybody would say "Well, of course!" Next they asked "Would you ever willingly hurt somebody?" "No!" Then they got it down to "Would you ever park in a parking space that wasn't legal?" "Would you ever not pay your parking meter because you thought you wouldn't get caught?" They got it down to very tangible day-to-day decisions that helped us understand the totality of an ethical life. It was part of four weeks a year of deep immersion into our value system.

In my very first week as CEO at Massachusetts Respiratory Hospital, I got a call from Paul Batalden [physician, noted quality improvement expert]. He asked me to join a program that he and Don Berwick [physician, former president and CEO of IHI, now administrator of the Centers for Medicare & Medicaid Services] cooked up—the National Demonstration Project on Industrial Quality in Healthcare. They had the idea that in other industries, if the executive team didn't like their performance— cost, customer satisfaction, product quality—they knew how to improve it. In health care we had this helpless feeling as if quality happened to us. The project matched twenty industry leaders and twenty health care CEOs for eight months to see whether the hospital executives could learn from other industries. Paul paired me with Florida Power and Light, the electric utility in Miami. I was a new CEO when I went to visit them. I asked "How do you improve quality?" They did not answer; they only asked me questions, and the questions were so enlightening that over the next month they guided me to work through a problem I had had at the hospital and got an amazing result. The problem was about agency nursing. The reason I picked it was because as I looked through the budget I found the largest line item variance was agency nursing. The people from the electric company guided me toward eliminating agency nursing within eight months. At the end of the journey I sat at my desk and I remember thinking: If I hadn't done this, what would I have done instinctively as a CEO with the budget variance? And I realized it would have been 180 degrees different in every way, in every process, and with poorer results.

The first question the Florida Power and Light executives asked me was "Why do you have this big variance?" I said "I don't know." So back at the ranch I started to work with the team about why we had this big variance. We had so many nurses leaving that it led to an increasing reliance on agency nursing. I started talking to staff nurses, head nurses, and the VP of Nursing, asking "Why are the nurses leaving?" They were leaving to go work for the agency because they could get higher hourly rates and they could pick their own hours. We then started to parse the process, looking at the hourly rate issue, hours issue, work situation issue, and relationships with the doctors. I interviewed the medical staff, and they said they couldn't stand it when agency nurses came in because it was not reliable. The patients didn't like it because they never knew who they were going to get. And the nurses didn't like it because the agency nurses were making more money. Nobody was happy except the agency nurses, and even they weren't that happy. I asked the union "Will you partner with me on this?" I offered to give a three-year raise if the union would partner with me on recruiting the nurses back. We eliminated agency nursing, recruited nurses back, outcomes were better, doctors were happier, patients were happier, and nurses were happier.

At the end of the day, I sat there at my desk and thought: Suppose I had called in the VP of Nursing and I had said to her "You're a million dollars over budget. How do you propose to fix this?" and she said "I've got a great idea, let's give everybody a raise," I would have thought "Get out of here!" In no way would I have gone on that journey. I would have very likely said "Let's bring in somebody who knows how to manage the budget." They would probably have used fewer nurses, which would have increased complications and decreased satisfaction. It was a great learning experience from an electric company.

Maureen's story of solving a financial problem and addressing quality, safety, and staff engagement problems at the same time shows the interdependency in complex systems. And the optimal solution was counterintuitive. *If you were to draw two columns labeled "Standard" and "Maureen" to contrast the two approaches, what three characteristics of problem solving would you put in each column? What column best illustrates your problem-solving style? Is it the one you will continue to choose having had this reflection?*

I was a firm believer that improvement worked in health care; I had a clear sense that we could do better. I was at this tiny chronic disease hospital, and executives from Henry Ford [Health System, Detroit] and Sister Mary Jean Ryan from SSM [Health Care, St. Louis; see chapter 9] asked if we could share information so their senior teams could learn from us. I started to get a sense that there was a lot of curiosity and that the story of what we had built, together with people from the demonstration project, could help a broader number of people.

Pathway to Health Care

I went to nursing school because being the oldest of nine kids, I had to pay for my own college. My mother was a nurse, so I looked at my mother. I looked at my father, who had a different degree. Nursing school at that time was $300 a year, so I could afford that with a loan.

My first job in a hospital was working as a unit secretary to make the money to pay back the nursing school loan. My second year of nursing school I was a nursing assistant. I did those jobs as I worked through my nursing school career. When I graduated with my diploma I began to think that I wanted to get more education, so I got an associate's degree, then a bachelor's degree, and then a master's degree.

When I first started working, I wanted to be a midwife, but it wasn't legal then, so I went to work in the operating room and I volunteered as a doula, a labor coach for women. I learned different methods of providing health care: in the more traditional methods by working in the operating room and then being a labor coach at night working as more of a healing, non-traditional health care resource.

Pathway to Leadership

I went from operating room nurse to the intensive care unit to staff development to vice president of nursing and then became chief operating officer, all at the same hospital where I started as a unit secretary. Fourteen years after I graduated from nursing school I went off to become CEO of another hospital.

I had this passion to innovate, but I didn't have a position by which I had the kind of credibility to do so. I was surrounded by people who trusted me, and that surely shaped my leadership style. For example, I was an ICU staff nurse and heard about this new thing called progressive care. It was one step down from the ICU but more care than on medical-surgical units.

We didn't have that, so I met with the CEO. I said "I'm hearing about this, and we've got bottlenecks at the ICU. I know if we invested some technology and higher levels of nursing care we could move those patients more quickly." In my own experience, my father had had a myocardial infarction [MI] when he was forty-nine, and I knew how safe he felt in the ICU and that when he was moved to a medical-surgical floor he was terrified. He was so afraid when hours would go by with no staff in the room, he was sure he was going to have another MI and nobody was going to be there. These personal experiences and the courage of the leaders to let this staff nurse walk into the CEO's office and say "I think we could do this" was amazing. They said "Okay, go ahead and do it." I was always struck by the trust that the leaders had, the faith in the people who were willing to try things.

Trust—based not on a position or title but on the merit of the idea and its link to patient care—is a common theme among the leaders profiled in this book. *Who in the past year in your organization would say you took the risk to trust them when they had a novel idea to solve a problem? If someone three levels removed from your role approached you with a novel idea that required an element of trust to accomplish, what would you do? What have you done?*

My early years were probably characterized by two things. One is amazing people who trusted me to try things. Two was always a sense of optimism and possibility. I could never figure out why people were afraid of things. I thought that failure might happen, but the upside possibility was just so attractive to me. It might have been a part of growing up. You grow up with very few resources and lots of competition for those there are, but we all succeeded.

My CEO at that time was not from health care. He had been a politician, and he was appointed CEO of this city hospital. Some leaders, particularly from outside of health care, are looking for people who are confident and innovative and putting them in positions where you would never think they would thrive. They do it because they themselves didn't come through a normal career progression.

A few years later, our city-owned hospital was in very bad financial trouble. The mayor put together a task force and asked me to join it—I was assistant director of Nursing, very middle level. The next thing you know I'm meeting with politicians, with health care leaders, and with people around the city. We did open meetings and decided we didn't want to close the hospital, nor did we want to sell it; we wanted to rescue it. That meant bringing in a management company. It was an amazing experience for a young person!

Did I set out to become a CEO? No way! I never in a million years expected it. I think probably the number one question I get asked from young women is How did you do that? I'm sure they assume that there was a tactic that I used. I didn't ever aspire to be a CEO. I only ever aspired to joy in my current job.

"Joy in my current job" is rarely voiced as a career aspiration. *Do you think this aspiration opens different career doors? Do you know someone who finds joy in his or her current job? What actions and behaviors communicate that joy?*

I have loved every job I had. I worked hard at it, enjoyed it, and I found that frequently I had an idea that I could do my current job a better way. Looking back, every time I did that, although I wasn't planning a change, somebody would say "Well, what about this opportunity?" It was all serendipity, none of it planned.

I met Dr. Joseph Juran [quality improvement pioneer], and in 1991 he recruited me to set up a global health care practice at the Juran Institute. I set up the health care practice globally and started working around the world in guiding innovative leaders to improve results.

Don Berwick recruited me to come to IHI at a time when the organization was young. I remember sitting with Don in the interview and I asked about the job. He said "Whatever you want to do." It was very clear from the first meeting that we would partner in making the Institute a success. That sense of trust and freedom was an amazing gift to me. It has influenced my leadership style, to know that people do best when you open up the doors and allow them to make their own mistakes.

"Whatever you want to do" is a compelling concept. *What would you do in your current organization if someone made that offer to you?*

What's Important to Me as a Leader

Culture

One key fact is that Don [Berwick] and I have managed IHI as a team. Don and I approach leadership of IHI as a team— we manage the culture and processes of leadership always as a team. We focus very strongly on the culture that we believe in. We have a set of operating values and what we call The Reputation, which is what we hope people from outside would say about IHI. Those two documents, the values and The Reputation, became touchstones for us. We surround ourselves with people who can thrive in this culture. We focus very strongly on a culture of engagement and joy in work. At IHI we have a very strong culture, and we work to find like-minded, like-value people in the world, and we have used that approach to change, as opposed to growth.

The culture trumps the individual skills. The most important thing is the mission of the organization and the culture. We hire people who enjoy the culture, then we let them use their own gifts, their own approaches, their skills, freely with regular connections between all of us. Some people walk in here and they get hives because they want their private space.

They wouldn't thrive here. When we interview people we use that set of values to ask "Could you thrive here?"

In one case, we were working in collaboration with another organization and the project wasn't going well at all. We had our team and theirs in a meeting. I suspected it might be a conflict of culture. I put up our values on the wall and I said to the other team "Tell me your values, and let's see how they match up." Our first value is teamwork and boundarylessness; we have one global brain. All of IHI has one big brain, and everybody's job is to pour their knowledge into that brain. The other organization said: "Oh, that's just the opposite here. You get promoted at this organization because you know something nobody else knows. So we would never share. You hold your assets, because it is your ticket to the future." I said "Our next value is speed and agility." They said: "We would never be fast; that's reckless. We're contemplative. We make sure we're right. We make sure that we prove a case, that we've got trials, that we've studied something before we publish it." The exercise helped people understand each other and why it was proving so hard to work together.

Maureen described a conversation in which she aided in discovering the differences in two cultures with openness and intent to learn, not judge. *What cultures are you working with that could benefit from a conversation about what culturally stands in the way of true collaboration? What about between a group of physicians, a group of nurses, or a group of administrators?*

You lead through the culture and values. You can't have processes for every eventuality in a complex organization, so you give a sense of direction through the culture and people will know what to do. I nurture the culture on a daily basis, especially with new people and programs. It can erode very quickly.

Helping others innovate is letting them be with time, space, and funding along with freedom and trust *and* also having a structured approach for research and development so freedom and structure operate at the same time. When people lean on traditional management tools, they put people into boxes and they underutilize their assets. When people ask me "Can I look at the organization chart?" I say we don't have one. I ask them why they need one. People say "We need to know who reports to whom." If you need a chart to tell you that, then you have a deeper problem of communication that a chart will not fix.

Voices of Others

Senior managers always say they give support but rarely do. She does.—SB

She advises me so that the systems I help develop are consistent with the culture, that the paths to the end results are consistent with the culture. It's not about the systems; it's about what the systems are supporting.—SB

As part of paying attention to the culture, she pays special attention to the professional development of young staff by mentoring and coaching. It might be just two minutes in the hall, but it adds up.—SB

She really cares about others. She puts feelings of respect for the individual in the forefront, even with tough issues. She won't avoid tough issues; she takes them on directly.—SB

She's taught me to think about how I want people to feel when they go out of the room rather than focusing on having an agenda.—CM

She can read a room and know what's needed at that time, when there needs to be necessary tension.—CM

She pairs emotion with action, and she is attuned to red flags.—CM

She translates what a topic means for everyone. She makes things practical.—CM

She obsesses about the culture of the organization—at the individual and team levels. She has a sense of the organization and worries about what changes will mean.—PC

She takes the time to personally be with people.—PC

Connecting to Mission

People very much need to be reconnected to why they came. People tell stories about patients that had been healed by us, patients that had been failed by us. We find motivation in reconnecting to the mission. I have learned how to say no when people ask me to work with a group and used the words *convince* or *persuade* or *change* another group. When they say we're curious about how to get better; when I can give them a sense of what the picture could look like, it fosters a sense of optimism and possibility, which is a more natural way for me to go.

It's the mission that is the number one thing that gives me energy. The idea that we can improve health care is very powerful and motivating for me. That is why we're here. My friends say to me "I have a job, but you have a mission." In the crush of daily work and frenetic pace, we can end up with a heads-down task focus. We don't lift our heads up to see and understand how important health care is to people. We need the space to tell the story, the meaning this has in our lives. As leaders, we need to hold a view of the larger system, to see the organization in a larger context.

Connecting to the purpose of the organization is consistent with these leaders. They also developed skills in connecting people to the purpose and help them see where they fit in the larger picture of the mission. *What skills do you have to connect others to purpose? How have you tested and developed those skills over the past six months? How well are you doing? How do you know?*

Voices of Others

She's always asking questions. She is clear on where IHI is going and pushing to the next level. She's thoughtful and challenging so you can apply it to your work.—CM

She doesn't provide solutions; there's rarely a mandate. She respects the expertise at all levels.—CM

Transparency

Transparency is very important because the number one value is teamwork and boundarylessness, which means that everybody works together as a team. Our physical co-location is very helpful in making sure that we are on the same page.

The culture's very strong. We try to represent that visually in the work space. In our office there's Don, me, three IHI fellows, and senior fellows that come in and out. We have seven people on average in an office that's the size of a normal executive office. Nobody here has their own office, and everything is glass so the view is open to all.

The way it works is if Don and I are having a meeting, any of the IHI fellows who are in the room and are interested are welcome to turn their chair around and join in the conversation. They always add value—always. When they turn their chair into the meeting, we turn up our ears to what they are going to say because it's going to be great.

Strategic Nongrowth

We have a huge mission at IHI to change health care worldwide. Don and I decided on a strategic approach that we would not grow. We would stay small, and we would operate through leverage and through our culture. We studied other organizations that grew very quickly. We saw that growth, not change, became the objective. Where revenue or growth became the aspiration, organizations started to become beholden to themselves and they lost sight of the mission. Growth becomes the conversation, the number one strategy. It takes over from "How are we doing with the mission?"

The right column in our strategic plan is the aging column. We put programs in the aging column when we are doubtful about their contribution to the mission. It's very hard to do. I have to force things into the aging column because staff are working on projects they like. If the program is in the aging column we have a year to either reconceptualize or it goes into the furthest right-hand column, defunct. My job is forcing things to the right. If we're not going to grow, we're going to have to make room for new concepts, so we've got to keep pushing stuff to the right in order to give staff the leeway and the freedom to take on new projects. Leaders in other industries are better at stopping things than we are in health care.

It gives me courage that a tiny organization with a hundred people can reach millions effectively. It gives me courage to stay small. Otherwise, as a leader I may be tempted to try and force our way into different terrain in order to keep revenues up. It's the optimism and the effective application of new ideas that give me courage.

Strategic nongrowth is unique to most organizations, especially in health care where growth is an engine that feeds the definition of success. *If you adopted a nongrowth strategy for your organization or part of the organization, in what ways would you need to think and act differently?*

Voice of Others

She has amazing financial discipline. She manages growth very carefully; exceeding our revenue is not a good thing. It's about the growth and scale of the organization, not just limiting resources as a means of preventing growth.—PC

Creating the Future

In the next office is a group of eight staff people from every area of IHI. They are working in a glass-walled room called Future Works. Their job is to design the future. They've got sticky notes all over the walls, Magic Marker writing all over the windows, and they're creating the future of IHI. It's fun to look in there and see what great things are going to come out.

Leadership as Learning

My philosophy is that leaders need to learn every day. I assess that by looking at how often leaders ask questions versus how often they give answers. Leadership is learning. It's being open to the gifts of the people who work in your organization.

> Leadership is about learning from everyone—inside and outside the organization. Maureen assesses the appetite for learning in a leader by looking at how often they ask questions versus give answers. *We invite you to keep a log for a week with two columns—(1) asked a question and (2) gave an answer—and note the frequency of each.*

The more that we as leaders open ourselves to what's really happening on the front line, we are closing that gap between the front office and the front line. It gives leaders courage and ideas. It is an honest inquiry, creating a culture that says we value everybody's assets in this organization and together we can solve these issues faster than any one person can by themselves.

We wanted to learn from executives outside health care. The lesson learned was that as health care leaders we can't afford to stay in the front office. We can't afford to avoid the rich interactions with the front line. It has reinforced the need for executives to meet with patients. Once they have developed the methods and processes for doing that, it engages and energizes them like nothing else I can think of.

There are some other leadership lessons to be learned. Leaders can become less patient with the status quo as they connect with patients and with the workforce and when they really see the full impact of defects—the harm, the human cost of defect, as well as the financial cost. I believe they will more and more reach out to try and find new ways to lead, as are courageous leaders who are making huge differences in today's systems.

What we learned about successful leaders was systems thinking—a clear picture of where they stand compared to the best and of the gap in performance. They will do what it takes to understand the gap and have a picture in mind of how to close it. They will expect big changes, not one small project. When I talked about an infection and the human costs, other leaders would say "We didn't do it on purpose." I said "Yes, we did." We are responsible for the systems that made that happen.

Voices of Others

She's wicked smart and thinks deeply about issues. She's a fantastic storyteller who uses narrative so well.—DB

She thinks above and outside the moment. She frames a more powerful view that offers more daylight.—DB

The twenty-four hour rule shows how she uses time well. She knows when to wait twenty-four hours to make a decision.—DB

She's really smart and reads and scans a lot. She studies other organizations to learn from them.—PC

It's about Team

I'm embarrassed to be even sitting here because I don't think leadership is about a person. It's about the team. It's because of the rest of the leadership team and the culture of the Institute that we engage the energy of all.

It is a group of people who have different skills and different backgrounds but who enjoy working in the same culture. Sometimes people will want me as the COO to make a decision. When they're asking me to make a decision it's oftentimes because they want to go in one direction and somebody else on the team wants to go in another direction. I often resist jumping in and making the decision because it is the easy way out. It doesn't create a greater sense of teamness. We'll often work through those kinds of important decisions painfully slowly to make sure that everybody is heard and that people can get on board with the decision.

It's why I shouldn't be sitting here by myself; it's a partnership. When people come into IHI they expect a normal division of labor, and when they don't see it they find it a little bit confusing. People who come here learn that sense of teamness.

And that sense of teamness extends to the joyous people we get to work with around the world. Together something amazing is going to happen. I can feel the sense of possibility and promise for patients and communities. For example, we have been working on a project with Common Ground, a 501(c)(3) organization whose mission is to end homelessness. We are working on the homeless in New York City with an incredible group of people who give us energy. Just look into the next room and you can see these young people, mainly from other industries, who are sitting with those with clinical expertise talking about how to improve health care, how can they help the homeless in New York City.

Voices of Others

It's pairing the right team, knowing what is needed to balance your skills. She understands different styles and matching styles with needs.—CM

She's the bridge between the practical, in the present, today camp and the visionary, tomorrow, future camp. With the bridging she gets people excited about the future and decreases the anxiety so you can handle it. She gives us the room to change.—CM

Values

We developed the IHI values. They're not personal values, they're organizational values. Don and I developed them in one long car trip and presented them to the staff. We didn't go through one of those year-long processes. The staff added one value: celebration and thankfulness. They saw that we need to look back and celebrate what we have built and be thankful with one another.

We have the IHI Olympics, where we create teams of people who don't normally work together. I was on a team with a person from IT, with a new co-op student, and somebody from finance; all levels were mixed together. Six weeks before the Olympics each team got a value and assignments. We had weekly meetings with our team with activities that made us very bonded. It's fiercely competitive with lots of fun—we celebrate our values as a team all day at the Olympics.

Voices of Others

The most important aspect is the operating values she uses. It is the way to be in an organization.—DB

There's a "thereness" when she's with others. She will swivel her chair, move in, and doesn't look at her computer while listening.—DB

She is always interested in you as a person before the task. It is the basis for the task work. She has a great sensing ability about you as an individual.—DB

She is terrific at leading with the positive. It gives the good feelings and confidence to tackle the tough issues. She will then move to where we can be better by saying: "We need to think about this" or "Did you try this?"—DB

Some might say you use economic downtimes to get rid of "deadwood." Maureen would not tolerate that. She would say if we have people not doing their job, we need to work with their supervisor to help them.—PC

A Good Day

Every day's different, which I love. I don't have a routine or a rhythm. Today's a great day. Yesterday was a great day. I love to come in early in the morning and have quiet time before anybody gets here. My whole workday is with people, and I find that energizing, not draining. A good day is experiences with different projects around the world. Friday was a great day because the leaders from the National Health Services Institute for Innovation and Improvement were here and we were planning how to work on improvement in all of England, Scotland, and Wales. One of the leaders brought his daughter, who's going to medical school, and I had so much fun with her thinking through some projects she's working on in health care: How do you create social change? How do you get activation across the country? My day's great today because I met with the Future Works team.

A Bad Day

Two things come to mind. One is the economy and watching everybody in health care struggle. It's tough. It forces us to be creative and think about new ways to work. Watching people suffer because of the economy is tough but inspiring in a different way. Second, the bad days are around conflicts in culture or a failure of the culture or when we're working with people whose cultures are very different.

Voices of Others

SB   Steve Brown, *vice president, Human Resources, IHI*

CM   Christina Gunter Murphy, *project manager, IHI*

PC   Penny Carver, *senior vice president, IHI*

DB   Don Berwick, *former president and chief executive officer of IHI, now administrator of the Centers for Medicare & Medicaid Services*

5

Much Done, Still a Long Way to Go: Mike Murphy

Mike Murphy was named president and chief executive officer of Sharp HealthCare in 1996. Sharp is a not-for-profit, multi-hospital, integrated health system with more than 14,000 employees and 2,600 affiliated physicians in San Diego. Mike joined Sharp as a chief financial officer (CFO) in one of the hospitals in 1991. Prior to joining Sharp, he spent thirteen years working as a certified public accountant.

In 2000, Sharp HealthCare looked in the mirror and acknowledged that it was a good organization in an underperforming industry. This acknowledgment set it on the road to transformation through what became known as The Sharp Experience. Sharp was a recipient of the Malcolm Baldrige National Quality Award, Health Care Category, in 2007.

Growing Up

I have lived in California since I was two and San Diego since I was five. I have five sisters and a brother, a family that was very close, and still is. Our parents were very supportive, very loving, and worked really hard to make sure that all seven children could do things that they felt were important to do, whether it was sports or cheerleading or dance. The influential people in my life growing up were clearly my parents, my brothers and sisters. I think some of the formative stuff that went on around me was related to sports, related to teamwork in sports, related to hard work. I had some great coaches along the way who focused me on hard work and the need to work together as a team.

Background Information

CEO,
Sharp HealthCare,
San Diego
www.sharp.com

Organizational Vision

To transform the health care experience and make Sharp the

- *Best Place for Employees to Work*
- *Best Place for Physicians to Practice Medicine*
- *Best Place for Patients to Receive Care*

And ultimately to become

- *The Best Health Care System in the Universe*

Organizational Mission

To improve the health of those we serve with a commitment to excellence in all that we do. Our goal is to offer quality care and programs that set community standards, exceed patients' expectations and are provided in a caring, convenient, cost-effective and accessible manner.

Sharp Information

- Sharp HealthCare is the largest integrated delivery system in San Diego County, California, and the parent company of all Sharp entities. The Donald N. Sharp Memorial Community Hospital opened in 1955 to provide general hospital care for San Diego residents. Today, the Sharp system consists of four acute care hospitals, three specialty hospitals, two affiliated medical groups, a health plan, four long-term care facilities, a liability insurance company, and two philanthropic foundations.
- Licensed to operate 1,870 beds, Sharp provides care to approximately 785,000 individuals annually, including more than 350,000 health maintenance organization enrollees.

Selected Results for Sharp

- 2010: Sharp HealthCare was recognized by *Modern Healthcare* in its 100 Top Integrated Healthcare Networks ranking as number six in the country and number one in California.
- 2009: For the third year in a row, readers of the *San Diego Union-Tribune* recognized Sharp HealthCare as San Diego's Best Hospital in the newspaper's Best of San Diego Readers' Poll.
- 2008: Sharp Memorial achieved Magnet designation.
- 2008: Sharp HealthCare ranked fifth in the large company–size category of California's Best Places to Work.
- 2007: Sharp HealthCare received the Baldrige Award for health care.
- 2007: Sharp Grossmont Hospital achieved Magnet designation.
- 2007: Sharp Coronado Hospital was honored as one of the first five hospitals nationwide to receive the Planetree Patient-Centered Hospital recognition; Planetree is a not-for-profit organization at the forefront of the health care industry's patient-centered care movement.

Individual Recognitions for Mike Murphy

- 2009: Named Non-Profit Corporate Director of the Year by the Corporate Directors Forum
- 2008: Received the Heritage Award from the American Ireland Fund
- 2007: Received the CEO Information Technology Achievement Award from *Modern Healthcare* and the Healthcare Information and Management Systems Society
- 2007: Received the Leadership in Action Award from the Mental Health Association of America of San Diego
- 2005: Served as chairman of the San Diego Regional Chamber of Commerce
- 2003: Served as grand marshal of the San Diego St. Patrick's Day Parade

Big factors growing up, I think, were one, seven kids; two, we were, and do remain, very attached to our faith, which is the Catholic faith. My dad ran, and my brother still runs, a car dealership. I think I just had great role models in both my dad and my mom. My mom was, until I got out of high school, more of the traditional stay-at-home mom, making sure the seven of us were on the right track. My dad worked lots of hours to make sure we had enough to do the things we needed to do.

I think I was fortunate to grow up in the family I grew up in. Fortunate to have the parents I had and the values they instilled in all of us. What our parents modeled the most was working hard to do the right thing for their children and to do the right thing in the way they interacted with people.

Influences—People and Situations

When we moved to San Diego, my dad bought an automobile dealership that my brother still runs. Automobile dealerships don't necessarily have the best reputation, but I would say that in the business community in Oceanside and Carlsbad, where his business was, my father was seen as someone of high integrity, known for valuing his employees, valuing his customers, valuing his community, and most of all valuing his family.

I always admired the way my dad treated his employees. I also always admired the way he treated his customers and the way he was engaged in the community. There is no question that he has been my role model. If I could live my life the way he lived his, I would be happy, and that is what I try to do. My mom was very influential, especially in instilling in all of us how to treat our friends and others in the right way.

My sisters, my brother, and I are still close and very supportive. I had the luxury and fortunate ability to stay here in San Diego, get married, and raise three daughters. And family is what I am focused on in addition to my organization, what we do here at Sharp HealthCare.

The sport I played the most was football, and I was an offensive lineman, a position in which you are certainly not there for yourself. You are a key cog in the team, and you recognize that everybody needs to do their part or the quarterback, the running back, or the wide receiver is not going to be able to score the touchdown. No one told me that I needed to learn teamwork; it was always there.

Learning to work successfully in teams often begins early in life in a variety of activities. *When you were growing up, was teamwork a strong presence, or was individual achievement more of a presence? In what ways do those experiences shape your leadership even today?*

Pathway to Health Care

I went to college at Long Beach State [California State University, Long Beach] and played four years of football. Fortunately, my family had instilled in me that I'd better get a degree, and I majored in business. I had aspirations for football to last longer than it did. When it ended I got a job working for a large public accounting firm on the West Coast that specialized in health care in its San Diego office.

I began my public accounting career in San Diego at a regional firm that specialized in health care. The more I worked in health care—and I worked in health care finance—the more I enjoyed it. I became good at understanding the intricacies of Medicare and Medi-Cal [California's state Medicaid program], understanding the way a hospital operated or a health care provider needed to operate. I became very familiar with the people who work in health care, who I think are special people. The more I interacted with them and played a role in what they were doing to try to be successful, the more I saw health care as having a special purpose with worthwhile work that was making a difference. As I worked with organizations to try to either finance something or get involved in building a new cancer center or do a joint venture together with physicians, I became intrigued by the people, what they do and why they do it. I continued to get more clients and continued to work across more health care organizations. I became a health care guy even when I was with a large accounting firm where there were not many people fully dedicated to the health care industry.

When it came to decide what I wanted to do next, I had an opportunity here at Sharp. I also had some opportunities outside of California, but my wife and I decided we wanted to stay here. It was natural to go to Sharp, and I started as CFO of Sharp Grossmont Hospital. Seeing more closely what actually happens there each and every day—the way people interact, touch, impact patients and families, and have the ability to make a difference—solidified my commitment to health care.

My work has become even more energizing and fulfilling, and, as I've said many times to others, although truthfully I am over there on the sideline, I get gratification by helping our organization do things that allow our people to make a difference for the patients and the community that they touch.

Pathway to Leadership

My progress in leadership was not an intentional career plan. I do not feel that I have been called to be a CEO. I believe I have been called to do my best whatever I am working on, inside or outside of work. And I expect that of myself. I question myself every day. Am I doing the best that I can do? Am I doing the things that I should be doing? And I know I can be doing better and should be doing better in all aspects of my life—as a father, as a husband, and as a CEO.

There was a reorganization at Sharp in 1993, and all of the CFO positions in all of the hospitals were eliminated, including mine. Because I enjoyed Sharp and wanted to stay in San Diego, I applied for the system vice president of Financial

Services position at Sharp, and I got it. Over the next couple years some of the leadership of Sharp who did not know me well began to see that I could bring more value than they had recognized before. I was promoted to senior vice president of Business Development, which put me in charge of all of the big financings, all of the exploration of deals, buying or disposing of big segments of our business, and gave me exposure to the board. And still this wasn't a career path. I didn't say I wanted to be senior vice president of Business Development. The CEO offered it to me and it sounded exciting.

Mike believes he is called on to do the best in whatever he does—he demands much of himself and sees that he can do better. *Do you demand a lot of yourself as a leader and often find yourself falling short in your eyes? In what ways is this an inspiration, and in what ways can it be a drain on your energy?*

In 1996, Sharp was in the midst of a difficult time. We had lost money for a couple years and the organization was considering entering into a partnership agreement with Hospital Corporation of America. The CEO stepped down and the board called me and asked me if I would step in as interim CEO while they did a search. As the search went on, I think both the board and I started saying that we have lots of great people who could do much of what an outsider could do. A few months after I became interim CEO they asked me to take the position permanently.

Even when they asked me to be interim CEO I went home saying "Do I want to do this?" There is some family history to this. In the early 1970s during the gas crisis, my dad had to downsize his car dealership to just a few people. He was going to night school to figure out how he could get a real estate license so he could continue to afford to support seven kids, three of whom were in college. I saw how taxing that was on him, and I told myself that I never want to be in charge, that I never want that pressure. But the fact is that when anybody in my family gets into something, they can't be a "9- to 5-er."

We are wired to give it our all. I accepted the CEO position. I believed I could do the job well.

Right away we had to make very hard decisions. I was doing the kinds of things I had said I did not want to have to do: We announced we were closing a hospital; we announced we were selling a hospital; we closed a skilled nursing facility; we closed our residency program. It was very challenging. But it was the right thing to do to help the organization get where it needed to go.

Fortunately, we didn't have to continue to make those kinds of decisions for long before we returned to financial stability. However, there are always challenging decisions to be faced; we recently sold a medical group. It pained me to have to stand in front of those people and tell them "You are not going to be part of Sharp anymore." I am sure many of them still don't really understand why. But the leaders of Sharp, including the board and the leadership team, believe it was the right thing to do to put Sharp and the medical group in the best position for the long term.

> Making difficult decisions that you believe are right yet affect many people in a very personal way are some of the toughest leadership actions. *When it comes to doing the right thing by making hard decisions, how much do you draw strength from within, and how much from others? How do you approach a difficult decision—what steps do you take to ensure it is right?*

What's Important to Me as a Leader

Integrity, Being Real, and Visibility

I think it is crucial to have integrity, to be real to your organization, and to be visible and accessible. [That means] remaining open and honest with the organization—about where we are and where we're going; when it's hard, being okay saying it's hard; when we're doing well, congratulating the team; telling them we've got to do better when we've got to do better, helping them understand decisions when they might not seem to make sense to everyone in the organization; acknowledging our mistakes—because sometimes we screw up, and sometimes we do make bad decisions. When that happens we have to learn from the experience.

Leading and living with integrity is important to me. It means being fair with people at all times; treating people with respect, regardless of who they are or who you are; being a part of the community, knowing that we have a responsibility to it. That it is more than just about you. I do think it's extremely important to act with integrity, and I think the biggest challenge is to make sure you keep doing so, because if you violate trust once or twice you will never get it back. I expect the entire leadership team at Sharp to have integrity, not just me.

Being open and accessible is just who I am. I could walk through any hospital or go anywhere in Sharp HealthCare and I don't think that you would find employees are nervous walking up to me to talk or to ask me a question. I know some executives stay in their office, but that's just not me. I go to the same cafeteria all the employees go to. We host an annual all-staff assembly where we bring the entire organization together to recommit to our vision and celebrate our successes. At the assembly the senior leaders get up and make clowns of ourselves. People like to know that you have the ability to have fun. I don't really see that as a CEO I am all that different than anybody else who works here. And I think the people feel that way. When I walk down the hallway I expect our employees to say hello to me and I expect myself to say hello to them, regardless of who they are or what role they play.

Accessibility to everyone in the organization is core to most successful leaders. *How open and accessible are you to your staff, not in your opinion but in theirs? How do you know?*

Voices of Others

He has an innate integrity, and people around him want to do the right thing.—KL

He has a real willingness to listen and has created an environment in which people are willing to give their opinions.—KL

He is vulnerable, open, and authentic; Mike has led this organization with an open heart.—SR

He is so human, so real. It is an amazing experience to be around him.—SG

To hear him when he was with us was remarkable. He wasn't guarded, or arrogant, or full of business lingo; he asked us questions and made everyone feel important.—SG

The Power of Team

I am just a part of the leadership team. It takes a collaborative effort to run an organization this large and this complex. I see my role as helping everyone get the job done. Staying focused on what matters—our people and the purposeful work they do every day taking care of patients. My job is to help them get the resources, the technology, the equipment, and the systems to allow them to do really, really well.

I rely on a great leadership team. Most of us have been together since 1996. We work well together. I would say the vast majority of the great ideas that have moved Sharp Health-Care forward have not been my ideas. They have been other people's ideas that we collectively figured out how to prioritize and how to implement.

I was talking to somebody about our strengths and our weaknesses and how our strengths are our weaknesses. I am a consensus leader, and sometimes that creates a delicate balance. If necessary I will make a solo decision, but it is not my preferred style. My style is to figure out what the right answer is together and, while some may not prefer the decision, we all are going to support it because we have made it collectively and we are going to go in that direction. So how do I balance that? It is a delicate balance. We are a diverse team, so within my own team I have people who want to move faster, and there are people who want to slow down. There are people who want to turn right, and there are people who want to turn left. But really it is about coming together to do what's right for the organization.

I think that one of the important reasons we have succeeded at Sharp and done the things we have done is because we have a great leadership team that asks the tough questions all the time. I have leaders who are questioning why we aren't doing more, and I have leaders questioning why we are doing so much. One of our big talents is to balance those two points of view. I hear we need to be pushing more and there is so much more to do. And I will also hear people say we have been pushing the pedal to the metal for eight years without coming up for a breath, and we can only take so much. In reality, both points of view are right. So my job is to keep us pressing forward without burning people out. It is a forever balance.

Holding the tension and balance of how much to do, and how fast, is a challenge for most leaders. *Do you experience the "forever balance" Mike is talking about? Is there at least one way you and/or your team could be more effective in managing it? What is the conversation you would need to have, and with whom, to make this happen?*

Voices of Others

He has an incredible sense of collaboration and a desire to seek input to ensure the right decisions are being made.—DG

When I think how much he cares, I get emotional; he makes me want to do whatever I can to make Sharp strong.—SG

He never accepts a community position for himself. It is always because it will serve Sharp and the community.—SC

We always have a war with him about compensation. We have to force his raise down his throat. He keeps telling us to give it to other people.—SC

In his work with the board he is really inclusionary. He makes us part of the solution and truly cares for our input. He is a great listener; he is a proactive CEO, coming to the board on issues early rather than late.—SC

He is driven to make a difference and surrounds himself with great people.—SC

When Sharp experiences success or an achievement, he will put himself last as a contributor.—DG

Striving to Get Better

I do want to stress what we've done at Sharp is because of a lot of good people beyond my senior leadership team who have been successful in energizing and engaging the organization to do better—good people at every staff level, our physicians, board members, and volunteers. Before we started The Sharp Experience, our community told us we were no better or no worse than anybody else in an industry that had much room for improvement. I'm thankful that we had employees who were willing to hold up a mirror and say we could do better than that. They are the ones who made it better. Many of them are still saying we need to get better and challenge me all the time on that.

Voices of Others

He wants to hear what is important to people and their successes; he wants better lives for them.—DG

He truly assists those around him to be better individuals personally and professionally.—DG

When we launched The Sharp Experience, he said: "I am not interested in why it won't work but how it can work. We don't have all the answers, but I am convinced that the wisdom is in the room with each one of you for what we need to do."—SR

Focusing on What Matters

Everything we do at Sharp is focused on the vision we created in 2001 as we set out on this journey. Our vision is to transform the health care experience and make Sharp the best place to work, practice medicine, and receive care. We have our commitment to excellence in the six pillars we operate under: quality, service, people, finance, growth, and community. When we set our goals or undertake initiatives, we screen their contribution to the six pillars and how they help us to be the best place to work, the best place to practice medicine, and the best place to receive care. It has to be in all six pillars; it can't be one. Sometimes people get pretty frustrated with that. Yes, we have got to be successful financially, but at the same time, we have to ensure we are providing the highest quality, safest care for our patients. We believe that achieving our vision requires us to create an exceptional health care experience. We have to create a great employee experience so that employees can, in turn, provide a great patient experience.

The reality is, there are lots of great ideas that move us forward and our leadership team has the challenge of saying which ones we are going to execute on. At the end of the day the leadership team has to confront what we can and cannot do based on our prioritization of what is best in the long term for the organization to deliver on our vision.

Part of my talent and our leadership team's talent is to make sure we select the right priorities, we go in the right direction, and it's moving us where we need to go. Because you can't go twenty different directions all a hundred miles an hour; that's part of the balancing act and part of the questioning: Are we setting the right priorities? Are we setting the right number of priorities? Can we actively and appropriately move the organization, successfully engaging people in those? I have those internal conversations. I have people saying: Murphy, you're implementing a time and attendance system. You're implementing a just culture. You're implementing all these things; we can't keep up. And I have other people saying we need to advance, we need to move faster, we need a patient portal, we need to enhance learning. The reality is that those are both true. It is indeed a challenge to balance our need to create a better organization while keeping everybody engaged. The bottom line is, we have to push ourselves, or we'll never be what our team members and patients want and deserve.

Focusing on what really matters is an essential strength for leaders. Identifying what matters requires information from a range of sources. *As you look at decisions being made in your organization, can you say with authenticity "Everyone involved was heard" and "We heard from those closest to this work"? If not, what change is needed? How can it be implemented today?*

Voices of Others

The toughest decisions we face are never made hastily and never made alone. Part of his process is to ensure that others have been heard.—DG

He has a restless discontent; he is always pursuing something much greater. For him the journey never ends.—DG

He carries a phenomenal sense of ownership for the organization, the people, and those we serve.—SC

The Greatest Gratification

Receiving the Malcolm Baldrige National Quality Award was very gratifying. Being named by the Human Resources Association in San Diego as the best employer of any size company was a nice recognition. But the greatest gratification is in the day-to-day examples of caring in our organization that make me so proud to be associated with our people and what they do. It affirms that this is the kind of company we want our people to work in and reminds me this is why I do what I do.

I found out about this example a couple of days ago. A four-year-old kid got hit on the Mexican side of the border, dragged under a car, and ended up being taken across the border to our Chula Vista hospital. The child and mother were both Mexican nationals. Although our emergency department went overboard to try and save this child, they could not. The mother grieved, and all of the employees in the emergency room grieved with her. They also understood that the mother was incredibly poor. In five minutes they had raised $700, with every employee giving something, so this mother could bury her child with dignity. I could tell you many stories of everyday patient care—caring above and beyond. They tell me we are doing the right thing, that we have created a different organization in which people feel different about what they do.

I love it when employees come back to the organization, which happens a lot. I got an e-mail a week ago from a nurse who left a year and a half ago to work somewhere else, and now she is back because, she said, there is no place like this.

Stories are an important way to affirm organizational priorities and values. *What stories do you tell about your organization? In what way can you strengthen the power of storytelling in your organization?*

Voice of Others

He attracts people who share Sharp's sense of values.—KL

On Growing as a Leader

Yes, there's been development regarding how I work with people, how I collaborate, how I tackle issues. But I haven't changed my core beliefs and how I fundamentally operate.

Have I learned skills? Absolutely, and I continue to learn skills every day. One of the most important lessons we have learned on The Sharp Experience journey is that to be a better organization we need to be better leaders. We created The Sharp University to specifically provide critical leadership development at Sharp. Those development sessions are for all leaders—and believe me, these are skills we all need. I've learned so much and grown in so many ways. Leading is learning.

Voices of Others

He expects perfection of himself but is generous with others.—DG

He can learn exponentially with extraordinary speed; [he is] an avid reader who is constantly educating himself.—DG

He is a leader willing to learn and the greatest role model for a learning organization.—SR

When we were going on site visits on our way to The Sharp Experience, he attended all twenty-seven sessions, was the first in the room, the last to leave, and took voracious notes.—SR

Courage

It takes courage to be a leader. For me, courage as a leader means doing the right things in an honest way, including both the difficult situations and the easy ones. It also takes courage to acknowledge and learn from mistakes, to do all of this with openness and visibility.

Voice of Others

As a leader, Mike demonstrates the importance of getting comfortable with the uncomfortable—personally and professionally.—SR

A Good Day

A *good* day, which is the vast majority of my days, is when I have the privilege of hearing or witnessing through an employee, a physician, a patient or their family that what we are doing is making a difference. That they recognize that what we are doing is making health care better for all stakeholders, and that the journey we are on is the right one. When I see pride and excitement from our people about the work they do, at every level of the organization, regardless of role, and the recognition that they make a difference. When I see their eagerness to continue the journey, the recognition that we are not done and that we need to constantly work to get better and continue to pursue our vision.

A *good* day is when we celebrate the completion of a project that moves us forward as six-pillar leaders. These run the gamut from department quality and patient safety goals and enhanced cost efficiency to implementation of major electronic health records systems and the opening of new facilities. A celebration of progress to be the best we can be.

A *great* day is when we celebrate our people for all they do to make a difference for Sharp and the people we serve. A *really great* day is when we bring together all 14,000 employees, along with our physicians and our volunteers, for Sharp's annual all-staff assembly sessions. The sessions are designed as a time of celebration for the great work we do, education on where and how we need to improve, and inspiration to fuel our fire and, as we continue the journey and the hard work, that will transform the health care experience.

A Bad Day

A *bad* day, which is certainly the exception, is when an event occurs where I believe our performance has not appropriately lived up to our standards and our values; when we have disappointed an employee, a physician, a patient or their family; that we have not performed at a level that we strive to achieve. We try to turn all of these into learning opportunities; and that we have a recognition that The Sharp Experience and the pursuit of our vision is a marathon, not a sprint, a journey that will never end; and that the good will always want to get better.

A *challenging* day, after contemplation, not really a bad day, is when we are faced with a number of wonderful projects, ideas, and opportunities to move our organization forward with the recognition that we cannot do everything we would like to do, and we must prioritize to live within our human resource and financial capacity. Similarly, when we are faced with these priorities and we recognize a need to change course or eliminate a program or service so that we can perform better or place higher priority on other areas. These are challenging and often emotional decisions that can lead to great people being disappointed with the outcome. The ability to communicate effectively with the organization and these people and help them to understand the priorities and the organizational constraints is critical to move us forward. Critical, yes, but it does make for some of our more challenging days.

Voices of Others

KL   Ky Lewis, *senior vice president and general counsel*

DG   Dan Gross, *executive vice president, Hospital Operations*

SR   Sonia Rhodes, *vice president, Customer Strategy*

SG   Suzanne Griffiths, *clinical lead, Behavioral Health Clinic*

SC   Stephen P. Cushman, *chairman of the board*

6

The Ability to See the Truth: Patty Gabow

Patty Gabow is a nephrologist who joined Denver Health (DH) in 1979 as director of Nephrology. She was asked to be CEO in 1992. Founded in 1860, DH has for most of its history been a component of Denver's city government. In 1997, led by Patty's vision and persistence, it became the Denver Health and Hospital Authority, separating its governance from the city government in order to better sustain its public safety net mission while still serving as the city's health care system.

Under Patty's leadership, DH strives not merely to survive as a safety net health system serving the community's most vulnerable people but also to be a model for U.S. health care as an integrated, efficient, high-quality health care system that serves all.

Growing Up

If you have a gift and you don't use it, no confessor on earth can absolve you.—Patty Gabow's grandfather

I grew up in rural western Pennsylvania in an Italian immigrant family. My father was killed in World War II when I was a baby. My mother moved back to live with her parents, so my first ten years I grew up in a family with my grandmother; my grandfather; my mother; an unmarried uncle; and my grandmother's two unmarried sisters, who lived two houses down from my grandparents. Both sets of grandparents came over from Italy at the end of the nineteenth century as part of a major European migration.

Background Information

CEO,
Denver (Colorado) Health
www.denverhealth.org

Organizational Mission
- *Provides access to quality preventive, acute, and chronic health care for all the citizens of Denver regardless of ability to pay;*
- *Provides high quality emergency medical services to the citizens of Denver and the Rocky Mountain region;*
- *Fulfills public health functions as dictated by the Denver charter and the needs of the citizens of Denver;*
- *Provides health education for patients and participates in the education of the next generation of health care professionals; and*
- *Engages in research which enhances its ability to meet the health care needs of patients of the Denver health system.*

Denver Health Information
- Founded in 1860, Denver Health is an integrated public safety net organization that serves 151,000 individual patients each year—approximately one in four Denver residents—many of whom are poor, uninsured, or disenfranchised. Denver Health admits 26,000 patients a year who receive treatment at DH Medical Center, a 500-bed acute care hospital with a strong trauma service and one of the most high-tech and busiest medical intensive care units in the state. The hospital delivers 37 percent of babies born in Denver.
- Denver Health uniquely combines all aspects of the care continuum—public health, family health centers, school clinics, 911 system, acute care (including Level I trauma care), a call center with a regional poison center and patient advice line, a health maintenance organization, and an employed physician model.
- Denver Health is committed to providing technology to support its integrated care model through the investment of $320 million and full use of computerized provider order entry and standard order sets.

Selected Results for Denver Health

- As a member of the University HealthSystem Consortium (UHC)
  —Denver Health received UHC's Star in Safety and Quality award in 2009 for significant improvement in UHC's rankings in quality and safety in academic medical centers. The award is based on a composite score of performance in patient safety, timeliness, effectiveness, efficiency, equity, and patient-centeredness.
  —In 2007, DH received the highest ranking for a public safety net hospital with regard to patient safety and quality in the eighty-three-hospital database.
- In 2009, Denver Health was the recipient of the Colorado Performance Excellence Timberline (CPEx) Award for continuous performance improvement. The award was the highest CPEx award granted that year.
- Denver Health is Colorado's largest Medicaid provider and the provider of the largest amount of uninsured care. In 2008, 46 percent of DH users were uninsured. The value of its care for the uninsured was $275 million in 2007, $318 million in 2008, and $362 million for 2009 (unaudited). Despite this role in caring for the most vulnerable, DH remains fiscally sound, having been in the black financially every year since 1991.
  —Denver Health charges lower-than-average fees for medical services for metropolitan Denver peer hospitals in all but one of the thirty-five diagnosis-related groups; DH's charges were the lowest of any peer metro Denver hospital in twenty-five of the thirty-five categories (source: Colorado Hospital Association).
- Denver Health was one of three finalists for the 2008 Foster G. McGaw Prize for Excellence in Community Service. The organization was nominated for its innovative programs to provide its community's most vulnerable populations—including low-income children, newborns, and the uninsured—with high-quality health care. The Foster G. McGaw Prize is presented to a health care organization that provides innovative

programs that significantly improve the health and well-being of its community.

- In 2009, HealthLeaders Media named Denver Health one of the Top Leadership Teams in Healthcare. The Top Leadership program is designed to celebrate outstanding teamwork that occurs in health care organizations each day and to share what makes executive leadership teams successful. Winners were judged on the team's overall leadership culture, its ability to overcome challenges, and its ability to demonstrate successes that result from outstanding leadership teamwork.

Individual Recognitions for Patty Gabow

- 2009: Selected by the American College of Physicians (ACP) as a Master of the College. This is the highest honor bestowed on ACP members. Of the ACP's 119,000 members, only 546 have attained the distinction of Mastership. Master status recognizes outstanding career accomplishments such as teaching, outstanding work in clinical medicine, contributions to preventive medicine, improvements in the delivery of health care, and/or contributions to medical literature.
- 2005 and 2009: Recognized as one of the Top 25 Women in Healthcare by *Modern Healthcare,* which noted she was "an outspoken advocate for accessibility, affordability, and quality in healthcare."
- 2009: Recognized as one of the Top 100 Most Powerful People in Healthcare by *Modern Healthcare.*
- 2009: Honored as one of five Women Who've Changed the Heart of the City for leading one of the nation's most highly regarded, extensive, and integrated health care systems and seeking to improve care for the underserved.
- 2008: Received the National Center for Healthcare Leadership National Healthcare Leader Award for her significant and lasting contributions to health care.
- 2007: The Patricia A. Gabow Endowment for Vulnerable Populations was fully funded. The endowment provides funds for faculty members at DH to perform research that would lead to improved access, affordability, and clinical outcomes for patients from vulnerable populations.

My mother remarried, to a school teacher, when I was ten. She was a school teacher. My two uncles were school teachers and my grandfather was a school teacher. How I became a doctor remains a mystery to all of us. It is said that the most important and enduring influence on a child is the family, and I would certainly say in my case that is true. They were very religious Catholic immigrants, very much into doing the right thing for others. One of my grandfather's old sayings is that if you have a gift and you don't use it, no confessor on earth can absolve you. In a nutshell, this was the philosophy of the family.

My mother and stepfather taught in the school I attended, a small country school. I had both as my teachers. My mother was very tuned in to the poor and disenfranchised and was always saying "Now Patty, you have to be nice to those poor kids." My mother was always the one who would see a kid who couldn't go on the school trip and find someone who would send them. If a girl didn't have a gown for the prom, my mother would figure out how to get one—she was always out there doing that. My mother is going to be ninety this year, and she still has former students stop by to visit her. She made a large impression on the people that she taught. I would say certainly my first mentors were my family.

My uncle, who was single and lived with us, had me reading philosophy when I was ten years old. Family has been a very important substrate for the rest of my life. As a physician I think I was a good diagnostician and I think I was a good observer, and that ability has matured through the years. I think it started with my uncle encouraging me to think about ideas and concepts.

Influences—People and Situations

My grandfather was a very big influence in my life. His picture is on my office wall, along with some of the hundreds of his Italian sayings. He came to the U.S. when he was sixteen and began working for a circus band because he had a lot of musical talent. He actually had gone briefly to a conservatory. He was very, very poor in Italy. Then here he put himself through school to become a school teacher, and he put my mother and her two brothers through college during the Depression at a time when first-generation Italian women weren't being sent to college. My grandfather always used to say to me "My girl, if you get an education in America there isn't anything you can't do." He was one of those many immigrants who believed that the opportunity in America was highly linked to education. I went to a small Catholic girls' school for college that my father picked for me. I'd never even seen it until the day I got there.

My next mentor was Sister Florence Marie Scott. She had a PhD in biology. She was head of the biology department, and I was a biology pre-med major. She was tougher than nails. She was the quintessential nun. She took me every summer to Woods Hole [Oceanographic Institution; Woods Hole, Massachusetts] to the Marine Biological Laboratory as her research assistant. She was the first woman to ever be on the board of the Marine Biological Laboratory and of course, the first nun.

In those days nuns still wore those long robes. I can still see her, robes tucked up in her belt, out there wading in the water with all these male scientists collecting the specimens. She was a great example that you don't have to change who you are to be successful and that a woman can be successful in a man's world. I think as I proceeded through my own leadership that's where fairness but toughness and a very high bar came from. She set a very high bar. If you wanted to be in her department, you had to meet the bar.

Pathway to Health Care

I wanted to be a doctor from the time I was ten years old. My dad thought "This was just a passing thing; what does she even know about being a doctor?" But then it became clear that it truly was what I wanted to be.

Sister Florence Marie Scott was adamant that, if I wasn't going to be a nun—which she really wanted and I had no desire to be—and I went to medical school I had to go to what she believed to be the best medical school in the country—the University of Pennsylvania. So I went there to medical school. I was one of 5 girls in a class of 125, and after having been at a girl's school I thought I'd died and gone to heaven! Penn overall was a gracious environment, and I was blessed with several mentors there. One was one of the few woman faculty members. She was a nephrologist and a fantastic teacher, very folksy and down home. I think that's probably why I ended up going into nephrology. The chief of medicine there, Dr. Arnold Relman, who went on to be the editor of the *New England Journal of Medicine,* had a very idealistic view of what a physician should be and what the ethical and moral responsibilities of a physician are. He was very much committed to the well-being of the patient and was a major influence. In fact, I just had him here as a visiting professor. He's eighty-seven now and just as sharp and as idealistic as he was thirty years ago.

I did my internship at Penn, my residency at Harbor General in Los Angeles, a renal fellowship at San Francisco General, and back to Penn for another year of renal fellowship, and then came to Denver because I wanted to be at the city hospital. Penn, in those days, had two levels of service. They had big, open wards and luxury suites. I always gravitated towards the disenfranchised.

When I came here, Denver Health didn't have a position in nephrology, so the [National] Kidney Foundation paid for a half-time position. I worked full time for half a salary for almost two years. Then, seeing the need, Denver Health created a position for me.

Pathway to Leadership

I became the chief of medicine and then medical director and CEO. I've been CEO for seventeen years. I never applied for any of these jobs. For the chief of medicine position, one of my mentors said "You need to do this." Becoming medical director for the enterprise was a tough decision for me. It meant leaving the mainstream of clinical medicine, which I loved, and moving into administration. It took me three years to move completely to my new office. It was a crossroads moment for me.

Several of the leaders we talked with faced serious crossroads in their career journeys. The themes of having a positive future orientation, aiming high, being able to help, and challenging the status quo are part of this willingness to take the new path at the crossroads. *Have you faced a serious crossroads point in your career—either by choice because an opportunity was offered or forced due to a change in your setting? How did you sort through the options and make the choice? What advice would you give to others?*

Later in my career the mayor of Denver then asked me to be the CEO. I have no idea why they chose me. My son, who was a teenager at the time, and you know how teenagers are, said to me: "Mom, how are you going to take a job for which you have absolutely no training?" I said: "Good point. I don't know." But I felt I could help.

I've come to believe that being trained as a doctor is good preparation for leadership. I was also a researcher and a scientist. I had a large NIH [National Institutes of Health] project for fifteen years. I feel that being trained as an investigator and a physician were good training for leadership because I've always treated administrative problems just like I treat patient problems. You need to make a diagnosis. You need to create a treatment plan. You need to monitor the treatment plan. If it's not working, you need to go back and change the diagnosis or change the treatment. To me it's pretty straightforward.

One of the things that I see in management is that often a diagnosis of the core issue is not made; instead there is treatment of symptoms. I always was a big data girl, so being able to look at data was important to me. At first I had to demand it. This was partly because there was no reliable data and partly because people didn't understand how to use data. I think my medical and research training on how to approach problems has actually served me well in this environment.

What's Important to Me as a Leader

Seeing the Truth

Lord, grant me the ability to see the truth, and when I see the truth,
give me the courage to use it.—Prayer from one of Patty's mentors

Sister started every lecture with a prayer that I still say every day because I think this talks about leadership: "Lord, grant me the ability to see the truth, and when I see the truth, give me the courage to use it." That is a lesson that I never forgot.

I very much believe you do have to try very hard to understand the truth. I said to the mayor recently "I long for the day when there were only two sides to every story." It's not always easy to find out what the truth is. The second part of this saying is also important. You have to have the courage to use the truth. It's not always easy to follow what you believe is the correct thing to do.

At Denver Health we take risks for the sake of doing good. We are more interested in doing good than doing well. I think some of American health care has sold out because the leadership are more interested in doing well than doing good. Money is just a way to accomplish what is good. It's not an end in itself. I think profit has become an end in itself for some components of health care, which is why we are probably going to have difficulty getting real health reform.

Recognizing that every story has more than two sides and diagnosing the core problem rather than treating symptoms are two skills Patty brings to her leadership. Leaders sometimes find themselves in situations where the decision is not between right and wrong but between two "rights." *How do you approach complex issues to ensure you understand the core issue, not just symptoms of the problem? How do you approach complex issues when the choice is between two right choices?*

Hiring People Who Have Integrity, Are Smart, Work Hard, and Love Denver Health

When I'm interviewing people for jobs, everybody asks "What are you looking for from the person in this job," and my answer is always the same: The things I'm looking for are things I can no longer teach a person. First of all you have to have integrity, because without that there's no place for us to have a relationship. Secondly, I'm looking for someone who's smart. If you're not smart, it's pretty hard to teach you what I need to teach you. Thirdly, you have to be a hard worker, because if you don't have a work ethic, by the time you're looking at the jobs I'm interviewing for I'm not going to teach you that, either. And then you have to have the commitment to and love for Denver Health, because I don't think you can really give your all if you don't love something.

Voices of Others

I came here to work for Patty after twenty-one years somewhere else. With her experience in patient care, teaching, and research she walks the talk and sees things from her experience.—RA

We talked about the hospitalist model when it first started. She sent me articles, we talked. We could not make it work financially at that time. She said "Go ahead, it's the right thing to do." A typical bean counter or MBA wouldn't do that.—RA

There are many leaders with longevity here, and that has very good aspects to it since it means people want to be part of this organization.—ST

Leading as an Intimate Relationship

I believe that leading an institution is an intimate relationship. It's really caring about the well-being of the institution and the people that are here; wanting the best for the institution and having goals that are noble.

When I say it's an intimate relationship, I don't see this as a job. It is a relationship between me and this organization that has gone on for more than three decades. I think it is hard for me to draw a line between the enterprise and me in many ways. My son always used to say: "Denver Health is another kid. You think of it as another kid, Mom." I have two children, a daughter and a son, and I guess a third—Denver Health.

I love Denver Health because it does the right thing. I feel that some of health care in America has been taken over by greed, that money has become more important than mission. In some health care institutions, the mission statement has nothing to do with actual behavior.

We always say Denver Health isn't for everybody, but the people it's for, it's for life. It's an extraordinary institution, and the people who work here are extraordinary. And it's easy to love.

Voice of Others

I love her! She is the quintessential leader—a multidimensional leader; I marvel at her ability to balance the many demands.—BA

Leading as an intimate relationship with the organization and loving the institution is language not often heard from senior executives. *How would you describe the feelings you have for your organization? What would it take for you to feel love for the institution? If you feel love for your organization, do you express it freely to others?*

Creating a Model in Denver

It works for me to be at a safety net organization. I'm not sure I would be as successful somewhere else. Spending thirty years at one place, I know everybody in the community, everybody in the enterprise, everything about the enterprise—this is where I can make the biggest contribution. With the Obama election, a lot of people were asking me if I was interested in a national position. But I really believe that I can do the most good by creating a model that the country could learn from, a model that the country desperately needs.

A number of years ago our goal was to be a model for the nation in health care, and I think we are there. I think we have influence by demonstrating that a safety net organization can have very high quality because we serve everybody; it is a goal for health care that I have wanted. I've never been tempted to move.

Caring deeply about the organization—that intimate relationship—is richer and has more texture to the relationship as the years go by. It enables you to make good decisions for the long term of the enterprise. If you come from the outside, it may be hard to develop deep relationships.

Doing What Is Right for the Mission

To get to the truth, I like to talk to people and I put a situation up against what is the right thing for our mission, which is to care for people and to care for those who are disenfranchised. For example, years ago some physicians were upset that we didn't have an MRI [magnetic resonance imaging device], that we were the only hospital without an MRI. Because we are an integrated model we have the ability to do things in different places. That same year we actually opened school-based clinics in schools in poor areas instead of buying an MRI. The ethical principle that Denver Health tries to follow is: How do we do the most good for the most people, as opposed to doing the most good for the sickest, which is an equally valid ethical principle? Clearly, if you use that principle as your template—to do the most good for the most people—then having clinics in all the schools is going to have a bigger impact than doing an MRI on a thousand patients, some of whom may not really need it.

I like to see people do well. I like to see Denver Health do well. When we win an award and when we achieve something that is really good—like the American College of Surgeons releasing data that we have the best trauma survival in the nation—I am very pleased that the enterprise has done something good.

Voices of Others

She creates a standard of high expectations of the board. There is a fiduciary and spiritual responsibility expected from the board. The spirit of leadership is really [that of a] servant leader. I admire what good leaders can do and how average leaders can mess up.—BA

I'm wedded to her vision.—SP

Ethical principles that guide decisions provide a foundation for a disciplined focus on patient care rather than a reaction to the issue at hand. Patty translates the noble purpose of Denver Health to do the most good for the most people into decision criteria. *What ethical principles consistently guide your decisions?*

Learning from All

One of the things we did at the start with our Getting It Right initiative [the beginning of Denver Health's cultural transformation] was that I held focus groups with all the employees, starting with the housekeepers. We did it by groups because I didn't think that if surgeons and housekeepers were together the housekeepers would ever say anything. We gave them questions to answer in the meeting, and those questions were not the usual focus group questions like "How is your pay?" or "How are your benefits?" The questions were: "What do you see happening to patients that you don't think is right?" "Do you know who to tell if you see something not right happening?" "What keeps you from working efficiently?" "What part of your job should someone else be doing?" "What part of someone else's job should you be doing?"

I decided to do the conversations in our Getting It Right initiative for two reasons. One, I wanted to get input regarding our transformation journey, and two, I wanted to create a willingness for transformation. And it served both purposes.

Diagnosis of problems using the mission and values is certainly part of the diagnosis, but it can be much more mundane than that. For example, take the question "Why are you on divert?" A simplistic answer is: "The emergency department is full." Well, clearly. But that's not an answer. This is a complex question, and you're not at the root cause of the problem. And there is no way in a complex environment to get to the answer without using complex analytics. I'm big about using data as well as asking people to try to find out what is really up.

People send me e-mails, and I answer them all personally. For example, I got an e-mail that we had scheduled the employee picnic on September 11 and they couldn't believe we had done that because it was insensitive. I said "I hadn't thought about that, but let me talk to my executive team." We decided that it was not a good idea, so we moved it. I sent her back an e-mail and thanked her for pointing it out.

Questions that provide a source of dialogue and mutual learning add to a leader's capacity to understand the root cause of problems. Patty shows the capacity to engage all organizational members to hear beyond the surface of issues. *What is the most provocative question you have asked, or have been asked, at work? Where did the question take the conversation, and what was the outcome?*

Voices of Others

She's like a sponge. She absorbs information.—PG

Patty has smarts and is an outstanding communicator. She comes from a family of teachers, and she's able to translate complicated issues. She's a dynamo with the energy of three. That energy is infectious and challenging.—ST

It's new for me. I've never worked for someone who knows the work and aligns the tools. She believes that everyone has to have the tools and ongoing learning. She knows that accountability fosters interdependent problem solving.—ST

One Brain

I spend a huge amount of time with my executive team as a whole, and I meet with them all individually. I do think that the way to develop a common vision is spending time with people and listening. You would probably tear your hair out if you were at some of our meetings because they're not as focused as they could be—we have a great deal of dialogue. I think that is a good way to get to the truth. We have a journal club that we do twice a year at my house with physician and administrative leaders. We read things like *Good to Great* [Jim Collins, HarperBusiness, 2001] or *The Spirit Catches You and You Fall Down* [Anne Fadiman, Farrar, Straus and Giroux, 1998]. We read a whole range of books that are relevant to the role we play. Our physicians and administrative leaders do everything together; we spend a lot of time together; we do our retreats together; we're one family, and that's important.

Voice of Others

At the senior management team we talk things out and get to agreement with everyone from the integrated system at the table. We moved from the city to a new structure to speed decision making and increase operational flexibility. Since then we've doubled in size with no change in organizational structure, so we're now asking ourselves whether we are sluggish in decision making.—ST

Persistence

It takes a lot of persistence. This is not necessarily courage, but persistence. I felt for a long time that we had to get out of the city government if we were going to survive, and I started working on the mayor. Imagine going to a mayor of a big city and saying "You know, I think your second biggest department in city government would be a lot better off if it were separated from you." Most mayors are not going to embrace that as their dream direction. It took me a long time to persuade him. At one point he said to me "Are you ever going to get over this?" And I said "As soon as you say yes."

It took four years of effort and involved talking to everybody. There weren't two people standing together in Denver who I wasn't talking to about why this was necessary. It was clear to me that this had to be done to make this institution survive. It wasn't easy to do. There were a lot of political barriers to overcome. There were a lot of internal issues to overcome and a structure to create. The easiest thing would have been to say "Well, the cards will fall where they will." But once I get something in my mind that is important to do for the enterprise, I'm very tenacious.

After we were independent, I said to the board: "I'm going to ask the mayor to issue a $100 million bond for Denver Health," and they said "You're crazy! He just let you go independent, and now you're going to ask him to do a bond? He's never going to do that." But he did, and it was for $149 million.

Voices of Others

She has extraordinary political skills because she has remarkable vision—she knows where she wants to go, has the reasons and the data.—RA

We built a new corporate structure from the ground up when we moved from the city. The mayor threatened that "If I get one call from an employee complaining about this." We had a huge communications plan with forums at which staff could bring their spouses. These were city employees who were used to complaining to newspapers or the mayor before us, but there was not one call to the mayor.—ST

She wouldn't let up! High expectations, high standard; the accountability factor is extraordinarily important in transformative work.—SP

Patty is persistent! She appreciates the patience it takes to get things done. She will let things play out and appreciates it's not linear or smooth. An example is the rationale for going with Lean as part of our Getting It Right initiative: Lean was the link to the mission; we knew that our patient needs were increasing and our resources were decreasing and that the way to deal with that was to get more efficient.—RA

People who are persistent can be called by other names—stubborn, inflexible, unrealistic, pigheaded—you get the picture. Choosing disciplined action in service to patient care, part of the constancy of focus, is clear in hindsight but less clear early in the journey. *Identify a person you know who showed long-term persistence to achieve a mission-based outcome. What reactions did you and others have toward that person? How would you now handle a similar situation?*

Culture, Not Structure

We had a long time leading up to the transition from the city. We were determined to raise the bar whether there was a change in governance or not—the structure change was not the focus—and to change the culture and behavior no matter what was the focus. We wanted to move to where the heart of most employees was. We had a commitment to accountability, to adult behavior. And we were determined that those not aligned with the vision would not continue to work here.

Voices of Others

Our focus on changing the culture focused on the 5 Rights—right people, environment, communication, reward, and process— and doing them all simultaneously. The level of performance transparency was difficult for some.—PG

Patty is a visionary—a Galileo type—she can see far and is progressive and creative. Becoming our own authority apart from the city was huge: moving that glacier and bringing the silos together. She said we need to redesign the basic functioning and change the culture.—PG

She knew that to change the culture we had to educate and uplift people, and for many it was the birth of a new intellectual life. I have absolute confidence in her constancy; she will not allow this to go away.—SP

The celebrations, ceremonies, and rewards are meaningful, and people feel recognized.—SP

Using structural changes or reorganizations to fix cultural problems in complex settings is a common leadership activity. This confusion of activity with outcome can result in changes but no improvement. Patty and her team were clear that cultural change was the outcome they sought and that structural changes would enable that outcome but were not the solution. *What have you learned from structural changes you have participated in? Were there cultural elements that were overlooked in those changes?*

Saying What Has to Be Said

Well, I'm pretty much known for always saying what I think. I am very straightforward. In many ways that takes some kind of courage in our society. There is a difference between being direct and having no civility. My COO always says I have perfected the ability to have whipped cream on battery acid.

I think I can say some very tough things in a way that is not hostile. That's served me well.

Voices of Others

She has a strong sense of integrity of what's right for patients—she lives and breathes it. It's not lip service. Her ethics are clear, especially when dealing with the city and in public forums. She has the courage to speak up when others do not.—ST

She has a delightful sense of wit.—SP

Not Being Held Hostage to the Environment

I do think that one of the things that's made us very successful is the ability to not be held hostage by the fact that we have a poor payer rate and are not a rich enterprise. My board chair once said that he thought this organization was schizophrenic because one minute we would be figuring out how we are going to manage this huge unsponsored care load and the next minute we would be talking about how we are going to do some joint venture to build a building.

We've put $320 million into health information technology (HIT). Levels of HIT sophistication are 1 to 7, and we're a level 5 HIT institution, one of 5 percent in the country. Others ask "Why would a safety net do that?" It is because it was the way to have quality, safety, and efficiency. Those are the kinds of decisions that take courage—to be willing to say we are going to put money into this. We issued bonds right after we changed from being a city hospital to start to transform our enterprise, to build single-patient rooms in a safety net hospital, because it's the right thing to do.

Voice of Others

Finance skills are another example of her multidimensional leadership. She found new revenues to subsidize indigent care. She formed a partnership with a health care organization that aligned their needs and ours. We have strategic partnerships with real estate developers to gain access to capital—another creative solution. These are not often skills found in MDs.—BA

Welcoming New Staff

I do new employee orientation every Monday, and I always start out by telling them "Welcome to the family." I tell them about Denver Health, our mission, and our values. I say that if the DH values are their values, they'll have a great career. If they aren't, they're probably sitting in the wrong chair. The people who come here self-select because they share our mission and values. You don't have coming to Denver Health as your dream job if you want to take care of the rich or famous. What's amazing about this institution is that everybody from the groundskeeper to the head of Surgery is committed to the mission.

Voices of Others

I wake up every day so glad to work where I do with the people I do.—ST

There's something about this place. I am privileged to work with smart people. I have total faith in Patty. Thoughts of disappointing her are unthinkable. She was on a rapid improvement event team recently, and by the end the staff would walk through walls for her.—PG

We have a system that prescreens all candidates for good fit with our values.—SP

Fairness

I try to have a sense of fairness. I think I am able to disconnect personal aspects from what's best for the enterprise. I can step back while others struggle with their personal feelings when we're dealing with tough issues, especially personnel issues. I think I'm able to be dispassionate because my uncle had me reading philosophy at a young age and that is a way of thinking about things. And the women in my family always took the issues they faced, put them in bigger context, and moved on them—they got things done.

A Model for Health Care

Our work at DH is about caring and being a learned profession. A mentor taught me that a learned profession took knowledge from previous generations and had an obligation to share with the next generation. If we can provide low-cost, high-quality care—what America needs—we are obligated to share those outcomes and the methodology with others.

There are four pieces that make us a uniquely integrated enterprise. Years ago, I saw that following the *integrated system model* would be a tremendous structural advantage. It creates multiple points of access; it gets people to the right place at the right time for the right level of care; and it enabled us to get different sources of federal money. I always say there's not a federal dollar I don't love.

One aspect of enormous potential in the model was *employing our physicians*; there is no misalignment between what the physicians are doing and where the enterprise is going, which is a core issue in American health care. Physicians are big decision makers in health care. We take out the toxic incentives—getting paid more for doing more. Whatever you incent is what you'll get. We don't have a physician practice plan here because it's toxic at the end of the day. We have more transparency across disciplines and better continuity for the patient; we can navigate the system for the patient versus the patient navigating the system. We have a formal affiliation with the [University of Colorado, Denver] School of Medicine; all our physicians are full-time faculty at the school, but they work for us.

Sophisticated *information technology* has been an important piece to this model. We had computerized provider order entry with standard order sets here long before it was in vogue, and most hospitals still don't have it.

Our *willingness to innovate* is part of the model. We are always innovating. Our people embrace it. For example, we have 200 black belts trained in the Toyota Production System, including the director of Medicine. We have orthopedic surgeons who are black belts. Go anywhere else and find an orthopedic surgeon who's willing to take 80 to 100 hours of training in Toyota Production. Denver Health people are willing to do that. If our physicians and nurses believe that an innovation is going to make for better quality, they are willing to learn whatever it is.

Finally, our model has *accountability and transparency*. If you are making money from state and federal payments but not sharing data, then there's something wrong. Being a public entity kept our values well aligned. Becoming independent from the city I saw as a very important step, but staying governmental was also important.

Celebrating our successes and having a high goal to be a model has helped us. We didn't start out thirty years ago saying we were going to be a model for the country. We started out with smaller goals, and along the way we said: We'll be the best public system in the United States. When we decided we had achieved that, we said we were going to be the model for the country. And when [U.S.] Senator [Max] Baucus [D-MT] had a press conference about health care reform and mentioned Denver Health along with three or four other places as people who really get it in health care, our employees were ecstatic!

Voices of Others

Politics is her second job. She sits on the mayor's cabinet, and we call on the Colorado congressional delegation in Washington; she's always looking to promote our model.—BA

In quality she has a relentless commitment to execution. She creates a culture of serving the underserved with a fierce loyalty. She recruits people from all over the world. She could work anywhere with far more resources, but she chooses to be here.—BA

She is creative, innovative, and proactive. The Lean process is a wonderful example. A public institution merged with an innovative approach so that it becomes part of the culture is a great example of transformational leadership—very different than your average public hospital. Patty has stunning vision, energy, drive, and passion; she inspires, challenges, cajoles to move things forward.—BA

Similar to other leaders profiled in this book, Patty is clear on the organization's model of care. She articulates four components of the model, and the organization's function illustrates those components. It is part of the disciplined action that helps DH to achieve its results. *Can you concisely describe your model of care for your organization or program? If you cannot, what do you need to do to develop clarity about your model and communicate it to achieve better results?*

A Good Day

I used to say to my husband that any time I thought I was having a bad day, all I had to do was walk out on the floors of the hospital and suddenly my day was much better. I'm a very optimistic person. Every day's a good day. My aunt who lived next door, my grandmother's sister, used to wake up every morning and say "Thank you, Lord, for another day in your beautiful world." I was raised in that environment. These Italian women weren't complainers; they basically valued what they had.

A Bad Day

I'd say the worst day is when we have something bad happen. But I'm very resilient.

Voices of Others

PG   Phil Goodman, *Lean facilitator*

RA   Rick Albert, *director, Medicine*

ST   Stephanie Thomas, *chief operating officer*

SP   Susan Proudfoot, *administrator, Radiology*

BA   Bruce Alexander, *board chair*

7

An Honor
to Take Care of People:
Larry Goodman

Larry Goodman is president and chief executive officer of Rush University Medical Center in Chicago. Rush is an academic medical center that includes a 671-bed hospital in downtown Chicago and a health sciences university. He is a physician who still teaches and remains clinically active as an infectious disease specialist.

Larry joined Rush in 1977 as a resident. He has been at Rush since that time, except for 1996–98, when he was medical director at Cook County Hospital. He was named CEO in 2002 at a time when Rush was losing $5 million a month. In addition to executing a financial turnaround, Larry trained his strategic focus on more tightly aligning the classic missions of an academic medical center with the goal of providing the highest possible quality of medical care.

In 2009, Rush completed a fifth consecutive year of operating profit and had earned an A category credit rating from all three rating agencies. Currently, Rush is nearing the completion of a $300 million capital campaign (the largest in its history) and is approaching the midpoint of a $1 billion campus transformation. Over the same period Rush has been named to numerous top-performer lists for outstanding quality of care.

Background Information
President and CEO,
Rush University Medical Center, Chicago
www.rush.edu

Organizational Mission
To provide the very best care for our patients

Rush University Medical Center Information
- Based in Chicago and chartered in 1837, Rush University Medical Center is an academic medical center that includes a 671-bed hospital, serving adults and children, and Rush University. Rush University has nearly 2,000 students in its four colleges, which include a college of medicine, college of nursing, graduate college, and college of health sciences.
- In 2008, Rush broke ground for a new 304-bed hospital that represents a design shaped by user input to improve quality and optimize the patient experience while creating an environmentally sustainable facility with the most advanced technology available. It will be the first hospital in Chicago seeking Leadership in Energy and Environmental Design (LEED) gold level designation. In 2009, a new, 200,000 square foot ambulatory building dedicated to orthopedics opened, as did a new parking facility and power plant for the campus. Also in 2009, Rush completed implementation of its inpatient electronic medical record system.

Selected Results for Rush
- 2009: For the fifth consecutive year, Rush has been ranked among the top performing academic medical centers in the country in the University HealthSystem Consortium Quality and Accountability Study, which evaluates ninety-three academic medical centers on the basis of risk-adjusted mortality, timeliness, effectiveness, efficiency, equity of care, and patient-centeredness. For the fifth year in a row, Rush attained a perfect score in the equity of care category, which measures whether patient outcomes differ due to gender, race, or socioeconomic status.
- 2009: Rush was the only Illinois hospital and the only Midwest hospital to receive a perfect score on the Healthcare Equality Index 2009 (HEI), an annual survey conducted by

the Human Rights Campaign Foundation and the Gay and Lesbian Medical Association. The HEI evaluates the nation's hospitals on their treatment of lesbian, gay, bisexual, and transgender (LGBT) patients; their families; and LGBT hospital employees.

- 2009: For the third consecutive year Rush was named to the Center for Companies That Care honor roll. Companies named to the list excel in ten characteristics inherent to a "company that cares." Some of these characteristics include establishing and reinforcing ethical standards, supporting work-life balance for employees, providing a great work environment and competitive compensation and benefits, and supporting company involvement in the community.
- 2009: Rush was named as one of the nation's top 125 hospitals by Consumers' Checkbook, a not-for-profit research organization that selects top hospitals from 1,467 acute care facilities in the fifty-three largest U.S. metropolitan areas on a number of quality indicators.
- 2009: Rush was selected by the Leapfrog Group as a national top hospital for quality. Rush was one of thirty-four urban hospitals that earned the Top Hospitals Award from among more than 1,200 institutions that were surveyed. The survey evaluates performance on safety, mortality rates, infection rates, and efficiency.
- 2009: Rush was recognized by *U.S. News & World Report* as a top hospital in nine specialty areas.
- 2007: Rush received the Exemplary Voluntary Efforts Award from the U.S. Department of Labor. The award recognizes federal contractors for exceptional efforts to increase employment opportunities for minorities, women, individuals with disabilities, and veterans.
- 2006: Rush was designated a Magnet hospital, recognizing clinical nursing excellence, for the second time. Fewer than 50 hospitals have received Magnet designation twice.

Areas of Interest for Larry Goodman
- Research focused on infectious diseases, particularly gastrointestinal infections
- Teaching and curricular change
- Clinical quality and clinical resource management

Growing Up

I was born in Detroit, and my family moved to Long Island, New York, when I was thirteen. No one in my family was in health care. My father was on the road a fair amount of time selling insurance. My mother worked in a department store as a salesperson. My sister became a teacher. I think that most people are a product of the people they grew up with. I came from a very loving family that encouraged me to do anything I wanted to do. My parents gave me absolute support. It was great growing up, a great atmosphere.

Influences—People and Situations

I think as you go through life you see all kinds of people: people who are outstanding and people who are not so great. But you can learn from everybody.

I was very much inspired by an individual who has been one of the key leaders at Rush and now is the chairman of Medicine, Dr. Stuart Levin. He is one of the best physicians and one of the best diagnosticians I've ever seen. He was inspiring to me as I went through training. You walk around thinking that there is so much I'm going to know and when I do I'll know as much as anybody else. Then suddenly you see someone who is really at another level. I guess some people might get depressed by it, but to me it was inspiring to know that someone can perform at that level. Maybe I will get there, maybe not, but it's what you want to shoot for—something that is really great.

Larry was not discouraged when he met someone who performed at a level beyond his current skills. He used that role model to spur him to work toward better performance. *Are there opportunities for you to strengthen your own capacity to learn from others by action or reflection on a daily basis?*

On the other hand, all of us have interacted with people who are very smart but don't work and communicate well with other people, and you can see the damage that can be done. You see a very smart doctor, but the whole sum of their behaviors is not leading to the best outcome for that patient or for that student. So that is also instructive, because you realize that an atmosphere that is mutually nurturing is a big deal, that everybody gets better in that environment. For example, if the training is very supportive, there's no reason why students should feel intimidated by anybody on the health care team. They should be questioned in a way that encourages them to think and talk without worrying that "this is my one chance to shine, and otherwise I'm going to get a bad grade." Every member of the health care team needs to be comfortable asking questions and speaking up. Intimidation and rude behavior are not just unpleasant or inappropriate; they contribute to bad outcomes.

Medicine is not something that you can get up the next day and think, I've got this thing licked. It's just not like that. Medicine is very humbling; just when you get used to thinking you're right, it turns out that, in fact, you're wrong. Everybody who takes care of patients has had the experience of waking up one day and looking at a lab value and realizing it's not just off, it's way off—potentially life-threateningly off, and it's been in the chart for twelve hours. You look at that and you start beating yourself up. Or you didn't consider the one diagnosis that, if present, was the one that needed to be treated yesterday. Going through those experiences—and everybody goes through them—you realize that horrific things can happen. When I was a chief resident I got a chance to talk to students and residents who were going through these experiences for the first time. I used to say when I was going home during the first year of my residency that I just hoped I get a chance to save a few people before I killed somebody. Because you never know what's going to happen first; and those things can really stay with you and have the potential to derail people, particularly those early in their training. So, the lesson is hard, but the atmosphere and the people around you can make all the difference.

Part of the reason I love to practice medicine is because it is challenging, intellectually stimulating, and very personal. There are few things more important to people than their health or the health of their loved ones. You put on a white coat, you walk in a room, and you meet a stranger who is often willing to tell you just about everything from surreptitious drug use to marital infidelities, and then they'll take their clothes off and you'll examine them. It's an incredibly intimate relationship with a patient, and it's a tremendously trusting relationship. It is a huge honor to be able to take care of people. It really is. There's nothing, or at least there are not very many things I know of, that are quite like it. On top of that it is very challenging and intellectually rewarding. Their illness may be related to where they work, who they have been in contact with, where they have traveled, their habits of daily living, or the genes they have inherited. In the field of infectious disease, the history is often more important than any blood test or x-ray. To do the best job, you need to get to know the patient.

At the time I became CEO, Ed Brennan was chairman of our board. I've never known a person who was more of a gentleman, and also more insightful on business issues. I'm sure he knew what to do and could have just said it, but instead he helped me develop and succeed as a CEO. I was a person who had never done this, had no financial training except on the job with the various budgets, and still he lent his expertise and reputation, but never tried to manage. And he was always available. He never, ever directed in the slightest way, not who to hire or what to do next. He was just supportive, and if I had a question he would immediately sit and we'd talk it through. He was outstanding. When Ed died, he was succeeded by Dick Jaffee, who had previously served as vice chair of the board. Again, I was very fortunate. Dick was the same kind of chairman, totally involved and committed, and also a great teacher and friend. Their leadership and mentoring at a critical time for Rush was a big part of our success—as was the tremendous involvement of the entire board. This job has taught me about the invaluable contributions that are made by committed civic leaders. The Rush board is packed with such individuals.

Some leaders like to create an atmosphere of anxiety to keep others off balance, to throw them in at the deep end to see whether they sink or swim, not really caring which occurs; they withhold rather than freely offer the benefit of their experience. In contrast, Larry and other leaders are invested in the success of others and share accountability for it. It is part of their genuine caring for others and their desire for others to fully express their talents. *What kind of leader are you? How do you know? What actions illustrate your preferred approach to working with others?*

Pathway to Health Care

I started right out in college as pre-med, but not because I knew I wanted to be a doctor. I actually thought I wanted to write, and so I was also an English major. Michael Crichton was a writer at the time who was just coming out with some popular novels when I was in college, and he was a physician. So I thought I could go to medical school and write. I realized that I couldn't go to graduate school for English and take care of patients, so I decided to go to medical school. It was that simplistic. Both things interested me a lot.

So I prepared to go to medical school without knowing much about what it meant to be a doctor. I purposely took the bare minimum pre-med courses that were required. When I started to actually take care of patients, I absolutely loved it. I liked every clinical rotation in medical school. I liked talking to patients of all types. I liked hearing about what was going on. I liked the challenge of trying to figure out what was wrong.

My specialty is infectious disease. This is a specialty that is more hospital based, since many of the patients are in intensive care units or are immunocompromised in some way. Most patients are very sick, and in most cases there will be an answer when the cultures and other tests are completed—usually over the next few days or weeks. However, many patients need to receive the correct therapy before the diagnosis is confirmed, so the history and physical examination are critical. To do that well at Rush, we round with four or five students, a similar number of residents, and a fellow. It is among the busiest consult services in the hospital. I enjoy trying to take things that took me a long time to figure out when I was in training and explain those things more simply. When I ask students to discuss a case, I expect their differential diagnosis to make sense based on their level of training. No matter how off base their final conclusion might be, if it is logical based on what they have learned to date, then it shows they are thinking and using their knowledge. If they are correct in the diagnosis but can't explain how they got there, that's much more of a problem. To be able to combine two things I am passionate about, taking care of patients and teaching, has been ideal.

Pathway to Leadership

I came to Rush for an internship, residency, and fellowship and have stayed here the whole time with the exception of three years in the mid-1990s when I was at Cook County Hospital as the medical director. County and Rush affiliated during that time, and that relationship has grown. We have many programs together and, ten years ago, jointly built the Core Center, an outpatient building for the management of HIV/AIDS. At Core, County and Rush physicians work side by side serving a vulnerable population and achieve some of the best outcomes in the nation. I loved working at County. I learned a great deal from my boss, Ruth Rothstein, and was continually impressed with the talent and dedication of many of the doctors and other health care providers. The governing body for County was the Cook County Board, a group of elected officials. I believe this is a flawed structure, but through it I learned a great deal about both the importance of oversight and governance and if that component is dysfunctional, how damaging it can be.

In 1998, I was asked to come back to Rush as senior vice president for Medical Affairs, a newly created position. A short time later, I became dean of the medical school. In 2001, there was a search for a new president and CEO. The search committee of the board invited me to apply, but initially I did not. I assumed that they would go outside the institution for somebody, since Rush was really having some serious financial challenges. I told them I would be happy to help whoever is selected for as long as they would like me to help, and if they didn't want my help, I would go back to practicing as an infectious disease specialist. I truly wanted to play whatever role was necessary to help correct things—and sometimes that role is to get out of the way. I knew I could be happy either way. As time went by, I was asked to apply again. I did, and I was eventually offered the position. I took the position not because I had some long-term career plan to be a CEO or by thinking that if I didn't get the position I would go elsewhere. I love this place. I enjoy practicing here. I enjoy my colleagues here. I knew very well that I had never managed anything as large as Rush, I did not have a ready recipe for how to reverse our problems, and this was not a game. I cared deeply that Rush was in difficulty. We were losing about $5 million a month at that time. All I knew was, I was more than willing to do everything I possibly could to help, and I also knew that other academic centers had successfully adjusted to new challenges and we should be able to, as well. I did have tremendous confidence that Rush could do this.

What's Important to Me as a Leader

Our Success Is Not about Me

At every level—from the board to admitting physicians to management to the frontline people—they chose to be constructive and act positively in a very tough time. That is why Rush was successful. This is not false modesty; this is the absolute truth.

When I became CEO I needed to make sure that I kept as many of the very talented people that were already in senior positions as possible and to recruit additional ones as quickly as possible. If there's one major message I would have about the story of Rush's turnaround, it is that anybody who thinks this is a story about me is just off. A very large number of people have contributed to the positive results here. It is many more than the senior management team, but they deserve a great deal of credit. It's the board, and it's so many clinicians, researchers, other administrators at all levels as well as employees who, particularly here in Chicago, with so many other academic centers, had multiple opportunities to leave. Nobody would have to sell their home or pull their kids out of school. There are a lot of other big hospitals and academic institutions around here. But they didn't leave. People stuck it out, dug in, and helped. That is what the big deal is here, and so it is not in any way, shape, or form the story about one person.

The team of people that is here now in management has been critical to our success, and fun to work with. To be able to have a group of people like this stay at Rush as long as they have in senior management has been terrific. Certainly, the overall trajectory of the organization from where it was to where it is today has been outstanding. And it is great to see a lot of hard work by a lot of people pay off. I think it is remarkable that senior managers took a chance with me and with Rush and joined the team when things were most challenged. Catherine

Jacobson became the senior vice president [SVP] and CFO during the darkest time for Rush. Today she is also in charge of strategic planning for Rush and is the head of the Healthcare Financial Management Association [board] nationally. Lac Tran joined Rush as the SVP in charge of IT—when we had no budget for IT. He had been in charge of IT at several other institutions and agreed that it was easier to do this job with a lot of money but more challenging to do it with a limited budget. He came with the idea that we would invest in IT—but not for several years. He took a chance. Peter Butler joined Rush after serving as CEO in two other organizations, including an academic medical center larger than Rush. He accepted the role of executive vice president and chief operating officer. He could be a CEO anywhere but wanted to help at Rush. The title was not the issue. Tom Deutsch left a chairmanship to become dean and provost—again during the time when Rush was distributing new funding rules and reorganization plans, not so many recruitment packages. Bob Clapp joined us from Duke [University Hospital] as the SVP for Hospital Affairs, and Avery Miller and Diane McKeever remained in senior key management positions. These individuals took a chance on Rush, and we all worked like interns.

Voices of Others

He is quite shy, not a small-talk kind of guy. He is also modest. He willingly shares recognition and equally willingly accepts accountability when things don't work; he does not blame.—JL

He is humble. Being interviewed for this book is the last thing he would want.—PB

An Effective Executive Team

It is important that we have the correct team with the correct mixture of views, especially for me as a physician CEO and especially for a place like Rush, where the university (research and education), the hospitals, the salaried physicians, and our community programs all report to one team and one president/ CEO. The strategic plans and the funding for these plans all have to be coordinated and make sense as a whole. Some team members need to know the business side well, but just knowing that is not sufficient to understanding and striving to achieve the full range of the mission that includes financial, research, education, and quality elements.

It is also critical to me that along with a strong variety of views comes a willingness to challenge each other, and that includes me. It is not a question of who is right, it is a question of whether the team member is comfortable enough to ask questions. No one can fake it in making and owning a decision, just as no one can fake the practice of medicine.

Relationship issues in the executive team are hugely exacerbated by CEOs who always have to be right. They act without sufficient input or thought. They convey a message that "I'm the CEO; I'm going to make a decision, and this is the way it is going to be."

That is absolutely not me personally, so if somebody said at the board level "That's what you have to do," I'd just leave. It would be so out of character for me; I just could not lead that way. I wouldn't be happy. It's the same as teaching medical students by screaming at them, which is no good. So, the only way I can enjoy dealing with tough decisions is to reach some conclusions, test them with people, try to get people to beat it up if they think it's wrong, and then when I feel like everybody's together, then we have a path forward. At the same time, there are times when some very tough decisions just have to be made and we don't always have the luxury of time. When we have to say we have come to the end of the road on an issue, and whether everyone agrees or not, or whether everyone has weighed in or not, an action needs to be taken. Firm, unambiguous action in those situations is also very important. By no means have we attained this level of balanced performance in making decisions—it is a goal.

Larry offers a great lesson for boards in appointing board members or hiring a CEO, or for anyone hiring for a position in health care: Is the person you are hiring driven by a spirit of service to the organization and its mission and values, or is the person driven by a spirit of self-service? *What drives you? And what questions would reveal whether an applicant is driven by service or self-service?*

Voices of Others

When he became CEO he decided he had to use his executive team, get the brightest people around him, and sustain his physician connection; he has created a spirit of inclusion in decision making. His invitation: "Come be a team with me."—CJ

He has developed into a strategic leader who has successfully learned to manage a team of executives; all this from someone who didn't know how a balance sheet worked when he became CEO.—CJ

He considers it critical to choose leaders who fit into the big picture and who act as owners of the whole organization.—TD

Developing Leaders

We have improved our succession planning, have a leadership mentoring program, have leveraged our 360[-degree feedback] process to identify and to close skill gaps, and have continued to improve our evaluation of employees. I think we could be better at moving people "over" and not only moving people "up" by using horizontal promotions.

Voices of Others

He is our spiritual leader, setting the tone, modeling, listening, and making decisions.—JL

Values are pivotal to him. We rolled out our I-CARE values to every individual in multiple conversations and incorporated them into our performance appraisal.—JL

He demonstrates all of the Rush values naturally. For him it was not the what but the how of walking the talk organizationally. So 50 percent of our evaluations are based on our demonstration of the values.—PB

Making a Positive Difference in the Learning Process for Students

I taught in lots of different medical school courses. I met with our student advisers. I looked at what some of our best teachers were doing. When I was the associate dean of the medical school, I went with the students to every one of the promotions committee meetings when they were up for review. I looked at the differences between students who got feedback that was undeniably constructive versus the feedback that was more caustic, more intimidating. The ones who received constructive feedback received it better, appreciated it, wanted it, sought it out, and often revered those who gave it to them as the best teachers. They wanted to be told what they were doing wrong and how they could improve. Intimidation is not the way to teach. In the dean's office, we tried to make sure we were supportive of students, and we took great pride in the fact that many of the people who won teaching awards were members of the dean's office. After all, we were the ones being paid to be the stewards of the students' education and to provide a better experience for our students. It became a much more rewarding career for those of us in the dean's office and, I'm convinced, a better way for everyone involved in the educational process.

Putting Myself in Others' Shoes

If there's one thing I try to do, and I'm not perfect in any of this stuff, it is to put myself in other people's position. I try to think what it's like to do any of the jobs around here. It is important to me that people feel as if those of us that are trying to run the place have a set of behaviors and values that they themselves could be proud of. I know we've got to make some tough decisions, even let people go or stop programs that are useful. But I think that what people affected would like to know is that there is a chance that those decisions could get revisited if there is enough reason and that people would at least give them the courtesy of thinking of them and listening to them, and to do that with seriousness.

Voices of Others

When we had a patient suicide he led our investigation in a compassionate, thoughtful, blame-free, evidence-based way and encouraged us to report the event to The Joint Commission because it was the right thing to do. He came in during the middle of the night to make sure the staff were okay.—JL

He is not formulaic, he is genuine. He meets with staff, is concerned about the impact of change on everyone, including the housekeeper. He answers every employee e-mail in a thoughtful way.—JL

He is an extraordinary articulator who can shape his message to any audience.—TD

Helping People Feel a Part of Something Worthwhile

I think people really want to feel that they are an important part of something that is, itself, extremely important. I think that all too often people think that it's a big place, it's impersonal, it's just a job. "I love taking care of the patients; the rest of it, it is what it is." And that is what a lot of people *say* about working at big places, but it's not what they *want*. I think what people really want is to believe that the place they work at really cares a lot about them, the patients, the right things. You would think that would be easy in health care—but size has the potential to minimize the role of the individual and depersonalize the actions of the whole. Also, communication is an added challenge in large organizations. But we are not making widgets—what everyone does is incredibly important, and they deserve to be told that and thanked often.

Voices of Others

He is focused, results oriented, and attentive to the things that really count and matter: the culture of the organization; that every patient counts; that our field of work is a calling; that the little, everyday actions matter more than grand strategies.—PB

He is more than happy to spread the credit to everyone else, and he doesn't need to claim the credit.—TD

For him, patient care is primary.—DJ

Taking People Seriously and Treating Them with Respect

I want everyone who works here to believe that Rush is successful because of others. They are important. I'm sure it doesn't always feel that way to people, but it's very important to talk about it, to let people know. That's why at the many employee meetings I attend it's important that people realize that they are taken seriously. It's not that hard for me to push back on somebody's concern with five facts of my own. But it is much more honest, really more respectful, to say: "Here is the fundamental issue we are all dealing with"; "Here is what we are trying to do"; "Here's how it hasn't worked for some groups"; "Here's what we are thinking about doing now"; "And if you have got some other ideas, it is important that we take them into account."

I'm not concerned when others question me for spending so much time talking to employees and doing employee lunches where I can only meet with fifteen to twenty employees once a month in small groups. Or when they question why I do second- and third-shift town hall meetings when I get 200 or 300 attendees during the day but only 10 or 20 at night. Some ask me "Why are you going in at three in the morning for that? What are you doing that for?" I think it's a good thing to do. But it's not a prescription for everybody else. I just think it's respectful of the people who are working at night, and I think the ones who don't even go like to know that the CEO is there sometimes.

What I find is that students and employees are incredibly forgiving. It's the most amazing thing. They're so incredibly nice as they explain to you something isn't working well; you hear it and you think, my goodness, these students are paying tuition, or this employee shouldn't have to put up with that. But they are so pleasant and respectful in the way they are trying to express the problem and grateful that anybody's trying to help turn it around. People are very open if they feel like they're going to be heard. I have received a huge amount of positive feedback on this, and if, at times, I am less certain about whether having these sessions for a small group is a good idea, every single time I've done it I leave those sessions thinking that it is only ten or fifteen people, but I'm glad I did it.

Talking with employees in small groups or responding to a single employee's e-mail is something Larry values in his leadership work; he believes that the conversations inform his decisions and reflect the organization's values. *Do you consider it a waste of your time to meet with very few people, sometimes on off shifts? Or is it a valuable use of your time? And what personal values are shaping your point of view?*

Voices of Others

He is accountable, compassionate, transparent, and smart.—JL

He is a tremendous learner and listener.—PB

He is consistently positive, supportive, and thankful.—PB

He makes people feel that he cares about them personally, because he does.—TD

He has taught me to be a better listener and more respectful of others' opinions, to be calm (and calming), to develop the ability to think through decisions as opposed to reacting. He leads people to their own insights.—CJ

Everybody Is Mission Driven, Value Driven

I always get concerned when people say that the way they do this CEO job is to say "I'm mission driven. I'm value driven." Well, I think everybody is. I'd like to think everybody is trying to do the right thing and do their best. I assume right off the bat that I don't have the corner on being value driven. There's no reason why I suddenly have a different set of values than anybody else who works in this place. To say that I have some value-driven approach is not respectful of them. I do think they care a lot, and I do think that caring is going to make the institution a lot better.

It is not uncommon to hear health care leaders complain that employees and other stakeholders, like physicians, are not committed to or care about the mission and goals of the organization, usually leading to the question "How can we get people committed to what we need to accomplish?" Larry offers a different point of view, that people are mission driven, leading to a very different question: "What can we do to help our people express their commitment to the mission and goals? *Which question are you asking most often? Which is the better question for you to be asking?*

We were fortunate when I started as CEO that this had been an organization that was clinically strong. So we were able to say that we wanted to be among the best and to measure that on clinical quality. That resonated with people. They felt it was attainable, and they didn't mind the fact that we were telling them we are not there yet, even though people took a great deal of pride in what we were already doing.

When I became dean I decided early on that I was going to try to be as available as possible with open meetings and that I was going to take questions just as I did when I was an assistant and an associate dean with the medical students. I went on rounds at every single site that we send our students to. I would do clinical rounds with them. I would also always sit and talk with them and ask them "How it is going? Is all this happening the way it's supposed to happen?"

Voice of Others

When his appointment as CEO was announced to a group of managers, the room erupted with a standing ovation. It was a great day. We knew he would have the best interests of Rush at heart.—JL

Having the Hard Conversations

The harder things sometimes are to go to people who you have great respect for and know are working very hard in a positive way for everything in the institution and yet have to tell them that something they are doing or something in their program is contributing to a problem and needs to be corrected.

You get back to transparency. I don't much like the word *courageous*, but I think the difficult thing is forcing yourself to face the facts as you know them, lay them out for people, seek to understand the root causes of the problem better, and to engage in very difficult conversations. It can be hard because people who have spent a lot of time trying to manage these areas aren't very happy when somebody comes in from somewhere else saying "Let's open up your books and look at everything you are doing."

What makes it easier is to focus on the fact that, first, it is my absolute responsibility to make sure that to the best of my knowledge things are working the way they're supposed to, and second, it is silly to make decisions based on a current situation that can be changed and resolved. Early in our turnaround this did require much more hands-on time by administration in a lot of areas. It was hard for people in an institution that was traditionally more laissez-faire and more decentralized. It feels like you are questioning how they do their jobs, which is not easy, especially for somebody who's been in the organization their whole career doing something a particular way. Again, it was wonderful that, even though I'm sure they were put off by that, people stuck around and worked through it and did a wonderful job and became a big part of Rush's success. When decisions are made that are individually inconvenient but better for patient care, everyone can agree on them.

Voices of Others

Unusually for a CEO, Larry chaired the Sentinel Event Committee and created an analytical no-blame approach.—TD

Underneath it all he is supremely confident because he knows he will figure out if he doesn't yet understand it.—PB

When he created a culture of accountability it was a big change.—TD

He is able to put his own ego aside and truly think through what is best for the organization.—DJ

We were losing $5 million a month. When he was appointed CEO, key leaders hung in because of Larry: "If he's in, I'm in."—PB

An Open Style—Important, But Insufficient, for Partnership

I think people here welcomed an open style. They welcomed transparency: Here is where we are and here, to the best of our knowledge, is why we're here. They appreciated being told what was going on. But I learned that there's a lot more to all this stuff than just transparency. It is not enough to say Here's exactly what's happening, and so here's why I'm doing this to you. Being told what is going on doesn't make you a partner. That takes a lot more understanding; it takes bringing everyone up to speed. For example, you start explaining why the medical school loses money and people say "Wait a minute, what is overhead? How did you decide that I should have to pay for this much overhead?" Well, you have to get into a discussion about how we distribute overhead in an organization such as Rush, and if that's never been part of anybody's language, you need to have discussions and debates about something that's really not very important in driving to better performance but still necessary so people can decide for themselves that these are legitimate costs and that overhead is distributed in a fair way, or at least an acceptable version of fair.

Similarly, the mission is consistent with what Rush has always stood for, which is a focus on clinical care. But anybody, particularly a CEO, can be subject to misinterpretation. It doesn't matter how long they've known me. We say patient care is number one and that research, education, and community service are also important but they're driving that goal. I believe the best patient care can only be sustained in an atmosphere of active research and education, so we planned investments in these areas.

These are not things that can be easily communicated in writing, although written materials can be supportive. They are things that are best communicated when you can be in a room, talk to the people, explain, and respond to questions. By far and away the best communication is when you can get into either small or medium-sized groups and actually talk to people, answer them, look at them. I did that from the beginning and still do a lot of that, as do many other people on the management team, and still the number one challenge is always communication. It's the hardest thing.

Voices of Others

He is candid and open. In town hall meetings he will admit a problem, ask questions, admit when he doesn't have an answer, and respond in a way every employee can understand.—JL

He has no hidden agendas.—DJ

He is a learner who will go out of his comfort zone.—JL

He is so smart, and he is a quick study. He doesn't accept things at face value and never jumps to a conclusion.—JL

The Power of a Vision

In the past, many people on the clinical and the research end would say that the financial performance is not their issue, unless it impedes what they can do. When everybody realized that financial performance was everybody's issue, we were able to clarify the gap in financial performance. People began to see more clearly where we were headed when we laid our finances out and explained what this means; what steps are happening; why we are doing this; how endowment spend-down works; why we are spending money on this program; why we are marketing, and the results we expect to, and do, get from marketing. We also developed a consistent way of describing where we were along the path. We incorporated all that into our annual milestones and corporate goals, showing how they all contribute to realizing our longer-term financial and strategic plans.

It was important to us that we picked a year (2015) to attain the vision rather than some indefinite time out there. We picked 2015 about five years ago for a number of reasons. First, we wanted to make the point that we are not there yet. Second, we needed to show that just building a new hospital (due for completion in 2012) doesn't get us there—if people think we are just a new hospital and electronic medical record away from being among the best in the country, take a breath, because that's not it.

Also, it required developing metrics moving forward and the measurement of performance. Each year when we present the budget, we look back on the year, get clear answers to the questions "Did this get us moving as we expected towards reaching our vision both in the financial aspects and, much more importantly, the clinical aspects and the quality outcomes, or did we lose ground, or just tread water? And does next year's budget take us a sufficient step closer to our 2015 vision?"

So far, each year we've been able to look back and say we did. We made the progress or more than the progress that we expected, and we just submitted and got approved the budget that, if we're able to execute on it, ought to get us yet another step closer. I think that has been an easier way to describe it to people because they can see the tangible pieces, the electronic record and campus transformation, which really helped. When people see these physical changes it feels like they are seeing the fruits of their hard work, that they're going to have a much better place to work in.

Voices of Others

With all the success Rush has enjoyed, he is still himself. Other successful CEOs might become overconfident and out of touch. Not Larry. He never loses sight of what really matters.—PB

I trust him with any decision he makes because he will always make it for the right reason—and he will not accept otherwise.—CJ

He expects us as leaders to drive towards the vision and mission.—JL

He is good at understanding whether something is a big deal or not.—TD

I have known a lot of very accomplished people, and he is one of the most outstanding human beings I have ever known.—DJ

He is one of those leaders with staying power. Not a hit-and-run artist.—DJ

Leaders committed to vision and mission in their daily work demonstrate outcomes consistent with their commitment. *Are your vision and mission operationalized, or are they, while well intended, disconnected from the goals, metrics, and everyday work of the organization? Would an employee or other stakeholder anywhere in the organization be able to tell you how their actions are moving the organization toward the vision and mission?*

What Is Non-negotiable for Me

If we reached a point where Rush had to change focus entirely, for example, become a place without a university, for me it would not be Rush anymore. There are things like that which are a big deal for me. Similarly, if somebody came to me and said: Here's what we want done, and we want you to do it in the next two weeks by laying out some edicts as the CEO that would fundamentally alter the relationship and commitment I have with everyone that works here, I couldn't it. You never want to need a job that badly.

A Good Day

What is a good day? Just about all of them, to tell you the truth. There are not too many jobs that expose you to so many different things in the course of a single day that are all so fascinating. I might go to lecture in the medical school in the morning, meet with the employees at lunch, hear about where we are with the debt and borrowing money, make a presentation to bondholders, talk to trustees, and maybe then make a presentation for a philanthropic request for dollars to a donor, and in the evening go do some other activity.

Then there's a bunch of regular administrative needs. I may be walking around, doing safety and quality rounds on the floors. Those days are fun because it is so interesting to see so many different aspects of a place. I work with people I really like and enjoy. These are terrific, terrific individuals who are very talented, hugely dedicated, work very hard. So there is no wasted time on petty complaints about other people. It is a pleasure, it really is.

A Bad Day

Well, a bad day is when you know for sure that somebody, or some area, or even a larger group, is really kind of miserable about something. There are places that we've been challenged and we have been slow to correct certain problems that impact people who work here. When that happens, I feel badly about it. You can only apologize so much, but it takes awhile to fix some processes that are difficult, and we look to redouble our efforts.

There are also days when something occurs in the external environment or internal environment that create[s] a perception that the risks facing Rush might have dramatically increased in a specific area or as a whole, because health care is a risky place. So we are always at risk that we may have tomorrow an unexpected problem that could derail a lot of the plans we have.

And, of course, the worst days are when something happens with a patient that just shouldn't happen.

Voices of Others

JL   Jane Llewelyn, *vice president, Clinical Nursing Affairs*

PB   Peter Butler, *executive vice president and chief operating officer*

TD   Tom Deutsch, *senior vice president, Medical Affairs, and provost, Rush University*

CJ   Cathy Jacobson, *senior vice president, Finance, and chief financial officer*

DJ   Dick Jaffee, *chairman, board of trustees*

8

Health without Boundaries: Phil Newbold

Phil Newbold is president and chief executive officer of Memorial Hospital and Health System in South Bend, Indiana. He joined Memorial in 1987 as CEO. His background is in hospital administration. Memorial is a 526-bed regional referral center, including a Level II trauma center; a children's hospital; a home care entity; and the Memorial Medical Group, with 3,500 employees and 500 physicians.

Phil is a passionate advocate for innovation in health care. Memorial was one of the first hospitals in the United States to establish an innovation research and development (R&D) policy. An example of its innovation efforts is MEDPOINT express® retail clinics. Developed by Memorial before retail clinics gained popularity, they are now wholly owned by Memorial Health System in partnership with Walmart and are located in regional grocery stores. Another innovation is Memorial's tithing program. Endorsed in 1992, the tithing is above and beyond the traditional charity care provided for patients who cannot afford health services. Each year, a portion of excess revenues is set aside to help local organizations develop innovative programs that address a vast range of risks to community health.

Growing Up

I grew up in Dayton, Ohio. I would characterize my upbringing as very typical, middle class—walked home at lunch and after school; Cub Scouts, Boy Scouts, Sunday School, sports, all the usual kinds of things growing up; and it was a wonderful, carefree time. I had great parents, a brother and a sister. There were interesting activities in the evenings and on the weekends; it was just a great childhood all around.

Background Information

President and CEO,
Memorial Hospital and Health System, South Bend, Indiana
www.qualityoflife.org

Organizational Mission
Memorial is dedicated to improving the quality of life for the
people of our community.

Memorial Hospital and Health System Information
- Memorial Hospital traces its roots to 1894, when the Women's Home Missionary Societies of the Methodist Churches of South Bend, Indiana, founded Epworth Hospital and Training School. By 1901, the hospital had grown from three patient beds in a converted house to a fifty-bed "modern" hospital—complete with a maternity room and an operating room—in the first building in South Bend designed specifically as a hospital. The name officially changed in 1945 to Memorial Hospital of South Bend.
- Memorial developed an innovative service, BrainWorks. It is a program that focuses on a healthy brain lifestyle and is made up of three primary categories: physical health, brain fitness, and vitality. Among the related services are online cognitive development activities to maintain brain fitness.
- Memorial partnered with IDEO, an organization that understood the process of innovation and enjoyed a deep history of introducing new products and services. IDEO helped completely redesign the patient experience in the $40 million Heart and Vascular Center.

Selected Results for Memorial
- An early innovation (which predated the Board Innovation Policy) resulted in the creation of the country's first HealthWorks! Kids' Museum. This unique program and facility offer fun and interactive educational activities to help children learn to make healthy choices in life. Since opening, the museum has been replicated in Tupelo, Mississippi, and featured on Tom Peters' PBS special "Re-imagine!"

- Return on investment in innovation has been 130 percent to 300 percent for the last four years.
- 2008 Hospital Consumer Assessment of Healthcare Providers and Systems (HCAHPS) results:

Would patients recommend the hospital to friend and family?

Memorial   **U.S. Average**
  77%   68%

Rate this hospital overall?

Memorial   **U.S. Average**
  73%   64%

- 2008:
  - Operating Margin: 4.0%
  - Tithing investment: $1.5 million
  - AA− bond rating

Individual Recognitions for Phil Newbold

- 2004: Inducted into the South Bend Community Hall of Fame
- 2002: Recipient of the Exemplar Award, Coalition for Educational Success
- 2001: Recipient of the American Hospital Association's Foster G. McGaw Prize for Excellence in Community Service
- 1998: Recipient of the Community Service Award, presented by The Hotchkiss School

I had a very intact nuclear family with good values and from an early age always knew right from wrong. I had a lot of structure around me with school, Scouts, church, and many activities. I was also self-sufficient and a bit independent yet still had enough structure so I didn't get too far off course. My mother passed away when I was in eighth grade, and my dad remarried.

I went to a very good suburban high school, where there were about 140 in my high school class. All but two of us went to college. Going to college was assumed. It showed me the value of expectations and who you are associating with. I decided to go to Ohio State [University]. It was much easier on tuition than the eastern schools that had accepted me, and I was going to run track at Ohio State. I actually switched from track to lacrosse; I won three varsity letters and continue to participate in sports as a huge part of my life.

Phil identifies that those around him influenced his performance in a variety of areas. *How would you describe those who surround you, those with whom you choose to spend time? Do you surround yourself with people who have a positive view of the future and lead you to new heights in your effectiveness and growth, or do you surround yourself with people who affirm your limitations and those of others and harbor a pessimistic view of the future?*

Influences—People and Situations

Good, steady parent support was key, but I would say I was mostly influenced by teachers, coaches, and scout leaders. They were people in authority who were good role models, and most of them never let me down. They were right on target with life's lessons, doing the right kinds of things for the right reasons.

I developed mononucleosis and I was out of school for many months in my senior year of high school. Somebody suggested to my dad that even though I had graduated from high school, maybe I ought to take one more year at an eastern prep school to get ready for college. I applied and I got into a top school called The Hotchkiss School. There I was surrounded by kids who were mostly going to Ivy League schools. It was a great environment. In the year I was there I really learned how to study better. And I learned the value of surrounding myself with high-performance people.

Pathway to Health Care

Right after college, I went to graduate school at Miami [University] of Ohio and got an MBA. I had no clue of what I wanted to do, although I knew I liked leadership and management. This was at the time of the Vietnam War. I joined the National Guard and then transferred to the Army Reserves. The main driver at that time was to be able to stay in school. I kept transferring until I ended up in a medical unit. I went to Fort Polk [Louisiana] for six months for basic training. I joined a medical unit, and I went to Fort Sam Houston [Texas]. On the weekends I visited a couple of fraternity brothers who were in medical school at Baylor [University] in Houston, Texas. They are the ones that actually got me interested in hospitals. I followed them around on the weekends, seeing patients, and they spoke so interestingly and highly about hospitals and medicine. I knew I didn't want to be a doctor, but boy, those hospitals were really interesting places: how they were structured, put together, and managed.

When I got out of the reserves, I got a job right away at Children's Hospital in Columbus, Ohio. Again, I didn't have any idea of what I wanted to do. I did well in those next few months, and the person I worked for suggested I stay in Columbus, and he would see if he could get me into the hospital administration program at Ohio State, and I got in. Then I got married that August—my wife had an elementary school teaching job in Columbus, and I went to graduate school. That is how I got into hospital administration.

Pathway to Leadership

I was elected president of the High Y, which was the YMCA, somewhere between eighth to tenth grades. It was the first time I was in a leadership position, and I can remember clearly that I liked it. I thought that was pretty interesting, and we actually started organizing and producing dances. I very much enjoyed doing new things, things that hadn't been tried before. My first entrepreneurial activity was as a newspaper boy, getting up at 4:30 every morning and doing that for several years.

At Ohio State I became president of the fraternity and then president of the entire fraternity system at Ohio State. I was very active in up to a dozen different organizations I belonged to in college. I never wanted to just join. I always aspired to be president. I just enjoyed taking the organization and moving it in a positive direction. So I became an officer or had a leadership position in many of those groups, which helped me develop my leadership. I enjoyed trying new things, doing things differently, and going in different directions—not the contrarian way but to find exciting, interesting new ideas and do something about implementing them. That pattern continues today. I am on at least twelve boards or community groups today.

I worked for Children's Hospital for a couple of years while I went to graduate school. My wife and I, between us, had seven jobs during that time. I had a business as a DJ! It was a successful little business that required good organization. I got very, very comfortable speaking in front of a microphone. Getting in front of a crowd was like second nature, and that, as it turned out, was a big advantage when I got into management positions. It helped me to be good on my feet and able to handle about anything that came at me. It developed my ability to create, express, and entertain. It was one of those little things that help along the way.

Then I moved to St. Luke's Hospital in Cleveland, Ohio, and I worked there for eight years. The thing that drove me nuts there was that everything was cost-based reimbursement. There was no advantage to taking a risk because whatever you did you got paid for anyway. I got to a point where I thought I had learned about everything I could from that organization and that experience.

A search firm connected me with Jay Henry, the CEO of Baptist Medical Center in Oklahoma City. The whole Southwest was really exploding and growing, fuelled by the oil and energy business. That really appealed to me, and we moved out to Oklahoma City. For four years I had the most fun I have ever had in just about any organization. It was four years of go, go, build, build. We were the joint venture kings of the United States. We did more joint ventures with physicians than anybody in the country. It was an entrepreneurial environment. We started a heart transplant program and recruited Christian Barnard, who brought his whole heart transplant team from South Africa to Baptist in Oklahoma City. We started a big transplant program, and we were on *Good Morning America* five or six times. I joined Baptist as vice president of Planning and Marketing, and then I got a shot at being the CEO of the hospital, which I took. I was the first CEO in the United States who came from planning and marketing; most CEOs at that time came from finance or operations. I was thirty-six. When Baptist went through reorganization, I applied for the system CEO job but didn't get it. That led me to look around, and that's when the Memorial CEO job came open. I have been here ever since—for twenty-two years.

Risk taking is a component of leadership work. Often leaders do not consciously examine their view of risk taking and the failures that are bound to come with taking risks. *What is your relationship to risk? Is it something to avoid, or do you believe that taking risks is the key to significant positive change in health care? What is the impact of your view on day-to-day performance?*

I always wanted to be a CEO. I enjoyed working with CEOs, and I aspired to be like them. I worked for four good ones before coming to Memorial, and I really learned a lot from each one of them. I thought they did wonderful things in the community and for the organization; that was always my aspiration, to be in that type of a role.

The first few years at Memorial we spent focused on improving operations, building my own management team, and other basics. Since then we have had eighteen years of uninterrupted growth and have done very well. We have been through three major transformations: quality improvement, the healthy communities movement, and innovation.

The First Transformation: Quality Improvement

I saw early on that quality is something we really needed to excel in. We looked to learn from the very best in the country, and then in the world. We exposed ourselves to many quality experts and gurus, but we really resonated with the folks in the Juran Institute. The question then was How do we get to that next step up, that next breakthrough? They suggested that we go to Japan. We did, for two weeks, touring and seeing first-hand the Deming quality prize–winning companies. We also spent time at Motorola, Florida Power and Light, Milliken, and other big, successful companies. That actually set the tone for our work in innovation, which came later.

Learning from outside of health care is a consistent theme of leaders who achieve sustained results. *Do you spend time outside your organization and outside of health care, seeking ideas from best practice companies? Who have you learned from in the past year? What is the most compelling lesson you learned that affects your leadership practice?*

We saw that if we could really embrace this quality movement and understand it, it could transform the culture in the organization. It certainly was a skill set we needed, but our visits and conversations showed the importance of culture. Up to that time we really didn't try major cultural transformation. We would get excited about productivity or management by objectives, or there may be something we did in terms of management improvement, but nothing like quality. Quality is pervasive and it touches everyone. They helped teach us the value of a culture that is positive and supportive. The movement was about making sure that everybody was responsible for quality. They understood that all work is a process and the processes are what people do their work through. It's not that people are trying to do anything wrong; it's just that they're caught in bad processes. All that kind of thinking was new, and we had to learn it. We found that when you build quality into your culture, wonderful things happen. We had very good success, and we still have a focus on quality and process improvement today.

The Second Transformation: The Healthy Communities Movement

The second transformation was very different; it was the healthy communities movement. The question we asked was "How do you develop health in a community?" We used a variety of people around the country to plant some seeds about tithing and healthy communities. We brought in speakers like Leland Kaiser [a recognized futurist]. We were very active in the Healthcare Forum. We took our board members to national meetings and introduced them to national speakers. We brought other speakers in and arranged it so our board, the mayor's staff, all the other not-for-profits were literally enjoying and learning together from the same speakers. It was educational, awareness building, collaborative, and experiential learning. Even today when we invite a speaker, we always have community seats and always share that person with others so that everybody gets better together.

We very quickly learned from our exposure to what was happening in the country that it is largely about the choices people make out in the community—not in the hospital, not in doctor's offices, but in neighborhoods, schools, faith-based places. And we realized that if we are going to help people stay healthier, we had better be out there helping and [educating].

When it came time to develop the tithing policy, it was not even controversial. Our board had been involved all along, so their response was "Of course!" The tithing policy was approved seventeen years ago, and it continues to this day. Specifically, 10 percent of our bottom line is tithed to the community. In that way, through tithing, we have generated resources that enable us to go out into the community, to partner, and to create health. It has set off a whole series of initiatives in the community driven by thinking about health, where it is created, why it is important in people's lives, and what role the hospital or our health system plays, with schools, with neighborhoods, with other not-for-profits and organizations, to help create healthier choices and health. Because our efforts were funded, we did not have to rely solely on a volunteer effort. As we have done better financially, our healthy communities tithing fund has grown in many years to the same size as our local United Way [contribution fund].

In Memorial's second transformation, the organization looked beyond its walls in creating health, not solely health care. Phil began to see the organization as one without walls. *What is your organization's relationship to the communities it serves? Is it deeply involved in a wide range of health issues in the way Memorial is? If not, should it be?*

We operate our fund completely different from a traditional United Way. There are no forms to fill out, no committees to go through, and no deadlines to meet. If people have good ideas, we just put them together into a plan. We have criteria, of course. We take on the more unusual, the more entrepreneurial, ideas. We have tried an awful lot of things, and then we put them on the Internet in something called Learning Histories.

Becoming a tithing organization is probably the best thing we have ever done. That whole movement helped us get out of only worrying about the bricks and mortar and technology. It gave us license to literally involve ourselves in everybody else's business and in every part of the community. That has been very, very helpful. It has shown us the way to build strong, collaborative relationships with our community; it has enhanced community health; it demonstrates both our tax-exempt status and our place in the community; it has helped others look towards Memorial as more of a life partner or a collaborator, not so much as a place but a force that can help them stay healthy and improve the quality of their life. That is a whole different type of relationship.

The Third Transformation: Innovation

About eight or nine years ago we started seeing Leland Kaiser again. He is one of my very top mentors. He asked a question fourteen or fifteen years ago: Why don't hospitals have innovation and research and development policies like every other business in America and set aside some dollars to invent its future? But hospitals and health systems don't seem to have anything like that. We got wondering about that. That is when we started visiting leading companies—we have visited about thirty-five of them so far—to ask them about their R&D and innovation work. They couldn't have been more gracious and giving of their time, energy, and talent. We brought all that learning back and, about six years ago, crafted our first innovation policy. I am not aware of too many other hospitals that have an R&D or innovation policy. We thought it was so important to set some resources aside to begin to make sure that innovation impacted every area of Memorial and, as much as we can share, in the community as well. We have been on that journey ever since. As with other transformations, this one is based on getting out of comfortable surroundings, comfortable offices, and familiar things that you know in the hospital and health care and getting into the terribly unfamiliar, and sometimes uncomfortable, world of innovation and learning from the experts, learning from those who have gone on before you, and learning from anybody and everybody you possibly can, and then bringing all that learning back and making it work in Memorial, South Bend, and beyond.

Discussion about the need for innovation in health care organizations is becoming more frequent, but as the saying goes, "After all is said and done, more is said than done." *How true is this saying of you and your organization? What example of innovation can you identify in your past work?*

Some of our innovations have had a broad impact outside of the hospital. The first MEDPOINT express care centers that you find in Walmarts were created and are owned by us. Some of our leaders took a secret shopper trip to an urgent care location out of state. They loved the concept but the experience was poor. So they put the concept through the prototyping and development process we learned from IDEO. We called Walmart [headquarters] in Bentonville [Arkansas], went there, and pitched our concept. That's how we ended up in Walmart as their first in-store convenience care clinic. We also created HealthWorks! Kids' Museum, an educational experience for children to promote awareness about health in a fun, hands-on way. We have a location here in South Bend and have built another one in Tupelo, Mississippi.

Innovation means different things to different people. *What does it mean to you? Is everyone on the same page when they talk about it in your organization? How do you know?*

What's Important to Me as a Leader

Teams Create Success

I played a lot of sports, mostly team sports. What I always enjoyed was the camaraderie—the team elements. Teams all the way through are what win, including winning at work, meaning good performance and being able to have high quality and good results in services and outcomes. It has always been important to me to bring teamwork to what I do. Plus, it's a lot of fun. It is important that we get to celebrate team success in large organizations like winning teams in any other field. All improvement comes by way of a project because it gets people to work together focused on a common goal.

Having different skill sets enhances team performance. When I am interviewing [candidates], I look for someone different, someone who has a broad background coupled with a deep expertise we are looking for.

Voices of Others

He fosters collaboration in the community and collaboration internally.—JC

It is not about him, it is about the team. He walks his collaboration talk.—MO

He is not a command-and-control leader. He selects competent, developed individuals and supports them as needed to get the job done.—KG

He encourages the board's participation.—RW

Create the Environment for Innovation

All of the uncertainties we are facing are a blessing. There are so many things we could not have predicted, like 9/11, the rise of China and India, the housing and stock market collapse, health care reform. Leadership is not about trying to predict the future as much as it is about making sure the organization and its people have enough capacity, leadership, and agility to make the best of any situation, expected or not. Innovation is one of those capacities that will get you beyond a challenging situation.

Part of the job of a leader is to learn and to be a good teacher. To do that leaders need to hang with the right people, those who will stimulate new ideas, to entertain and balance different points of view, and to become a semi-expert so they can model and teach those competencies to their organization as a body of work, like quality improvement, for example.

Another part of the job of a leader is to create a culture that supports and engages others with new ideas, allows room for experimentation, helps others understand the expectations and rewards, and recognizes that culture.

Leaders must themselves step out and [be] willing to be uncomfortable with risk, never doing it by themselves, learning along with others what does and does not work, and making sure that organizational courage is rewarded.

This has a lot to do with lifelong learning, which is critical for a leader. I think in terms of three piles of knowledge: (1) things we know for certain, (2) things we are uncertain about,

(3) things we know are not true. In my opinion, the secret to lifelong learning is to keep as few things as possible in piles 1 and 3.

Leader as learner, teacher, capacity builder, and role model is an alternative to standard definitions of leaders. *When you think of your knowledge, how does it divide among the piles: (1) things we know for certain, (2) things we are uncertain about, and (3) things we know are not true?*

Voices of Others

He rewards the ability to react quickly to what is coming at us, learn-ing from the outside, and creating a win from the situation.—JC

He is incredibly inquisitive.—KG

He shares success and does not want to take credit. But he takes responsibility for failures and debriefs events for learning, not blame.—MO

He is so up to date, so well read, always thinking things through. He went on sabbatical and came back full of ideas.—RW

Sustaining Improvement

It is critical to stay with things, like our transformations, until they are embedded. Then they don't need the same excitement, enthusiasm, and energy as when you start, and they may have a changed emphasis. Patient safety is now in our focus, and although we are applying a different methodology and different tools, it is in the same context of quality improvement, healthy communities, and innovation.

A positive culture is key to making improvement stick. For that to occur, leaders need to (1) create a dissatisfaction with the status quo, to take a realistic view of where the organiza-tion is and acknowledge that we need to do better; (2) create a shared, clear, and compelling vision for the future: "If we are successful, then . . ."; (3) provide a vehicle for the journey, a design for change, tools, processes, methodologies; and (4) articulate a personal "What's in it for me? If we pull this off, what impact will it have on me, our group, our organization, and the outcomes important to us?"

Voices of Others

He is the consummate continuous learner.—MO

He is highly respected, creative, and innovative and has imbued the whole hospital system with those attributes.—RW

Every one of our meetings begins with an educational component. He wants us to understand the background and nuances for areas for which the board has a responsibility. At a time when there are so many changes in the offing, this has been an invaluable addition to our meetings.—RW

Focus on Strengths

I am a very optimistic person. I tend to always see the good side or the better side of people and situations. There are some things that I steer clear of because they are not a fit for my skill set and talents. I think you make your career and your life on your strengths, not by trying to shore up a couple of weaknesses you might have.

I think the only time you really spend a lot of time on weaknesses is when they are either very toxic or career limiting in some way: things that are really going to hurt you. But other than that, rely on the strengths because where you make your life and your biggest contributions are with your God-given talents or greatest interests.

Building on strengths and capitalizing on the strengths of those around you is a consistent message from Phil and other transformational leaders. *What are your top strengths? How do you build on your strengths to aid your work as a leader?*

Voices of Others

He is well respected for his ability to listen, take in information, debate an issue, reorganize his own thinking if he is wrong, and to provide constructive feedback.—JC

His theme is Be true to yourself.—KG

He understands his strengths. He lets others take the lead for parts of work he doesn't have a passion for.—MO

I was really concerned about work-life balance when I came here. He convinced me that it was important to him as well, and this proved true by his actions, the structures he creates, and his encouragement of exercise or taking time for reflection.—KG

A Culture That Expects Your Best

The question for me is: What kind of a culture do you create, and do you work and live within? I mentioned how impactful it was on me to be surrounded at school by people who had high expectations. The same thing holds true in an organization. If you catch yourself and others saying "That's not good enough for us; we could do better than that," that's a very positive culture, where you just don't settle for less than your best work.

You want to create a culture where people do their best work, and their best work also ties in to the best work of the organization. It's both as the individual and as a collective, the group and the organization.

If the culture is positive, supportive, nurturing, directional, and gives people enough latitude but enough direction as well, that's a wonderful place to work, and people want to work their whole careers there. Or if they do leave—and people do get hired away by other organizations—they always look back and say: "My experience at Memorial was just fabulous!" They feel very good about what they did, and that is what we want. For most people, they look back and say: I did something of great value, meaning, and purpose that had great impact, and I'm a heck of a lot better person for having been at Memorial, because of that culture, because of the leadership and the expectations.

"We can do better" is an example of challenging the status quo and of a positive culture in which you do not settle for less than your best work. *When discussing big challenges with colleagues, how much time is spent explaining why a challenge can't be met by the organization, and how much time is spent exploring new solutions and in positive action?*

Voice of Others

He doesn't fall back on traditional values and will challenge us if he sees us doing that.—MO

Big Ideas Attract Big Resources

If you look at any of our community health initiatives—we have between twenty and thirty in our Learning Histories that we try to continue to work at—we developed initiatives in a collaborative way; it is not something that just we are doing. It involves community organizations, neighborhoods, schools, and other groups. When we collaborate, we begin to develop less risk because everybody is in this thing together, and we are in there all learning together. As long as you capture those learnings and have some criteria for improving health, boards and community people are not only supportive, they are extremely enthusiastic, and you end up having people volunteer, step forward.

Big ideas always attract big resources: talent, people, ideas, money. If an idea is powerful enough, impactful enough, and fun enough, people will self-select. We see that all over the community, and so we have a lot of partnerships, a lot of folks who want to work with us. That is the secret sauce, the fact that big ideas attract big resources.

Voice of Others

He has a clear vision, an abundance mentality, and a "we can all do better" attitude.—MO

Experiential, Collaborative Learning Is Vital to Success

The whole healthy communities movement was one of breaking down silos, making people interested in health, and more of an end game where people really aspire to be. Our vision statement says we want to create the healthiest community in the country.

Well, I don't want to do it by myself, and more important, I can't do it by myself. We want every school, every Boys and Girls Club, every church, every neighborhood helping us work on that. That's what gets me out of my office. Walking the streets and neighborhoods and talking to folks everywhere, trying to find out what gets in the way of them being healthy and what role we might play. Sometimes it is a leadership role, sometimes not, and one of the ways we do that is through community plunges, where we take four or eight hours and actually plunge ourselves into a problem—homelessness, spousal abuse, drug dealers, or too many guns and firearms in the community—whatever the problem is. The idea is that you have the mayor sit next to the Boys and Girls Club director, sitting next to a minister, sitting next to a physician, and everybody gets on a bus and goes to listen to personal stories, to try to understand an issue. When we did a community plunge into the drug problem in our community, one day we piled into a bus and visited a crack house—not driving by, but speaking to active users and absorbing what was going on, which was very graphic. When we involve ourselves in an issue that way, everybody is learning firsthand so we can smell it, taste it, feel it, and see it, even if it is sometimes hard. Then, with an expanded appreciation, we try to work on those issues and do something about them. It is not so different from going to Japan and walking through a factory and seeing people in their jobs, trying to get things done, and you can see it, hear it, taste it, and feel it again. Experiential learning is an important way to get people into a whole different mind-set, into a whole different way of dealing with a problem or an issue.

Experiential learning takes on a new perspective when it puts us into uncomfortable settings and exposes us to situations in which we are inexperienced. *Have you had an experience that placed you in uncomfortable settings, where you were inexperienced? What if you sat with a patient and his or her family for a day as the patient received care; would that put you in uncomfortable settings, where you were inexperienced? What prevents you from testing new experiential learning?*

That is why we always tell people you have got to get out and visit something and somebody if you're going to get some new thinking. That became *the* cornerstone behind our innovation work. If we want to be innovative we need to find the best and go learn from them, bring that learning back, and then share it as broadly as possible with as many people as possible. Not just our own organization but everybody in our community learns from that as well. Every transformation started with experiential learning: quality improvement, healthy communities, innovation. We believe that everything we will ever need is already available to us; we only have to ask, and others will spend time and share with us. We will share what we have learned with anybody who wants to show up in South Bend from any organization. That sharing really does get everybody up to a whole different level.

Voices of Others

What distinguishes him is his thoroughness and personal commitment to others.—RW

He is concerned for people on the margins of society. His service on local boards working with the poor and homeless underscores this attribute. Memorial became the first hospital in our area to tithe, and this action, fully supported by the board, has helped make our local community a healthier one.—RW

He has shown great solidarity with this organization and community. He has turned down the opportunity to go to other places.—RW

Intuition and Reflection

The longer I am in leadership, the larger the role of intuition becomes. It helps me synthesize, get more perspective, and feeds my imagination—which is critical to me because if you can't imagine something, you can't accomplish it. And when you can imagine, you can create the new, whether it is ways to be more effective with existing resources, out-of-the-box new products or services, or other innovations large and small. For us, innovation is not a twelve-step process; it is more about how to think, how to imagine.

I take time out on busy days to reflect so I can be more present to what is happening and to not be reactive. I do some journaling every day about what is happening, and I often see the future through that process. I will spend time in nature—going for a walk, watching birds—to experience the connection between nature and the big cycles of change, to observe and think how they can be seen and applied at the microscopic level. When I do this and stop thinking, I am more open to intuition.

It is hard in a day full of urgent demands and important work to step back. *Even so, what is one thing you can and will do on a daily basis to engage in reflection?*

Voice of Others

He is one of the most brilliant people I have ever worked with. He has an intuitive nature, a broad perspective, and he looks beyond health care for ideas.—MO

A Good Day

A good day for me is getting started early with exercise; getting to the office looking forward to what we're going to do; at the end of the day, feeling like I had some impact. That might be in relationships. It might be a performance metric. But it is usually a combination of all of those things, knowing we are really moving a step closer to our basic goals, and if I am continuing to grow and excited at the end of the day. Most days are good days. I do all of this with a good sense of humor, trying to have fun and really enjoying not only what we do but how we do it, was well.

A Bad Day

A bad day is when I feel like I have absolutely made no progress whatsoever, and probably those are around people problems. And although it may seem like a bad day, almost always there is a silver lining to it because something's telling me that I didn't do something or didn't pay attention to this and it isn't working for this reason. So bad days are very, very instructive.

Voices of Others

JC	Jeff Costello, *system chief financial officer*
KG	Kreg Gruber, *hospital chief executive officer*
MO	Mike O'Neil, *system chief operating officer*
RW	Father Richard Warner, *system board chair*

9

The Healing Presence of God: Sister Mary Jean Ryan

Sister Mary Jean Ryan began her career as a nurse in a hospital that was part of the SSM Health Care system, based in St. Louis, Missouri. She has continued as part of the system for her entire career and was named the first president/CEO of SSM Health Care in 1986.

When she assumed that role, the SSM system had transformed from an affiliated group of organizations into an integrated system with a new governance structure. She led its transformation over the next twenty-three years, during which SSM was awarded the first Malcolm Baldrige National Quality Award for health care in 2002.

Sister Mary Jean is a leadership role model for continuous improvement and innovation within a broad definition of accountabilities for health care organizations, including her emphasis on promoting women and diversity in health care and preserving the earth long before green and tobacco-free campuses became popular.

She transitioned to chair/CEO of the SSM system in August 2009.

Growing Up

I grew up in a small town in Wisconsin. I was taught through eighth grade by Dominican nuns and then went to a public high school. I had no idea in the world what I was going to do. When I finished high school those many years ago, there really were not that many opportunities for women. You could be a

Background Information
Chair/CEO,
SSM Health Care, St. Louis, Missouri
www.ssmhc.org

Organizational Mission
Through our exceptional health care services, we reveal the heal-ing presence of God.

SSM Health Care Information
- Founded in 1872 by five sisters and now sponsored by the Franciscan Sisters of Mary, SSM is based in St. Louis and owns, manages, and is affiliated with fifteen acute care hospitals and two nursing homes in four states: Wisconsin, Illinois, Missouri, and Oklahoma.
- The congregation that sponsors SSM opened the first Catho-lic hospital for African Americans in the nation in 1933. Not only did the hospital welcome African American patients but it also offered African American physicians and nurses the opportunity to practice their profession.
- In 2008, SSM cared for 1.4 million people through the work of nearly 23,000 employees, 5,400 physicians, and 3,000 volunteers.
- SSM University provides educational opportunities for all employees within SSM Health Care. One of its components is School at Work, which is designed for entry-level employ-ees who have not graduated from high school. By taking the course, employees build the skills they need to pursue further education and advance in their careers within the organization.

SSM Selected Results
- In 2009, SSM hosted its thirteenth annual Showcase for Shar-ing, where more than 350 employees and physicians shared their improvements with an expectation that others steal shamelessly and replicate. The presidents of each hospital iden-tify what they will replicate in their organization the next year.

- Since 2002, various hospitals within the SSM system have received thirty-four state quality awards.
- In 2009, St. Anthony Bone and Joint Hospital, Oklahoma City, achieved 99th percentile physician satisfaction, and Good Samaritan, in Mt. Vernon, Illinois, reduced sepsis mortality from 25 percent to 11 percent.
- Between 2004 and 2009, SSM invested more than $1.154 billion in SSM Health Care facilities, compared with the value of $799.208 million for those assets at the end of 2004. In other words, SSM has rebuilt itself almost one and one half times within this five-year period. In 2009, the SSM system's days cash on hand was rebuilt to 204 after 2008 investment losses caused them to decline to 166 days.
- 2002: SSM Health Care was the first health care recipient of the Malcolm Baldrige National Quality Award.

Individual Recognitions for Sister Mary Jean Ryan
- 2009: Received the Joseph M. Juran Medal for distinguished performance in quality leadership from the American Society for Quality
- 2005: Received the American Hospital Association's Award of Honor
- 2004–2009: Listed among the 100 Most Powerful People in Healthcare in *Modern Healthcare*

---

secretary, but I had failed typing in high school, so I felt that that was probably not a good career path! My parents were not wealthy enough to send me to college to become a teacher. So I went to nursing school in Madison.

Influences—People and Situations

I've said this any number of times, and I will keep saying it because it's absolutely the truth: Those three years in nursing school were probably the most influential years of my life. The friends that I made then are my friends yet today; we recently gathered for our fiftieth reunion. When I was in nursing school, we lived together, we worked together, and we played together. We did everything together, so those were very meaningful years.

I got an opportunity at that time to interact with the sisters, and there were some that I really admired a great deal. And because I was really not settled in any kind of a career path and because I was so inspired by those sisters, I made the decision to enter the convent. Basically I thought I would spend the rest of my life being a staff nurse in some hospital, probably in the Midwest.

Pathway to Health Care

I entered the convent in 1960, and about two days later I was told that I would be going back to St. Louis University to get my baccalaureate. And I said "Okay." That was my very first act of obedience, and I can't name too many more since then! Nevertheless, that was the first and probably the wisest. My baccalaureate was interrupted at one point by a semester off to relieve staff at our hospital in Dillon, South Carolina. Since I knew nursing, I was perfectly positioned to do that.

Pathway to Leadership

When I graduated, I became the assistant supervisor of the operating room at our St. Mary's Health Center in St. Louis. When the supervisor went off to study to be better prepared, I became a supervisor. It didn't take long for me to understand that that was not where I wanted to spend the rest of my life. I wasn't very good at it, and I didn't particularly like it. One of the biggest problems that I had in the operating room was some of the surgeons. We had several who were absolutely lousy at what they did. In those days the medical staff was not nearly as willing to take some of those people to task. I felt that in administration I could have a greater influence on those types of situations. So I asked to go back to school in administration, and I was granted that request. I went to Xavier [University] in Cincinnati [Ohio].

At the end of the health care administration master's program, we were required to do a residency. I didn't have a clue as to what I was going to do, but I thought about California because the West Coast was beginning to experience some new litigation. Jeff Chandler, the actor, had died of an infection at a hospital in California, and his family had sued the hospital. It was the first time charitable immunity had been lost. Subsequently, there was an increase in litigation, and I knew that what happens in California tends to move east. So, I thought I could benefit from a residency there. I blanketed the West Coast with resumes, and I got a call from an administrator at a for-profit hospital. I didn't have a clue what a for-profit was, but I agreed to go there. I can't say it was the greatest year that I ever had, but it was one of those times when the learning of what *not* to do is as valuable as learning what *to* do.

Subsequently, I began my administrative career, of all places, back at my nursing school, St. Mary's of Madison. After awhile, one of the sisters said: "We're going to create a new position of property and construction. How would you like to be the director?" I have always particularly liked construction (for many years, I built doll houses with Sister Susan Scholl) and so I said "Sure." Again, I didn't have a clue what I was going to be doing in this job.

Jumping into a situation you know nothing about appears in many of the profiles in this book. Today, information is more easily available than when Sister Mary Jean was applying for her residency, yet even with abundant information we may find ourselves stepping into situations that present unknown factors. *What is your most recent experience of stepping into the unknown? What was most interesting about stepping into uncharted territory? What did you learn from that experience that can benefit others in their own careers?*

I also began service on what was the old SSM board. It was probably one of the worst governance models you could ever imagine. We were both governing and managing, but we basically had absolutely no authority over anything. And the presidents who reported to us had even less. In the previous structure, hospital presidents did not even have authority to spend $5,000 without board approval; that's just how ridiculous it was.

After several years of deliberation with long-range planning, in 1986 all of the hospitals that were part of SSM came together as a health care system. We had determined that the first president and CEO would be a sister, and a whole range of circumstances led to my being asked to be the first president. It was a brand new job, so we knew we had to make it up as we were going along. It really was starting over in many ways.

I knew that one of the first things I had to do was to get the operations going, and that meant hiring a chief operating officer. In those early years as president/CEO of SSM Health Care, I spent all my time and energy getting things to work internally.

I'm a really strong introvert and shy, so being in that position was sometimes difficult for me. The good news is that I have always had an abundance of good advisers and close friends whom I respect and admire and whom I rely on a great deal for help. One of the things I've never been shy about is admitting what I don't know and what I would like help with.

What's Important to Me as a Leader

Our Mission

As part of our Baldrige work, we collected twenty-one single-spaced pages of mission and values statements from all around the organization. Then nearly 3,000 people at every level of the organization and from every facility participated in a year-and-a-half process of facilitated conversations and came up with a new mission statement. When they showed it to me, I was in awe. It's only thirteen words, but to me, they are absolutely profound: *Through our exceptional health care services, we reveal the healing presence of God.*

Right now I would venture to say that 99 percent of our employees can quote that mission statement. It has been the basis of all of our planning efforts. It is the thing that drives us. We can show that every single day, every single employee has the ability to impact the mission statement.

One thing I feel good about is my ability to rally people around things. I can identify what people can relate to, and that's an important part of my job. If I don't continue to reinforce the mission, and why it is at the heart of everything we do, I wouldn't be able to sleep at night. That's my job!

Ultimately, it's about integrity. If our mission says exceptional care, how can we do otherwise?

Voices of Others

She is inspiring—and has a desire to improve health care. When she does her sharing sessions she has overflow crowds of employees who want to hear her. Why? They come to work because of the mission, and she reflects that. Employees want to work where they can live the mission.—TL

She is intent and intense about what she believes in—there are no half measures, no hesitancy. She articulates her beliefs and translates those beliefs into behaviors; there is integrity in her life.—RD

She links the mission to everything we do. The communication from her when you're in health information technology is: "You don't have to be a clinician to deliver exceptional health care." Our electronic health record is a clinical transformation project, not an IT project—there was never a question of that. We are not in the computer business; we are in the health care business.—TL

She is driven to improve quality based on a higher motivation. For her, quality is a vehicle to reveal the mission, not an end in itself. She has never lost the sense of the person in the bed.—RD

*She has a commitment to patients and the mission statement, and
she is able to hold that view through rough spots, highs and lows.
She never lost sight of her commitment to quality improvement
and to safety. Even when we are cutting in other areas, we are
investing in our safety culture training.*—BT

*She takes the long-term view of the mission and is preparing for
the future. She is transitioning the organization to nonreligious
leaders who have a sense of responsibility to carry on the
mission. The future of SSM is in our hands.*—BT

Translation as a leadership skill is recognized in Sister Mary
Jean's profile. She effectively translates the mission to every
role and helps people see how they fit in with it. Her passion
for the mission leads her to see that a big part of her role
is rallying people to the mission and role modeling that
commitment. *How do you help others see how their daily work
helps achieve the mission? Can most people you work with
state the mission? If they cannot, what is called for in your
leadership?*

Valuing People and Flattening the Organization

Any credit that I get is only because of the work that people
in SSM have done. When I give outside presentations, I use
employee stories to illustrate to the audience that change actually can happen. I am very, very proud of the people of SSM
Health Care. They are absolutely remarkable.

I told this story to a group of 800 operating room nurses
last year: In my early days in the operating room, there was a
surgeon who I knew was doing bad work. I went to an anes-
thesiologist who had assisted this person on many cases, and
I said to him: "We know that Dr. So and So is not doing a
good job. Would you ever testify against him for bad work?"
He said "Well, hell no." I said "I would," and he replied "Yes,

but you're only a nurse." That's that hierarchical view that to this day in many instances is alive and well—although it's better than it used to be. But it takes tremendous effort to be sure that nobody ignores our policy of "time out" that ultimately can prevent wrong-site surgery. We're still having wrong-site surgery because surgeons tell nurses "Don't tell me what to do." We have to be able to remove those barriers because this is ultimately about the care we give to our patients.

When I'm visiting housekeeping people, I'll say to them: "If administration's gone for two weeks, nobody notices, but if housekeeping's gone for two weeks, everybody notices." There is something about the work that everybody does that needs to be valued in a much greater way than it has been valued before. When we continue to have people in housekeeping who say "The work that I do is helpful for the safety of patients because it prevents infections," then I know that we are reaching them with our messages.

I think our work with multidisciplinary teams has broken down some of the silos; people have come to the conclusion that there's so much of the work they cannot get done alone. For example, we have tried to enhance timeliness in our emergency rooms. We can cajole, beg, plead, and threaten the emergency room people, but frankly, they have only a small amount of control over what they do because they have to deal with many barriers throughout the rest of the facility. They may not have a bed to put somebody in, or, even if there's a bed, housekeeping hasn't gotten to clean it yet, or a physician hasn't discharged somebody from an ICU bed, or x-ray can't get there. It takes a team from throughout the hospital working together to effect change.

We have replaced our old sense of hierarchy with a sense of interdependence. Our work with teams, combined with shared governance, has gone a long way toward flattening the organization.

As CEO of a large system, Sister Mary Jean demonstrates deep awareness of what stands in the way of or aids all team members in achieving high-level goals rather than simply demanding results. *Consider a current outcome that is less than ideal. What do you understand about the systems that stands in the way or aids team members to improve the outcome? How skilled are you in helping them to move beyond current performance? What skills do you need to be able to do so?*

What I want to know is: Do the people who do the work know that the work that they are doing has a purpose, and do they know why they are doing it? Why are you in health care? Why do you do what you do? Tell me why you're at this facility. I think we're at the point now where we no longer *invite* but rather *expect* engagement from employees.

When you come to this organization we expect you to have ideas. We expect you to have good thoughts, to be able to recognize when things are not working. Those are the expectations, because if we can't do that and if we have people who for whatever reason aren't getting what we're all about, even though they've been coached and worked with, they have to leave the organization.

I have friends who are at every level here in the organization. I just don't stand on ceremony. That's all there is to it. Anybody who knows how to get into the e-mail list knows I'm on there. They can, and do, write to me. And most times, I write back.

I definitely do have a deep-seated belief in the dignity and value of the human being, and some of that comes from my nursing experience. I can as easily talk to people in housekeeping and dietary as I can to nurses or people in the C-suite.

Why would senior leaders be treated differently than other employees? When all employees are seen as leaders, then we have leaders at every level of the organization and we can use the talents and gifts of all. We cannot afford to limit the participation of anyone at SSM.

Anyone who stands up for the right thing for patients, who says "No, that's not safe, and I won't do it" is a leader just as much as anyone with a title.

Health care organizations have a long and persistent history of performance-limiting and sometimes disrespectful hierarchy. Approaches to address it include respecting and valuing everyone's contribution; expecting everyone to contribute; fostering positive relationships for all, with all; and implementing systems for shared decision making. *What do you do daily to remove hierarchical barriers to engage everyone in achieving great outcomes? Is it enough?*

Voices of Others

There is a sense of heading in the same direction—that alignment means we have conversations with all employees about where we are going, creating a sense of team and a strong bond of trust.—EH

She is willing to make changes in a team to get the right skills in place when they are needed.—SB

Continuous Quality Improvement and the Status Quo

Early on we decided to bring together leaders from across the system at annual leadership conferences. In 1988, we focused on entrepreneurship, which is How do you achieve innovation within a large organization? In 1989, we introduced servant leadership because that seemed to be something that could really get to people's hearts and minds. But at the end of that meeting, Bill Thompson, who's going to replace me when I retire in a few years, and I were sitting around the pool having a beer talking and commiserating over the fact that throughout SSM Health Care there seemed to be this attitude that we were good enough—that the status quo was really okay. We were probably a little better than the national average in many areas. Our people would say "Well, we're better than the place down the street."

I mentioned to Bill that I had heard a presentation about work being done at Intermountain Health Care [based in Salt Lake City] that was making a big difference in outcomes for patients. And I said "I wonder if we could do anything with that work?" Well, coincidentally, Bill had been reading about total quality management (TQM). He's such an avid reader, bright, the classic sponge. We were sitting there, and I said "I wonder if this has some kind of application for us. How can we take what I've heard and what you're learning about this TQM and make it work for us?"

So we took the idea to our system management group, and we soon learned that Don Berwick [physician, former president and CEO of the Institute for Healthcare Improvement, now administrator of the Centers for Medicare & Medicaid Services] was also working on quality improvement. Several of us took a course in it, while other people took a field trip to a place that was being held up as a really fine organization dedicated to TQM. When we came back together, we decided it could work at SSM, and we made the decision to call it continuous quality improvement (CQI). We also were determined that it would be the way we work, rather than a program, because programs come to an end.

I took the concept to the board, and they were hesitant because they felt CQI didn't connect to the SSM values. So our system management group took half a day to do a side-by-side comparison of the principles of CQI and our values. Lo and behold, the connections were startlingly similar. Once I was able to make the link for the board, they gave us the green light to move forward. By the way, that side-by-side comparison became the first page of our CQI policy book.

We launched CQI as a system in 1990, and we don't have enough space in this book for me to describe what that was like. We have 23,000 employees in four states. Suffice it to say

that deploying CQI throughout our large and complex organization was not a job for the timid. To make matters worse,
we tended to use CQI to improve select projects that were not
necessarily strategically linked to our overall goals. And third,
our CQI work moved very slowly. So while employees grew to
understand the importance of working in teams, by 1995 we
had little to show overall for all our work with CQI. We needed
something that would help us focus on the things that mattered
most and that would help us get better faster. That something
was Baldrige.

Malcolm Baldrige National Quality Award

By 1995, we had heard about the Malcolm Baldrige National
Quality Award and how it helped organizations improve. Back
then, health care was not eligible to apply for the Baldrige but
was eligible to apply for state quality awards, which were modeled on the Baldrige. So we encouraged our hospitals to apply
for their state quality awards. The feedback gave us incredibly
helpful information about how we could improve. And, lo and
behold, we actually began winning awards, which gave employees a tremendous morale boost. So when health care became
eligible to apply for the Baldrige in 1999, we applied. However,
I have to emphasize that going for the Baldrige was never about
the award. It was about going through the process and saying
"By God, we are going to get better." I've told people that if we
hadn't received the award in 2002, we would still be applying.

Really the first step for us was acknowledging that we were
not as good as we needed to be. Once you do that, then you
say "Okay, what are the gaps, and what do we need to do to
fill them?" That's where a lot of our early work with Baldrige
came in. Baldrige helped us identify the gaps between where
we were and where we wanted to be in terms of results. Each
year, we would apply, and then we'd get the feedback. We
used that feedback—not to be cute—religiously. We would put
together a team from around the system, and they would look

at the things we could do from a system perspective to improve. Because when you get feedback that's fifty or more pages long, there's a huge amount to work on. Then we'd send the feedback to the facilities and say "Look through it and identify areas where you can improve."

One of the things that we made a commitment to do was to share anything that we could with anybody who wanted to learn. So we put our Baldrige application on the Internet. We told people to go on the Internet and look at our application because there really isn't anything in there that's confidential. This is about making health care better for everybody. Regardless of what comes from health care reform, I truly believe that if our quality is as good as it can possibly be, we will be able to weather whatever comes along.

"We're better than they are" is frequently used to describe performance in health care rather than "Here is how we compare to the best" or "Here is how we compare to our vision and mission." Moving beyond the status quo and aiming high are exemplified in SSM's CQI and Baldrige journey as a means to demonstrate its mission. *Whom do you know who is a model for challenging the status quo and aiming high? Compare his or her behavior to that of people you think are more comfortable with the status quo. Where do you stand in this comparison?*

Voices of Others

She has a persistency—a can-do, not-backing-off, challenging approach to her work. She knows what's essential and what's not. She's willing to listen and try alternatives, but the goal doesn't change—99th percentile in five exceptional areas: exceptional patient care in (1) patient/customer satisfaction, (2) safety, and (3) clinical/service outcomes; exceptional commitment in (4) employee and MD satisfaction; and exceptional (5) financial performance/growth.—TL

She is passionate about her work and brings consistency and a preoccupation with quality and safe care; she never gives up.—EH

*She will challenge us: "Why are financials the only agenda item?"
We are not allowed to just focus on dollars.—TL*

*We believe in transparency. A publication for both internal and
community audiences shows MD satisfaction in all our hospitals
from high to low—everybody sees it.—EH*

Three Areas of Commitment

*When one tugs at a single thing in nature, one finds it attached to
the rest of the world.*—John Muir (from a framed print in the
SSM offices)

In my more than twenty years as president/CEO, I have focused
on three main areas: CQI, diversity (including women in leadership), and the environment. All of these are not only morally
right but also right for business.

Diversity gives credibility to our view of the future. Steve
Barney in Human Resources has helped me build on our commitment to diversity. We have worked diligently to raise women
and people of color to new levels at SSM Health Care. People
of color in particular often have been relegated to entry-level
positions. That led us to create some educational programs
including SAW, our School at Work program; diversity forums;
mentorship programs; and other innovative approaches, all
designed to prepare minorities to advance in the organization.
Our School at Work program offers courses to people who have
never been to high school or went to school a long time ago.
The SAW program serves as the basis for them then to continue
to the next educational level, perhaps a technical school, nursing school, or college, so they can advance in their careers.

About fifteen years ago almost none of our hospital presidents were female. We realized that the common path to CEO
was first to be COO, and the COOs were all men at the time.
Within twelve to fifteen months about 50 percent of the COO
positions were filled by women, and now 50 percent of our
CEOs are women. Because if you only have a pool of white
guys, that's who will advance. Our search firms have to look
for a diverse pool of candidates.

And over the years, we've discovered many ways to do our part in healing our environment. We have Preservation of the Earth committees at each of our hospitals that are in charge of recycling efforts and finding other ways to be kind to the earth. Years ago we eliminated the use of Styrofoam with chlorofluorocarbon throughout the system. In 2004, we became the largest health system to go tobacco free both inside and out, and just a few years ago, we eliminated bottled water from our campuses. There are a variety of other ways we have contributed to the protection of the earth. Our corporate office even supported a wolf at a local wolf preserve.

Voices of Others

She has a single-minded commitment to improvement. She was an early pioneer, and she is unwavering, not swayed by current trends.—BT

She is very focused on patient care—it's first. She's never satisfied with average. She thinks we can always get better.—EH

For her, quality and financial management are integrated.—EH

She is in your face in a charming way. There is no hidden agenda; you always know where she stands.—SB

Learning and Trying New Things

Somebody said to me "I've been here twenty years, but I go home every night and I know that I've learned something new every day." And I said "You're the perfect kind of employee."

That story reminds me of the time years ago when I was looking for a senior VP of Human Resources. I did not want a *personnel* person; I wanted a *human resource* person. The difference is that a human resource person looks at ways to develop the full potential of the human person. The personnel person is more focused on policy and specific issues. The other people we interviewed besides Steve Barney were personnel people. We went through the usual interview process, and frankly, the people that interviewed the candidates did not rate Steve highest. And so I said "Well, I really appreciate your recommendation, but this is who I'm picking." And over time, I was proved to be right. A true human resource focus is still pretty nontraditional in health care. I knew I could find people who could help Steve with details about labor laws, pension, and other issues. What I really rely on Steve for is his thinking and his absolute commitment to diversity in every way, shape, or form.

For example, Steve was able to work out a way to apply employees' health benefits to legally domiciled individuals. That means an employee can have health insurance coverage for another adult living with them. It can be a significant other or an adult child [who] has come back home, or somebody who has a parent they're taking care of who's not yet eligible for Medicare—all are creative options for our employees.

Contrasting a *personnel* focus with a *human resource* focus is a unique part of Sister Mary Jean's leadership. She sought colleagues who could help make her commitment to developing the full potential of the human person. It provides an example of systems and structures—disciplined action—to move toward a single brain. *In your organization, how would you describe the approach to developing people's full potential? Is it clear to others?*

Voices of Others

She didn't look for the traditional path to this role I am in. For her it's about the quality of the person, not the ticket punched. My leadership path reflects her leadership—I was encouraged to try different things. I came from employee benefits and other roles, and not from a typical information technology background. She was open-minded about what it would take for me to be in this role.—TL

Human resources was the last executive position filled. She was looking for a human resource, not personnel, focus. I came through a nontraditional path.—SB

Baldrige was a means to evaluate the organization. There was a recommendation to not apply for one year to give us time to address the gaps from the most recent report. She said "No"; she wanted to keep the momentum going. That was the year we won.—BT

She recognizes when leadership changes are needed. The changes under way right now show she pays attention to the tough issues and when to change.—EH

We do things before others take them on, like preserving the earth, CQI, and a smoking ban. She knows we can always be better.—EH

She is always moving towards health, promoting health, preserving the earth.—SB

She has grown into her leadership. She doesn't stop learning and improving herself.—RD

The idea of looking for the quality of the person, not the "ticket punched," comes through in many profiles in this book—the ability to see beyond the traditional education and roles of a candidate to the personal assets they bring. *Do you have experience with hiring a nontraditional candidate? Why did you choose that person? What did you see that offered a unique contribution to the work? What would stop you from making a nontraditional hire?*

A Good Day

I see what people are doing and I say "Yes!" because they're getting it, they're really getting it, and it really doesn't get a whole lot better than that, truthfully. They get the connection between their work and our mission. They get the fact that what they're doing really does make a difference. I believe everybody wants to do that. Everybody wants to make a difference.

A Bad Day

At the end of every month, we get a report of sentinel and serious events. When I see some of the things that we have done, that is a bad day. If you want to have a sleepless night, take a look at those reports and try and figure out how many gaps in our processes allowed this to happen.

Voices of Others

EH	Eunice Halverson, *corporate vice president, Quality Resource Center*
TL	Tom Langston, *senior vice president and chief information officer*
SB	Steve Barney, *senior vice president, Human Resources*
RD	Sister Rose Dowling, *past chair, SSM Health Care*
BT	Bill Thompson, *president and chief operating officer*

10

Satan Shudders:
Julie Schmidt

When we interviewed Julie Schmidt, she was chief executive officer of Woodwinds Health Campus in Woodbury, Minnesota, a collaboration between HealthEast Care System and Children's Hospitals and Clinics of Minnesota. She has since accepted the new position of vice president and chief transformation officer for HealthEast Care System. She is a nurse and has a master's degree in business administration.

Julie was hired as the CEO of Woodwinds in 1997 when it was only a concept for innovative care. Leaving a secure role in another health care system to take this new position was viewed by many as a significant professional risk. She formed a senior management team and was responsible for the Woodwinds campus design and construction, employee recruitment, culture building, creation of the model of care, and relationship building with physicians and local communities.

Growing Up

Live your life in such a way that when your feet hit the floor in the morning, Satan shudders and says: "Oh, shit, she's awake!"
—A quotation tacked behind Julie's desk

I grew up on a farm in Wisconsin, the second of five kids. My dad was an entrepreneur and something of the black sheep of his family. He was very innovative, very creative, very driven. He left school when he was sixteen and got a job. Mom left school at sixteen also, graduating from high school as valedictorian, and is a lifelong learner. They always encouraged us to be the best we could be. They encouraged healthy competition. We are still very close—and very competitive.

Background Information

**Chief Transformation Officer,
HealthEast Care System
(since March 2010),
St. Paul, Minnesota**
www.healtheast.org

**CEO,
Woodwinds Health Campus, 1997—2010,
Woodbury, Minnesota**
www.woodwinds.org

Organizational Vision
To be the innovative, unique and preferred resource for health by fundamentally creating the health care experience in a way that has not been done before.

Organizational Purpose
To promote health and healing of body, mind and spirit for all, through relationships, choices, and learning.

Woodwinds Health Campus Information
- Woodwinds, an eighty-six-bed hospital, opened in August 2000 as a collaboration between HealthEast Care System and Children's Hospitals and Clinics of Minnesota. Located in a first-ring suburb of St. Paul, Minnesota, Woodwinds serves the southeast area of the St. Paul market—primarily suburban communities.
- The hospital has consistently demonstrated nation-leading results in patient experience, employee engagement, clinical quality, and financial margins.
- The partners sought to transform the patient experience by building an unprecedented health care campus designed around the needs of patients and families. The campus combines traditional and integrative services for patients and staff. In 2005, HealthEast aimed to "Be the Benchmark for Quality" in the Twin Cities by 2010.

Selected Results for Woodwinds
- HealthEast was named among the Thomson Reuters 2009 Top 10% of Health Systems
  —Measured in eight domains—mortality, complications, patient safety, core measures, length of stay, expense, profitability, and cash to debt.
- Hospital Consumer Assessment of Healthcare Providers and Systems (HCAHPS) rated this hospital highest in Twin Cities and Rochester hospitals and second highest in willingness to recommend—November 2009.
- Registered nurse engagement
  —Among the highest measured by Gallup
  —Ratio of 8.14 engaged to 1 disengaged—twice the Magnet ratio
- 2009: Best Minnesota Workplace—Minnesota Hospital Association.
- 2009: Perinatal safety—Received the Minnesota Hospital Association Innovations in Patient Care award. Met goal of 95 percent use of oxytocin bundles and reduced potential adverse events by 25 percent (as part of the HealthEast Care System).
- September 2008–August 2009: Zero pressure ulcers.

Individual Recognitions for Julie Schmidt
- 2009: Named a Nursing Sage by the University of Minnesota Densford International Center for Nursing Leadership. She was one of six persons recognized for launching bold new models of care with partners and in groups, transforming health care delivery
- 2001–2002: Vista Award from the American Society for Healthcare Engineering of the American Hospital Association
- 2000: Most Innovative Women Award, City Business, Minneapolis
- 2000: Recognized by the Minnesota Hospital and Healthcare Partnership for the "Vision to be the State's most influential, trusted and respected leader in health care policy and advocacy and a valued resource for information and knowledge"
- 1999: Recipient of a Regent's Award from the American College of Healthcare Executives

My parents encouraged out-of-the-box thinking and to always do the right thing. For them, "doing the right thing" meant putting others before yourself; having an ego wasn't important. What was important was to serve others and to make a difference, and that one's own achievement should never come at the cost of someone else.

"Out of the box" meant life is like a puzzle and situations are like a puzzle, and there is always a way to figure it out. We were told never to use the word *can't*, and we were rewarded for thinking of clever new ways to resolve questions or problems.

Influences—People and Situations

A big influence was my very first director of nursing. When I was in high school my girlfriend and I decided we wanted to be candy stripers. We had read about this, but there was no program at our little twenty-bed hospital. We knocked on the door of the administrator and said "We'd like to be candy stripers here!" Can you believe it? He sent us to the director of Nursing. We met with her and she said "I'll get back to you." When she got back to us she said "Instead of creating a candy striper program, why don't you create a nursing assistant program?" which became the first in that organization. I was one of the first five nursing assistants at Baldwin Hospital in Wisconsin. It was a great opportunity. That director of Nursing was very influential. I saw she was very powerful.

My first marriage ended in divorce at age twenty-eight, with two children, ages three and five. It was very difficult when I look back now. I was single for eight years, working full time, raising my two kids, and going back to school to get my bachelor of science in nursing.

I went to work in Holy Family Hospital in New Richmond, Wisconsin, and Don Michels was the administrator. He was the first manager I recall who talked about leadership—what it was and what his expectations were. He treated leaders in a very different way than I had ever seen before. He set expectations, and he offered education to leaders. He would share information. He would identify people whom he saw as potential leaders and take them under his wing, mentoring them.

I had some great mentors along the way who helped steer the passion I had to do the right thing. I never had the intention of being the leader, but I had people that were patient with me, who saw potential in me. Throughout my career I've had great mentors and people who were curious about what I thought as well as very open to sharing the way they think.

The really, really cool part of creating Woodwinds was that we were not micromanaged. It was almost as if we were told: "Here is 80 million dollars and fifty-six acres; go forth and do good!" We had a small team—there were three other women and myself for three years leading the planning. It was extremely stressful, but extremely positively stressful.

Mentors have shaped all the leaders in this book. Many of the leaders also talked about those they learned from as an example of what *not* to do. *List your mentors. What did they offer you, and what do you recall learning from them? What actions did they take that helped or shaped your thinking or behavior? What did you learn from those who offered a less-than-optimal leadership lesson? Reflect on how your leadership approach and career have been strengthened by your mentors. Do you give yourself freely as a mentor to aspiring leaders so they can receive the same gifts?*

Pathway to Health Care

It was pretty simple back when I was finishing high school and thought about working. I thought my choices were nursing, teaching, or becoming a secretary. Although my mother kept saying "You can be anything you want to be," it just seemed acceptable in the world that those were my three clear choices. My mother actually wanted to be an operating room nurse but was never able to go back to school. I attended a three-year nursing program at Lutheran Deaconess School of Nursing. I became an operating room nurse and found that it was a great fit for me. I loved it. I loved the teamwork, the skill required, and the tension.

In my junior year of nursing school, I decided to work as a student nurse in the operating room that summer. I remember there was a particular surgeon who was horrible to work for—very demanding, very rude and crude. I was scrubbing in a case with him one day. He was angry and threw a scalpel—he wasn't angry at me but threw a scalpel. After the case, I was shaking but I went to him and said "I'm never going to scrub in with you again because of the way you acted." Then I walked away. He requested me on his cases from that day on and never did anything like that again. When I look back now, that was a big deal to have the courage to do that. His behavior wasn't the right thing to do. It clearly was not right.

Where do you suppose she got the courage to speak up? Courage in daily actions is consistent among the leaders interviewed for this book—both demonstrating it in their own actions and supporting it in others. *Do you model that courage no matter what your position? How can you engender similar courage in the least senior of people you work with?*

A year after graduating, I became a head nurse. I don't know what they were thinking to promote me at that time! I had no clue what I was doing. My supervisor was on maternity leave, and I stepped into her role to manage the operating room and maternity areas.

The first ten years of my career were in rural hospitals, and those years were awesome. I became a good generalist. I always had trouble just doing one thing because I like to do a variety of things; I like to change and improve things. There were all these new ideas we could implement and improve, and that was exciting to me. I really liked new things, and I worked very hard. Working hard was something that was in my DNA.

Pathway to Leadership

It was never about seeking another position. It was about being sought after. People would ask "What do you want to be doing in five years?" and my answer was: "What are my choices?" I had no clear direction. There was never one point in time that I intended to be a CEO of a hospital. It was about creating change and creating improvement—always about the challenge of improving things. That's what drew me along the way.

I think getting into leadership was absolutely by accident. I believe I got that first head nurse job a year out of nursing school because I appeared confident. I was probably stupid, but I appeared confident. I did have courage and a can-do attitude. I don't know if that was for all the right reasons, but for me it was. It was all about learning. It wasn't about getting that next job. I never envisioned myself doing anything but being an operating room nurse.

I was willing to take a role on because I was needed. I wanted to be of value and be needed. That is a weak point, also. If I felt they really needed me and I had the skills, I felt an obligation to step in.

In the first ten years of my career I practiced leadership (or the lack of it) on a lot of people. The first year that I was a manager, it was all about having people like me. I realized at the end of the year that, number one, that was never going to happen because of some of the decisions I had to make. And second, it was not healthy for the organization. I quickly realized that leadership is a balance between gaining the respect of your employees and doing the right thing for the organization. Sometimes it's a very fine balance.

It was clear that I did not know everything, and it was the beginning of clarifying in my mind that you can lead but you don't have to know everything. In fact, it is always good to admit that you don't. It helps in bringing together people who add the pieces that I don't have or who have depth of knowledge that is needed to make some change. Yet I provide leadership influence skills. It is about leading but not necessarily having the depth of knowledge in every single area.

I had a great opportunity to be exposed to the strategic nature of health care in a small but very complex organization. During my stint at St. Paul Children's Hospital, I was a jack of all trades. Any time a leader would leave I would jump in and do their role or take on additional responsibility. I loved that. I was curious and interested in learning new things. That's why during my tenure at Children's, I went back to school for my MBA at the University of Minnesota Carlson School of Management.

After the interview for the Woodwinds CEO position, the selection committee's comment was "She was interviewing us more than we were interviewing her," which was true. I was not looking for a job, but what captured me were the vision and the challenge. There were dozens of people that warned me that Woodwinds might never make it, that it was a big, career-limiting risk. They warned me that this was an experiment that might fail totally, and they asked if I really wanted to take it. The risk part didn't bother me—that was not meaningful. It didn't matter because I would do something else if Woodwinds didn't work out. My thinking was "Wow, this is a really cool vision, and if we could make this work it could be really something else." I was open with the team I hired about the personal risks, and I told them they could leave with my support if they chose to. But they all stayed through it.

Transformation was what captured me and what kept me at Woodwinds. Here I was in a CEO position and I could instill into Woodwinds everything totally valuable and meaningful to me personally. How many of us have a chance to do something like that? The opportunity to build Woodwinds was the opportunity to really add to the industry what I personally thought was important and valuable.

I think all of my career was preparing me to lead Woodwinds. When I look at all the varied experiences I had, I can see the path I was on. The good news is, I listened and followed the path in my career without really even knowing where I was going.

The path to leadership is a unique journey for every leader we talked with. There was no clear leadership curriculum, experience, or set of actions taken that led them to their current role. *Tell a friend or colleague your career path, and listen to theirs. What curves or speed bumps along the way influenced your leadership today? What would you advise others who seek to be in your role in the future?*

What's Important to Me as a Leader

Leaders Put Everyone Else First

The management philosophy at Woodwinds is all about servant leadership. And it isn't just the words *servant leadership*; it's everything we do. The expectations of leaders here is to put everyone else first, including our employees, who we then expect to put their patients first. We round with our leaders, asking "Are there any barriers that I can remove for you so that you can do your work better?" It's all about putting everyone else first. That's the expectation of leading around here, very little about egos. It attracts a particular kind of leader.

I hire and develop leaders. The best of anything that I offer is a knack for hiring really good leaders. I have no idea why, it's like intuition. I interview each person a lot. I don't make a quick decision. Once they get on board, then the whole fun part of development begins: to help them be even more than they thought they could be. The leaders are the ones who attract or repel employees, so my time is spent mostly with leaders in this organization. Leaders and employees are the ones that make or break our relationships with patients and physicians.

It's the leaders I've developed throughout the years who are so gratifying. It's almost like we've raised the leaders here and then we've had them go, like seeds, to do great work—maybe other places in health care. I take great pride in that.

Voices of Others

There are coaches you'll run into a brick wall for. You love their vision and how they embody it. She's one of those people.—CS

Julie is impeccably true to her words. She is a servant leader—it is who she is—to help others be their best so they can do the best for patients.—CB

I am the best I can be because of the last twelve years with Julie.—CB

"Am I good or what!" That's what Julie wrote on my first-year performance review about how good she thought she had done in hiring me. She hired me with no hospital operations experience (my previous hospital operations experience was eating lunch in a hospital cafeteria!). She said she was looking for leadership skills and that operations could be taught.—TS

What Julie does as a leader is collect people as health care leaders, and it magically works. In my previous organization I was pegged in a role, and I knew I couldn't do that for another twenty-five years.—TS

She speaks to a deeper part of you. She's connected to me as a person and roped me in with the vision for Woodwinds at the first interview.—TS

Root beer floats: We got a broadcast page to all managers one morning from Julie to "meet me in the gazebo on campus at 2p."

*My first reaction was "Okay, I'll be there," and my second one
was "This will be fun." We just had a bad financial month—the
worst ever—and some of the other managers thought she was
going to talk to us about that. They were going with a sense of
dread. When we got there, it was a celebration with root beer
floats! We had our new employee engagement scores, and they
were even higher than the last time. Julie wanted to celebrate
all we did to make that happen. She also reminded people of
the beautiful setting that we had and to take advantage of the
healing garden. Not one word about the bad financials. She
knew we would fix that, too.—VL*

*Julie says "Health care is a calling" and "You've been brought
here"—it makes you reflect.—TS*

*Once, she knew I was really struggling with an issue, so she brought
me "lifelines." She and two other leaders arranged to meet with
me. She said "We're here to help you. Tell us what you're doing."
We used the power of a team, via flip charts and conversations,
to help me critically analyze the issue, develop goals, and create
action plans to achieve those goals. Through this process she
demonstrated that there are many ways to lead; there is no
"magic pill" to leadership. She taught me leadership by doing,
not just telling.—LL*

*The process of how she looked for leaders drew me in. She wanted
to understand me as a person. It was amazing to me. In
other settings it would be who you know and what you've
done.—LL*

*It's about servant leadership—a million little things. She values you,
and thus you're more productive.—LL*

Julie converts servant leadership from a trite phrase to a living
philosophy of daily life. The voices of others convey the depth
of commitment she has in her relationships with those she
leads. *Can you name any colleagues who would say about you
"I'd run into a brick wall for him or her"? What do your daily
actions convey about your commitment to others? What do you
look for in people you hire?*

Culture: Do the Right Thing—It's a Million Little Things

There are important culture examples at Woodwinds. It is the culture that we build. It's hard to separate leader development from culture, it's so intertwined. Compassionate care, innovation, a healing environment, and our model of care are examples of our culture.

Compassionate care. It's a culture of compassionate care to each other and to the patients. We live that out in multiple ways, and clearly all the ways that we live that out are not my ideas. It's stimulating others to come up with these great ideas, but the idea is all about compassionate service.

Innovation. Another part of our culture from the beginning has been a culture of innovation, empowering and rewarding people to be creative and to challenge the status quo. We say if there are no rules against it we probably can do it. We ask our people to come up with a great idea. We assure them that even though we can't use every idea they have at this point, we ask them to keep the ideas coming, to keep participating. People who visit will ask "How did you create your culture?" and they want us to say "If you do these three things your culture will be the same." It's absolutely not that—it's a million little things.

Healing environment. A person's environment is so important, and a lot of people don't realize how important it is to us. At Woodwinds it's all about utilizing the components of healing environments in the design. Like the connection to nature, creating positive diversions, eliminating environmental stresses, providing access to social support, and offering choices and options. Luckily, even before we knew a lot about this, some of what we did was the right thing for the Woodwinds philosophy. We keep the noise level down. We don't have overhead paging except for codes. We carefully chose colors that are not stressful. We incorporated extensive use of natural light. These things were not the norm in the late 1990s. It wasn't anything

I read in a book and said we should do. It was almost intuitive. I have a personal approach, meaning I think: "What would I want if I were a patient or nurse/staff person? How would healing look; how would it feel to me? What kind of environment do I want to work in?" I want to work in a place where I'm willing to work hard but I want to have some fun and I want to be challenged. By creating that kind of environment we attracted people that like to do that, too.

Model of care. Our model of care integrates traditional and complementary care. We have an array of healing options here. It has made a big difference, not only to the patients but to the staff who have access to all of the therapies. Our idea is keep the staff healthy and to help them take care of themselves so that they can pay that forward to the patients.

Staff that come here have the same workload they would at any organization, but I think the stress level is less. Last year our nursing engagement at Woodwinds was the highest in the nation according to Gallup. Employee engagement is important, and nursing is what it's all about. We offer holistic nursing classes free to all nurses. We reinforce and come back to the idea that it's all about mind/body/spirit—a basic principle that we learned in nursing school a long time ago and maybe have gotten away from. It has made a difference to the care that our staff give.

Culture is the lifeblood of successful leaders—it enables the results you seek or strangles the life out of the best of intentions. Julie is very deliberate in her approach to creating culture—she and her team do not leave their culture to chance but consciously focus on what they view as essential aspects. *What culture do you seek for your organization or area of responsibility? How would you tell the story of the actions you take every day to create that culture? What insights does Julie's story offer to support you in moving beyond cultural barriers you face?*

Voices of Others

We want to fill Woodwinds with people who are the best they can be. We are totally clear on our own values and align with others with the same values.—CB

We want to touch the spirit, mining the best in employees. If you don't focus on employees as much as patients, you won't get the patient experience you want.—CB

It's a delight working here. We love our work. We use the words love *and* compassion *around here a lot. We know we are fortunate to be part of this team.*—CB

It's that basic—she has respect for individuals.—JG

She knows there are some things you can't teach others—you have to come with the non-negotiables she expects to create the culture Woodwinds has.—JG

I found an exemplary organization, a stellar organization. It is remarkable. She's at every orientation.—VL

Since day one of Woodwinds, long before it became popular, Julie sent personal notes with positive comments from patients to employees' homes.—JG

She was inspirational. She could clearly say what Woodwinds would look like. She clearly articulated a vision and a purpose that resonated with me.—CS

Learning

Hypnobirthing Class

Mind-Body Wellness

Holistic Practice

Medication Reconciliation

Staff Meeting

—Daily meeting posting outside a Woodwinds meeting room

The exciting part of life is constant learning. It is never, ever, ever done. The more you know, the more you realize you don't know—that's why life is so fascinating.

Be Clear

I'm driven by feelings and emotions, and I've learned that when I'm in the midst of something tense that those feelings and emotions can draw me away from doing the right thing. Then I need to get away from it all. I either close the door of my office or take a walk to clear my mind, to be clear from any of the emotion that might drive the decision. In a very respectful way I decide the balance between doing the right thing for the organization and being respectful to the employee and the decision.

I've found that usually the right thing for me to do is inside of me. There are times when it's not a group decision, it's my decision. Then I have to clear my head and make that decision.

Voices of Others

We use our vision and guiding principles as a screen. We won't use a new approach or consultants if it's not a fit with our culture.—CB

She is very clear on what's important—we know what she needs to know from us.—CB

She is tenacious about achieving our metrics yet open to how we achieve them. She balances the big picture but is not removed from the work. If metrics are not in line, she will zoom in asking good questions to help us understand.—CB

Julie is clear—"This is the deal."—TS

Team

My preferred style is that I want the answer to come from the whole team. That's where the best decisions come from. I work much better, I'm more creative, and I'm a much better leader if I have a team. I would be like a fish out of water if I were in a job that would just be me. That would not work for me. I am totally stimulated, inspired, and do my best work in a team.

Voices of Others

We focus on the right thing to do, the value of ethical practice—any decision is based on why we're here. It's very powerful for us as a team. We believe there is nothing we can't accomplish, nothing we can't figure out.—CB

Julie has taught me a lot. She has the wisdom to know when the team needs to do the work when she could have easily said "I'm the CEO" and decided by herself. She collects and coalesces a group of leaders and does not feel like she has to have the answer; she trusts in the group to find the answer.—TS

We have faith in one another; there's a can-do feeling.—VL

Julie and the senior team are respected. Cindy Bultena, the chief nursing officer, called me and left a message: "This will be good for your heart and good for ours—your article was shared at the HealthEast board retreat. There are now fifty more people who value what you do."—VL

She's like the general contractor. We know the direction and how to do it, to build the vision, and she let us play our part. She got out of my way and gave me the freedom to do what I knew how to do, encouraging when there are barriers and redirecting when I'm off track.—CS

The Courage to Be an Anomaly

Those who take the first step to challenge the status quo are more likely to be viewed as an anomaly. A way to deal with being an anomaly is to stay connected to the current state as a way for people to not be so fearful of change. If you come up with new ideas too quickly it will feel like a hammer rather than allowing it to grow and evolve. You have a perfectly clear vision and then allow it to evolve.

A hospital with integrative therapies was odd, so I needed to stay very close to the MDs. Using influence, we developed an environment for creative ideas rather than for a dictatorship. We talked to the community, who wanted both traditional and integrative therapies. We wanted to bring credibility to the process. We knew it was the right thing and revolutionary, so we talked a year before we opened, educating physicians and creating education for holistic nursing. We created the Strategic Steering Team for Integrative Services to accomplish four things: (1) a visible focus, (2) involvement by other credible leaders in the community, (3) a focus on *how* and not *if*, and (4) generate support for the process and outcomes of integrative services.

I think you can't be courageous unless you know who you are. You have a stronger platform to stand on if you're being courageous about something you think is important based on your values or what you have a passion for. You can influence, lead, and be courageous if you know who you are.

The difference between a successful anomaly and a weird idea is often not apparent when you are in the midst of the anomaly. Integrative therapies are common now—a decade earlier when Julie and the team designed Woodwinds, they were seen as a serious threat to good care at worst and a costly distraction that alienated physicians at best. *Have you ever been an anomaly in your work? What was that like? What experiences come to mind when you think of being an anomaly? What current situations require anomalous thinking and actions?*

Voices of Others

How she designed and built the hospital is indicative of her leadership; she involved everyone, including the community and the MDs.—JG

She wants you to know that she expects you to challenge the status quo.—TS

We say "Let's try it"; we are trusted as managers.—VL

We can always be better. She's always asking "What's the next best?" She values what we are doing, celebrates that, and asks "What's next?"—CB

She raises the bar.—VL

Who Are You Inside?

When I'm mentoring people, I say that the most important thing is to figure out who they are inside. I think we're all influenced by what we think we should do. But who are you really inside? What really drives you? What's going to really make your career so fulfilling you are bursting because it's just so who you are and you're able to be the most fulfilled? It may not be something your parents want you to do or something you think you should do. It's who you are, really. Then line up with an organization that shares your personal values.

I would like others to say about me that she was fun, she was respectful, she was inspiring, she tried to do the right thing, she was authentic, and that her motto was "imagine the possibilities."

Julie advises that first and foremost know who you are—who you really are inside, not what others expect of you, what you ought to be, what you learned in educational programs, but what you know is your authentic self. *Answer Julie's question for yourself: "What's going to really make your career so fulfilling you are bursting because it's just so who you are and you're able to be the most fulfilled?" Does your current work bring that sense of fulfillment to you?*

Voices of Others

She helps us celebrate what's right with the world to give energy to deal with what's not; it's how we handle tough issues.—CB

She's authentic, mindful, prepared—not a false Disney-like figure. She knows me, my name, and my story.—VL

A Good Day

I have the respect for and of the larger organization I work in, and they depend on me for challenging the status quo in the system. I've moved into a role of influencing leaders in the entire system now, so that's very rewarding. That's a good day. Another good day is to come to work and have the leaders say "Guess what we did!" or "Guess what we're going to do!" or that they have come up with a new idea. I love that enthusiasm. To see that can-do attitude alive and well, that's a really good day.

A Bad Day

Doing the same old thing. I'm not a good plant manager. I do not like to do the same old thing. That's a bad day. It's being put in a position to try to make a change but not having the authority. Sometimes it's a bad day when I feel like I am a buffer between the larger system and Woodwinds because I want to keep the innovation, creativity, empowerment, and the culture living and breathing here.

Voices of Others

CB   Cindy Bultena, *vice president, Patient Care, Woodwinds*

JG   Joan Grzywinski, *board chair, HealthEast*

TS   Tom Schmidt, *vice president, Operations, Woodwinds*

VL   Val Lincoln, RN, PhD, *integrative services leader, Woodwinds*

LL   Lynne Lillie, *medical director, Woodwinds*

CS   Craig Svendsen, *medical director, Quality, HealthEast*

11

I Am Still Learning:
Tim Porter-O'Grady

Tim Porter-O'Grady is senior partner at Tim Porter-O'Grady Associates, based in Atlanta. He is a consultant, a university professor, and an author. Tim is best known for bringing the shared governance model to health care, a model that has had a transformational impact on the nursing profession and on cross-disciplinary collaboration.

He is a prolific writer and speaker who continues to expand his own understanding of leadership and his contribution to the field of health care. Tim is a nurse.

Growing Up

I was born in Canada, and I was given up at birth. I was predominantly in foster homes between the time I was born and five years of age. Then I was adopted at age five. My adoptive mother was a nurse, and my father was an Army officer who became an executive with the Canadian Pacific Railroad Company. They were clearly not prepared for parenthood or for me. I was fairly independent by the time I was five, and I was not a very compliant child. My brother was also adopted. My mother was looking for loving, expressive, warm, giving children who would appreciate being taken in by this wonderful couple, people who had really sacrificed their lives to adopt these two boys. And of course I was none of those things. So my childhood actually was rife with struggle and conflict and noise and painful parental relationships.

Background Information

Consultant,
Tim Porter-O'Grady Associates,
and
University Professor,
Atlanta
www.tpogassociates.com

Our Purpose
To provide consulting services for hospitals, community and health care services in the midst of major clinical service transformation and restructuring

Information about Tim Porter-O'Grady Associates
- Consult with systems and organizations with complex systems change
- Conflict resolution between individuals and systems
- Leadership education and development for organizations

Selected Results for Tim Porter-O'Grady Associates
- Shared governance structures in more than a thousand hospital and/or clinical settings
- Magnet hospital consultation in more than 200 successful Magnet-recognized hospitals
- Participated in production of validating research for empowered professional structures in clinical systems
- Conducted leadership development in more than a hundred hospitals

Individual Recognitions for Tim Porter-O'Grady
- 2010 American Organization of Nurse Executives Lifetime Achievement Award
- Seven American Journal of Nursing Press Book of the Year awards
- Honorary doctor of science degree from Medical College of Ohio for significant contributions to advancing the American health services community

----

- *Quantum Leadership: A Resource for Health Care Innovation*, second edition, co-authored with Kathy Malloch (Jones and Bartlett, 2007), is currently used in 220 graduate health administration programs internationally.
- Two earned doctorates: management in organizational leadership and education.
- 2005, 2007: Board Outstanding Service Award, Sigma Theta Tau International Honor Society of Nursing.

My father was a wonderful man but an impotent, passive parent. He was Irish, loved his drink, gentle, caring in his sort of way, but not a dominant player at home or in my life. When I was eighteen my mother told me that it was time for me to leave and made it clear that in spite of all her efforts I would amount to nothing. I told her I was delighted to leave and never return. That sums up our relationship. So I left home relatively healthy, but not completely. And I did not graduate from high school.

My adoptive parents are both dead. I connected with my birth family when I became an adult, and we've been connected ever since. My birth father died a couple of years ago, and my birth mother is still alive, as are all of my eleven siblings. I would have been happy being raised in that family. The downside is that I would likely be a farmer. I am the only one who is not a farmer and has moved far away from where he grew up.

But what offsets my home life growing up is that I had a wonderful set of school friends who had wonderful parents who understood my situation. They acted very much as surrogates and as models for me, because I saw in them the love, the connection, the communication, the expression, and the relationship that was very much missing in my own parental experience. And I was able to both live off that and learn from it. As a result, a lot of negative things that could have happened to me along the way never did. In fact, my childhood better prepared me for life than I could imagine being prepared otherwise.

> Growing-up experiences contribute to our lives in diverse ways. *In what ways have the experiences of your own childhood, positive and negative, shaped the assets and liabilities you bring to your leadership?*

Influences—People and Situations

I was seeing this woman who was older than me, a nurse. I married her when I was nineteen, long before I was emotionally ready. I wasn't aware of it at the time, but I married the mother I never had. She was a very loving, caring, passionate, expressive person; a wonderful human being; and a great nurse. I shouldn't have married her, but it is a blessing for me that I did because she was precisely what I needed to compensate for my lack of maturity and what I had not received from my parents. If it had not been for that experience and for her, my life may not be as it is today. With her I re-engaged with life, realized I was on a dead-end track with regard to education and work.

I got my [citizenship] papers together, and we emigrated to Washington state, where my wife's sister lived. I had no skills, so the first job was at a Weyerhaeuser wood plant. I was placed on the rejected door line. I was the difference between a door being part of a cabinet or being sent to the wood chipper. About my seventh day on the job, I had an epiphany. Briefly it was this: If I don't do something, I'm going to be on the rejected door line for the next thirty years of my life! I felt panicked and overwhelmed. That is when I said I really have to figure this out, but I didn't know what to do.

A counselor at the local community college was a PhD psychologist and a really great guy. He put me through batteries of psychological and behavioral tests, and at the end of this he delivered one line that was the seminal line for me at that time. He said: "Tim, you know, all of these tests indicate that there is absolutely no objective reason for you not being or doing whatever you want to do in life." And that was the first time in my life that I got a positive message. It was a sea change for me. I began to enroll in courses that I had had trouble with because he said it would be really easy for me to complete my high school diploma.

Pathway to Health Care

My friend at the plant was an engineer in the lab that was right across from the rejected door line. We had lunch together. He left the plant and went to nursing school. I said "Why did you do that?" He said "I wanted to do something meaningful with my life, something entirely different from what I've been doing, something that made a difference, and this is what I thought I would do." His wife was a nurse who worked with my wife. When I was sorting out what I was going to do, I was thinking maybe law school or something like that. We were at a dinner with them one night and he said: "Why don't you think about nursing school? You've got all the personal attributes. You want to make a difference in your life." We talked about it, and I got a little bit intrigued. They suggested that I talk to the nursing counselor, which I did.

She suggested that as I was finishing my high school diploma I could take a couple of pre-nursing courses and then I would know very quickly whether nursing was for me. I absolutely loved it from the moment I got in. It fit just like a glove. I liked the people. I liked the courses. I liked the direction. I liked the person-directed, health-directed focus, and the faculty was just wonderful. So I started, and I never stopped.

Tim knew immediately that his choice of nursing was a fit for him. Appreciating the fit with your choice to be in health care is linked to your authentic passion for patient care. *Does it matter to you and the organization that you are in health care and in a role that fits like a glove, or can you be just as effective in a job that is not that kind of fit?*

Pathway to Leadership

There are three things that when I reflect on it connect to leadership. First, when I was a kid, I was always dreaming up a play. The play was always counter to my real life. I was great at story creation, storytelling, directing, putting people together to live it out. Children on our block would actually play out the roles, and others began to turn to me. "Let Tim figure it out. What does Tim say? What does Tim think?" When I was with my friends growing up I was trying to find a place that wasn't defined by the experiences we had because I didn't share them. So I found a unique way to relate with them. I made it up just like the play.

Second, I think because of my circumstances I was more reflective than my peers. I was always looking for the why. And that was my mother's greatest problem with me. I would never give up the why. The same with friends, and eventually I became the why person for the group.

Third, from as early as I can remember I knew I would have to make my own way. That was just the way it was always going to be. That came out of the foster experience, because in that experience I knew I wasn't there because they loved me. I was there because that was the place I was put. They were paid. We weren't fed well, and they were not emotionally present. That was the foster experience. So whatever I got out of life was up to me. The good thing about that was that it really developed self-reliance. The eleven years with my wife, some of her family and my friends helped me connect emotionally. She died of a cerebral hemorrhage right about the time we separated.

At work I had a great mentor. As a nurse, she was remarkable, a role model. She had that edge. She was the kind of person who doesn't take any shit but has a heart of gold, who understands people and what they need. She had a highly developed level of intuition. Where I would have to follow the nursing process and do a logical, systematic assessment of the patient to get to a conclusion, she would go into the room, sniff the air, tell you exactly what was wrong with the person and exactly what you needed to do. Invariably and annoyingly she was right! I would ask her "How do you do that?" She would say "Well, I've been at this a long time." I would ask her "Are you saying, then, that if I'm at it a long time, I'll be able to do it?" She would say "Probably not, but you'll be able to do it better than you're doing it now."

I got promoted into a leadership job under her tutelage. She got me interested in the impact and value and meaning of leadership. She explained that as a leader she touched all kinds of lives in part because of the opportunities her leadership position provided her. I could make a choice as to whether I wanted to do that because the satisfactions are not so immediate, they're not so palpable, they're not so direct. Through her I got intrigued and interested in leadership.

There was something else going on, too. When I became a nurse I said there's something seriously wrong here, because what I was told I was going to be and do isn't happening. I was going to be a colleague with physicians. Well, I wasn't a colleague of physicians. They didn't respect me enough or weren't knowledgeable enough for this colleague stuff. Although I did notice another factor that was going on, in that the physicians treated me differently from how they treated the female nurses. I got to do more. I got involved in different conversations. I got away with a lot more. And I progressed on a career path quicker. I began to realize it had to do with inequity, although that wasn't the term that I used then. It was because I was male. Overall, I felt the system was not designed to support the work we do as nurses. My mentor said "Welcome to the real world." But it wasn't good enough for me. I wanted to know why it was that way, but I didn't know where to take it. She suggested I pursue more education or do something different.

The chief nursing officer, another fine person, recommended I get into the new master's program at the University of Washington. It was a brand new dual master's in business administration and nursing administration. I had been practicing as a nurse for four years, not long, when I decided it was time for me to go on and do that program. That was an important point in my leadership career because that was when I began to ask the question *why* as a legitimate, academic pursuit. I began to dig into some of these issues to understand what was wrong with the system that, number one, didn't value what nurses did and, number two, why nurses were not positioned to be key decision makers in what happened in care—even though whatever happened would depend on us to make it happen and, number three, how to address the gender issues.

Slowly, step by step, those issues became clearer to me. That is when our first work around shared governance emerged. It happened when we were studying theorists who discussed collective wisdom, group dynamics, and systems organizational questions. I began to codify a lot of their work around notions of ownership, investment and engagement, and related topics. That's when it began to resonate with me as a nurse. We were not engaged, owning, and invested, and we were not a part of that infrastructure; we were seen almost universally by key disciplines as laborers in the vineyard even though it was not the perception we had of ourselves. It is also when I began to understand the business construct for health care and the conflict between the professional construct and the business construct.

I was getting a ton of ah-has. If you want to get professional outcomes, you can't operate an organization like it is an employee group of laborers. What theorists I studied, like Robert Greenleaf and Chris Argyris, showed is that if you treat people like employee groups, you can only get employee group outcomes, not professional outcomes. You get exactly what you pay for and what the structure is; that is when I began to ask: If we are going to build an infrastructure for professionals and really operate it as a professional infrastructure, what would that require? That is when the whole concept of shared governance really took shape.

Tim identified a gap between the stated intent of health care organizations and how they are structured and led. *In your own leadership, how conscious are you of whether you are treating people like employees or as professionals, no matter what their level or role in the organization? What does it mean to treat others like professionals in terms of the way you lead? And what is the impact on achieving the outcomes you are committed to?*

My original trajectory when I got in leadership was to be a CEO. The issue wasn't whether I could be a CEO, because there were a lot of CEOs at that time who were not doing a very good job of it, which frankly is still true. But as I matured I began to realize that it wasn't so much the role that one had, it was the role that one played. To get anything to happen in an organization has nothing to do with position and everything to do with the capacity to lead. I got past the positional notion of leadership. If I was going to be a good leader I would have to have the capacity to lead, and if I did, it really didn't matter what position I held.

The other thing that was going on was that nothing I ever planned actually happened the way I planned it. What often happened was, something became available, and I became available to it. I would say sure, I can do that, and I did. That approach took me to places that I wouldn't have imagined because I wouldn't have known enough to decide on my own to go there. Opportunity is always there. The issue is: Are you available to it, and can you go where it takes you? It has been like that all of my career. I thought I'd be a good nurse manager. I didn't think I would be a good CNO, but I became one. Then the opportunity came up to be CEO of a community health system directed to serving the underserved in Atlanta. It was exciting and intriguing and different with a whole new story that could be told. And so I said yes. That led me to a whole community system for care of the homeless, indigent, the underserved, and to get a grant for three and a half million dollars. I never imagined that I would ever in my life get a grant for three and a half million dollars. Now I have my own consulting business. Along the way, these little pieces affirmed the message: I can do this. I can do this. But eventually I stopped having that message. Now the question for me is What is it I want to do, and how much difference will it make? That is a leadership question.

What's Important to Me as a Leader

Creating Your Own Path and Ignoring Naysayers

I think I have earned the right to be a "negaholic," but I don't have a negaholic bone in my body. Early in my career I was affected by the passive acceptance of our condition by our profession. I was surrounded by nurses who complained about it, but there were few who were going to do a damn thing about it, because it was always in somebody else's hands. And that intrigued me as much as anything else, because one of the things I wanted to know is Just whose hands is our situation in? If it is in somebody else's hands, as we all are saying, whose are those hands, and what are those hands doing? Because this is, after all, our life, and my belief was that you should have some control over that life, and nothing was going to change by accident.

I would hear from nurses: If only they would do this, if only it could be like that, the organization should do this, and if we only had this. My question was: What do we do to have what we want to have happen? Because, back to the play, I was writing the story. My questions were: "What can we do to make what we want happen? What can we put together to address that?" Their response to me was: "They won't let us do that. It's just the way it is. And Tim, you think you're going to change everything. It doesn't matter what you're going to do, you're only one person." My response to that always was: "Well yeah, I've always been only one person. What more can I be? I can only be who I am." The issue is do I want to be that person? That means not looking at our situation as if fate has sealed us into a room from which we can never escape. The answer back to me could be summed up as it's bigger than you. Well, in my mind, there isn't anything bigger than you. But what was bigger than me was that I didn't understand what it was. I didn't know the answer to why, and that wasn't satisfactory to me. I simply wasn't satisfied without pursuing the answer, some answer I didn't yet have that was just beyond my reach. That has been a critical element in my life and my leadership.

Shaping the environment in which you find yourself is tied to finding opportunities when problems are in abundance. *To what degree are you "writing the story" at work, and to what degree are you playing out someone else's story?*

Voices of Others

He thinks differently from other leaders and sees things that others cannot. He is a futurist.—BM

He poses out-of-the-box, nontraditional, creative solutions.—BM

You know where he stands; he is transparent, credible, and authentic, giving people confidence in his integrity.—KMc

He has brilliance and staying power; he never falters in his ability to stay true to his conviction that we can create change and lead health care to a better future.—JT

Setting the Table Well—an Appreciation of Brokenness

When I finished my doctorate, I was very disappointed. It really was a wonderful experience. But I realized at the end of it that what was really driving me was that one statement of my mother's when I left home, that I would amount to nothing and my need to show her and prove her wrong. I could acknowledge that I had accomplished a lot using that as my personal fuel, but I was not willing to lead the rest of my life driven by a need to prove my mother wrong. I received great counseling, and my therapist encouraged me to go back to visit my parents to have a frank conversation with them about what I think I deserved, what I think I should have had, what I didn't get. He told me the critical thing that I was going to have to do after I had done all of that was to tell them that I completely and entirely forgive them, and then let it go. I resisted mightily. The therapy continued for many more months before I committed to going back home, and I did.

That is when the anger stopped, and that's when I actually began to become a good leader, because my life was no longer about compensating for, or adjusting for, everything that had gone on before. It was now a clean slate that was about who I was and where I was going with my life, the choices that I was going make and the difference that I really wanted to make.

Another important thing this experience did was to give me a stronger appreciation and acceptance of brokenness in others, something in my anger years I didn't have a sensitivity or tolerance for. I was performing, accomplishing, learning, and getting degrees. And when someone would be struggling I would tell them to pull themselves up by their bootstraps, get on with it, take control of their lives, and start doing things like I was. By that time I had written five books that I put out like a Coke machine, and twenty-five juried articles. I had no appreciation for other people and their challenges. But when I came to terms with my own brokenness I really began to appreciate two things: other people's brokenness and the value of brokenness itself.

For me, brokenness itself is a leadership capacity, because when you embrace it, it exposes you to the realities of the normal human experience. I became open to a person's story and how that story contributes to their role in the group and in the workplace, because what you are dealing with as a leader is a whole complex issue of brokenness and trying to find a way in which to get people to be able to engage in their own lives, their own role, and to resolve their own issues.

Then, as a leader, when you are bringing people together you are setting a table so that the stories at the table can converge to make a difference. You must know a person enough to be able to know what they have to offer—what skills or talents that they bring, what things they don't bring—so that you're not asking from them what they don't have to offer. The result is that you are maximizing the opportunity for those at the table and for the organization. What happens a lot in groups is that leaders will set the table without due care and not realize that the reason the work didn't unfold well or succeed is because you didn't set the table well. You didn't think about what the table needs as you were setting it: who was there, what they bring, who they were as people, and how to match and blend those players to maximize the opportunity for success.

Tim identifies additional aspects to consider when assembling a team or setting the table in addition to their position title, experience, or technical skills. *When you put together teams, are you setting the table in the thoughtful way Tim is discussing? To what degree are you putting together a set of required functions or inputs without real regard for the individual and team dynamics?*

The last thing an appreciation of brokenness did for me was to change the way I work with people. Appreciative inquiry is very important as a technique of relationship and interaction when you recognize as a leader that you are working essentially with brokenness. Appreciative inquiry will free potential in people and enhance their contribution, ownership, and engagement. If a leader is unaware of that, it is virtually impossible for them to successfully engage a group around a goal over a sustainable period and make it real for them.

Voices of Others

You can know process inside and out, but the most successful leaders like him have the capacity to dream "team" and to motivate organizational change.—BM

His is a remarkable, authentic person.—BH

His dream is for a better health care system that uses resources without devaluing any individual or any group. He cares deeply about quality care and knows that it is possible to achieve.—KM

Remembering the Work We Are In

I think the role of CEO is characteristically nonreflective, and when I think about the reflective CEOs I know, they are intentionally reflective, meaning they incorporate reflection into the way they think and lead. I think the job is usually nonreflective because of all the time demands, the functional demands, relational demands, public demands, the structural demands, on the role and the expectations—demands that often are so strangling that people are sucked in before they hear that loud sucking sound. Then once they are sucked in it defines them.

In my own work consulting with organizations, the number one thing that I most notice at the senior level of health care organizations is that they often forget the business they are in. Or, horror of horrors, they never really knew. In order to really understand this field of health care you have to be reflective enough to understand that the work that we do is different from the business that we do. So many people in the C-suite are so subsumed by the business that they either never figure out what we do or they have lost track of what we do or they simply gave up what we do. What we do is we provide health care to the community.

I would say 90 percent of the time the organizations that I work with—and we work primarily with organizations that are troubled or challenged one way or another—have forgotten what their core business is. They have "businessed" themselves out of their core. When you lose your core, you lose everything.

You can see many of these health systems going into all kinds of trajectories of business, expanding all over the map, and then all of a sudden they're in crisis because there's no glue to pull them back to the center. They have lost touch with what grounds them. There's little left to bind them to who they are because they've become wherever the business went.

Leaders who demonstrate a passion for patient care as a personal value do not lose sight of what is their core business. *Are your actions as a leader shaped by the "business" we are in or the "work" we do? How would you know?*

If you listen to business leaders of any kind, the business leaders that are most likely to sustain success are the ones who never lose that core. A hospital needs a cycle of between six and eight years to build sustainability of a thriving trajectory. Most CEOs who are interested in advancing their careers are in a job cycle of three to five years because that is how they get rewarded. If you listen to how they are introduced it is by how many positions they've held, how many positions have increased in responsibility, and how they've ended up at a really great place that is a multifocal institution with lots of hospitals and networks and the CEO is making three million dollars a year. What they don't tell you, and what we can tell you because we are the ones who follow them in after they have left their positions for new opportunities, is the work at their previous place was unfinished. In three to five years they launched some major initiatives, got them to a certain high point, and then left at a time when the change was not yet sustainable. What you see happening in hospitals and health systems is that they end up limping their way through their initiatives leader after leader. The organizations and their people get so "backed up"—overwhelmed by initiative after initiative introduced by leader after leader. Even the ones that have some margin of success are often limited in that success, and it is often not sustained over the long term.

When CEOs define themselves as successful only by their career progression, those who stay in a place for a long time can be looked down on. He hasn't moved much, has he? She's stayed in that place a long time. Nobody says it, but that's code for: They haven't moved on much, have they?

Seeing the Whole

When viewing a situation, I "see" the whole thing. When somebody is telling me a story from their perspective I can see their part, but I can also see their part of the much larger story. Often as a leader I have the opportunity to develop them and the whole at the same time. It is not something I personally have had to work hard to develop but, developed or innate, it is very important to leadership.

Voices of Others

He remembers what it takes to change health care. He never gets rutted in everyday concerns as many do; he never loses his ability to think and to dream.—BM

He looks beyond what everyone else is looking at, puts together a world nobody else sees, and conveys that world to other people.—BH

He reconnects people to their dreams, to what floats their boat, and inspires them to continue to dream.—BM

Still Learning

I have a fundamental personal and organizational belief that when you are always looking for the answer, once you find it you stop learning. I think life is really lived in the question. If you're not living in the question, you have stopped learning and stopped living. When you are only looking for the answer, you stop once you get it. But when you live in the question, getting an answer becomes a springboard for the next question. By now I have three doctorates and have accomplished a lot, but I have a lot more to contribute, and I am going to find that by living in the question and by continually learning. That is why the tag line on my e-mail reads "I'm still learning."

Voices of Others

He has a commitment to excellence in himself and others; he is dedicated to learning.—KM

He sets very high standards for himself; he is always improving himself, always thinking, always exposing himself to diverse ideas.—KMc

Mentoring

I think being a mentor is essential to good leadership. And you can never be a good mentor if you try to get them where you want them to be, instead of get them to be better where they are and to be more strongly who they are. So I spend time in mentoring asking: Who are you? What does that mean to you? How does that translate into what you're going to do as a leader? Contrary to a lot of folks, I don't think leadership is a predisposition or a gift. I think there are people who are born with the potential to be leaders and that potential can naturally lead them. They could be Al Capones and still be leaders. Being born with the potential for leadership doesn't really mean that much.

For me, leadership is fundamentally learned, and it's also an intentional decision. Part of what I try to do in mentoring a leader is see how intentional their decision to lead is and what that intentionality means to them at that particular point in time. For example, I have one mentee who is a wonderful person with lots of energy and lots of commitment but not reflective. When we talk, he will dive into what projects he is up to in great depth, and in the middle of the project conversation I'll ask him "Tell me again, why are you doing this?" Because his problem is he is so busy doing it that he isn't reflecting on the value of doing it, the value that is driving doing it, and what that value means to him as a person. Then I'll ask the question "What would happen if you didn't do it? And what would happen in the organization?" because that drives him to reflection.

On the other hand I mentor someone who is a reflector rather than an actor. She has a very difficult time making decisions. Part of what I have to do as a mentor is help translate that reflection into action, and usually the question I have to ask is "What would doing this look like?" Together we build implementation scenarios that create a bridge from reflection to action.

The point I want to make is that a good leader works with people so those people will be more strongly who they are. It becomes an important part of setting the table well.

Tim describes how he effectively mentors others through helping them to be more strongly who they are, not changing them into someone different. *Is mentoring an important part of your life at work? Whom do you mentor? What have you done to help them in their life and work? To what degree is your own view of what constitutes successful mentoring consistent with or different from Tim's?*

Voices of Others

No one has had more impact on my professional career. I told him "You are my hero," and he responded "You are my hero because you make it all happen." I can't tell how much that has meant to me.—JT

He is incredibly supportive of other people and brings out the best in others.—BH

Letting Go of Control

I don't see an organization as a hierarchy but as a complex of nodes and networks with a myriad of interdependent roles. Thinking about it that way, it is vital that for a leader to see and strengthen the linkages between people who make up the organization's nodes and networks, to focus on the quality of the relationships and interactions that move action forward, and to let the stakeholders own what they do—to let go of control.

In my view, control is actually a failure of leadership. Yet what we teach in our graduate programs is control as one of the skill sets of leadership. But control is actually an indication of the failure of leadership. What you want people you lead to be able to do is act and operate in real time, in real circumstances, in real situations, and with a real capacity. So a part of the role of the leader is to help people evaluate just how real they are in their situation, in their circumstances, in their skills, in their activities, or in their life choices. That is why the leader doesn't retreat from honesty or actualization or confrontation or conflict. The good leader uses conflict as a vehicle for ownership, engagement, and actualization.

The final piece of this is for the whole to be able to appreciate its journey and to be able to express and celebrate themselves at work: their values, commitment, energy, and strengths. The soul of leadership for me is the non-negotiable desire to make life meaningful and to make a difference with that life, not only for themselves but to provide that opportunity for everybody.

Voices of Others

He has always had a tremendous vision: the ability to see things as they are and to see the possibility of what could be, fueled by his passion for the caregiver and the patient.—KMc

He can communicate his vision clearly enough and passionately enough that people want to follow.—KMc

Understanding the Part We All Play in Where We Are

In shared governance, one of the bottom-line questions we ask of everybody in the organization is "What part did you play?" Because ownership comes before engagement, and it is essential that everyone understands that the organization didn't arrive in this set of circumstances it is in—for better or worse—without everyone in some way participating in it. No matter how small your part, you played a part. So we ask "What part are you playing in the conditions and circumstances of your own life?" Often people who are part of an organization talk as though they are outside of the organization. It's like they are renters. As long as you are a renter, don't expect stakeholder and ownership rewards. People will tell us: They didn't invite us in. Well, did you really want to go in anyway? Or were you really feeling happy just complaining about the fact that they didn't invite you in? Because we know it's easier. It lasts longer. And it doesn't require anything on your part. So what part did you play in not being in? A pervasive sense of ownership is essential for a healthy organization. For any leader, don't be surprised if you call somebody an employee and they behave like a subordinate. Don't ask them ownership questions when you provide them an employee house.

This applies to the CEO as much as anyone else. I was leading a board retreat for a hospital in trouble, losing money, making all kinds of decisions that created issues. We were going around and around in the conversation. On a break, the CEO came up to me and said: "I just really can't understand how we fell into all this trouble. I just can't understand how it all kind of happened at once." And I said "The first thing that you're going to have to realize is that you didn't fall into trouble. You were actively led there and you were in front of the line. And we are not going anywhere in this meeting until you can say that." Dead silence. No response, except that look of why in the hell did I invite you here? But when we reconvened, and to his great credit, he said to the group "I need to say something." So he repeated our conversation and said to everyone "I need to take personal responsibility for the choices that I made that led us to the circumstance where we find ourselves in. And unless I'm willing to do that, I can't expect this room to do it." That was the breakthrough. Now we could do the work.

But if he had not been authentic enough as a person, willing to be vulnerable in front of the people who hired him, and been able to acknowledge the role he played, everyone might have left after two days feeling good and having accomplished absolutely nothing of value.

Everyone has a part to play in organizational functioning and outcomes. *How do you step back to see what part you play in your current results? What part do you think others play in contributing to those outcomes? When you are speaking to others in settings large and small, are you free to be authentic, or do you feel you have to play a part that is not your true self to satisfy yourself and others?*

Voices of Others

He enables people to see in themselves and in health care new possibilities, a better way to lead and act, so they are not afraid to leap into the unknown by acting boldly.—JT

He has a clear sense of his accountability in creating change and others' accountability; he doesn't enable others, he values them and assumes they will deliver on their promises.—KM

Teams without Equity Are Not Teams

I stayed away from talking about team, and I do it intentionally, because the concept of team has been so abused that we now have no concept of what it means. We hear people say all the time we need to operate as a team. Yeah, we do. But it will only happen if everybody on the team understands the mutuality of the contribution they uniquely bring to the team. One thing we know with absolute certitude is that in the health care team, one member of the team doesn't necessarily respect the value, contribution, or equity of another member of the team. And teams only work well and thrive if equity is operating. So what happens in health care is we have a dysfunctional hierarchy where we have, for example, the physician and then we have the nurse. The physician's perspective of the nurse hasn't got anything to do with the nurse's self-perspective. And the nurse's perspective of the relationship with the physician doesn't match the physician's perspective of their relationship for the nurse.

So you put the nurse and the physician in the same room in a team. You've got the physician thinking and acting by virtue of his or her history, experience, exposure, and social attitude. And you have the nurse thinking and acting by virtue of her or his experience, exposure, and social attitude. But that is never discussed, never laid out on the table, never made clear, and we still expect them to work together and we still say we are creating a team. Well, the ugly truth often is that they have absolutely no real intention of working together, and if you examine it really critically, and we have, who do you suppose does all the work and gets all the team assignments outside the team meeting? What usually happens is that, seeing themselves as the decider, the physicians decide, make that contribution, leave the equation as the guests they are, and then the people who are left to actually translate it, apply it, evaluate it are usually the nurses. So eventually the nurses say: I'm going to stay out of that meeting because ultimately I'm going to have to end up doing it all, following through, evaluating it, and chasing after the physicians to make it happen. Because from the nurses' perspective, the truth is, most physicians don't act like equitable members of this community; they behave most often like guests in this community.

The other elephant in the room is that most nurses are happy that physicians are only guests, because the last thing they want is for physicians to hang around the unit too long because when the physicians hang around they become a barrier to the work of the nurse. The nurses are actually thankful when the physicians leave the unit. The unaware, unreflective CEO will say "We are working in teams" without having done anything to address these many fundamental relation dysfunctions.

Teams are not really teams in health care—this is Tim's key point in this discussion. *What is your assessment of teams in your organization? What are the unaddressed elephants in the room in your organization regarding how teams operate and produce results?*

Voices of Others

He draws from what people are saying and synthesizes in a concrete, concise, and inspirational way and as a call to action.—JT

He embodies the principles of shared governance; he is collaborative, a great listener, loves what he teaches, and he can sit back and laugh as well.—KMc

A Good Day

When the people I work with are enthused and excited about a major impact on their life and work accomplished through their own efforts; when I experience a sense of having made a difference; ending the day with a good brew and an excellent read.

A Bad Day

When I let a negaholic get to me and bring me down; when I failed to act assertively or courageously in a moment that required it; and if I fail to make time for some private/personal reflection.

Voices of Others

BM Dr. Bernadette Melnyk, *dean and Distinguished Foundation Professor, College of Nursing and Health Innovation, Arizona State University*

JT Jolene Tornabeni, *health care executive; past client; co-author*

KM Kathy Malloch, *president, KMLS, LLC; clinical consultant, API Healthcare Inc.; clinical professor, College of Nursing and Health Innovation, Arizona State University*

KMc Dr. Kathy McDonagh, *vice president, Executive Relations, Hospira*

BH Bob Hess, *executive vice president, Global Programming, Gannett Education*

12

Guidance for Growing Leaders

In our conversations with these ten highly successful leaders we asked them what advice they would give to others in health care who aspire to become effective senior leaders. We organized their suggestions into the following major topic areas and offer them for your own use and reflection:

- Know yourself
- Know why you are in health care
- Career planning
- Be effective in your job
- Know what will be asked of health care leaders in the future

It is worth reiterating that only one of these leaders set out to be a CEO. For all of them, a major theme of their lives and careers has been to embrace often unplanned opportunities, excel, and make the biggest possible contribution in any role they chose. They are superb examples of how to "bloom where you are planted."

You will read in their comments here and in the profiles their passion for the mission of health care, their openness to a life that unfolds in unexpected ways, their willingness to take risks and seize opportunities, their commitment to excellence, and their boundless curiosity.

Know Yourself

These leaders are comfortable in their own skin. They demonstrate the ability to talk about themselves, their role, and what matters to them with a clarity that comes from self-awareness. They have healthy egos, firm points of view, and an appreciation of who they are inside, combined with a spirit of service; they are not wrapped up in themselves.

> *When I'm mentoring people, I say that the most important thing is to figure out who they are inside. I think we're all influenced by what we think we should do. But who are you really inside? What really drives you? What's going to really make your career so fulfilling you are bursting, because it's just so who you are and you're able to be the most fulfilled? It may not be something your parents want you to do or something you think you should do. It's who you are, really. Then line up with an organization that shares your personal values.* (Julie Schmidt)

> *Who do you want to be? What does your life mean to you? What do the decisions you make mean to you as a person? What kind of person are you, and what kind of person do you want to become? When you can answer those questions, they will inform your responses to these questions about leadership: What does being a leader mean to you? What does leadership look like to you? What do you need to develop as a leader?* (Tim Porter-O'Grady)

Who do you want to be? Who are you inside? What does your life mean to you? What really drives you? What is going to make your career so fulfilling you are bursting? *When you think about your career, are these the kinds of questions you have asked of yourself or others have asked of you? If not, do you see how important they are, and will you consider them in the future? If they are not important to you, can you really lead others in the vocation of health care? Is health care leadership the right profession for you?*

Know Why You Are in Health Care

The reason you have chosen a career in health care leadership is critical to your success and, much more important, critical to the welfare of patients who entrust their care to you, to those who care directly for patients, to everyone else in the organization, and to the community you serve. A passion for care is the high-octane fuel that drives these leaders. Anything less is a disservice to health care and is insufficient to producing and sustaining the exceptional results demanded from health care organizations now and in the future.

> *I can't imagine working in a field where you have an ability to make a bigger difference in people's lives. Not just the patients you touch, but also the people who work in your organization. You have an ability to celebrate great work every day and keep people focused on the great work that they do. That is so important. Even though you're going to have to go through a lot of hard things in life, the headaches, if you keep focused on why—the great work that's done in health care and why those people came into health care—and if you work to allow them to do what they do the best that they can, it will be extremely rewarding. There's going to be a bunch of change. A bunch we don't even know about yet. But if you focus on trying to create the very best environment for the people who work in health care, and the people you are serving, it will be very rewarding.*
>
> *On the other hand, if you focus on only the bottom line or focus only on making yourself shine or focus only on parts of the business instead of the whole, then I think what you will do is lose all of that purpose, and you will suck the passion right out of your employees along with the appreciation for why they got into health care and the difference they make. How sad that will be, or could be, and in some cases is. When people who are working in the health care field aren't being celebrated for the special work that they do, if they feel like it's just a job and that they don't really have an impact, that is damaging.*
>
> *When clinicians deliver better care, they're going to feel better about their work and themselves, and they're going to stay. They're going to create a better experience for their co-workers and for the patients that they touch. If we suck that passion out of them, it's going to be a job. There's going to be [an] "I'm here today, and I want to go home in four hours or eight hours" attitude. That would be a great loss if we got there.*
> (Mike Murphy)

Why are you in your job, and what's your passion? What are you trying to build? How has that been going for you? Are you happy? Because I think there are CEOs of hospitals and systems that have no clue, they're just doing it because they want to be a CEO. I have people come in here all the time saying "I would like a job" and I ask "What would you like?" If they reply "Well, I don't care what it is; I just want to be a vice president," I know it's not going to work.

I would say real progress in health care takes someone to stand up and say something bold that they really believe and let the chips fall where they may—to have the courage to do that, because I think you'll find more support than naysayers. Going through the whole Woodwinds project, there were a lot of naysayers in the entire community. I had to just put on the blinders to all of that because if I listened to all of the discussion going on in the community it would have taken us off course, and we would not have been successful. It is all about figuring out what you really believe in, where you are going, and if the answer is yes then nothing should distract you from your ultimate goal. (Julie Schmidt)

Once you have a path, and that path has been determined not just by you alone but it's a path the organization wants to take, I think you have to be persistent about it. I don't think that leaders can go off in fourteen different directions. Obviously there will always be those things that distract you, but you'll always have to come back to what's the center of this. The center of all that we do has to be the patient. If you are veering away from that, I would suggest that maybe you don't belong in health care. Because if you don't have that as the core of what you do, then I don't know why you would work here. I worry about finances, capital, and so on. But none of it matters if we can't provide safe care. (Sister Mary Jean Ryan)

You have to have integrity. You have to work hard. You have to love your work—I always tell people "Don't work where you don't love things." I was just at a panel discussion at the World Congress on Quality and Payment Reform and somebody from the audience asked: "What if you're in an institution where the CEO doesn't want to do any of these things? Isn't involved in transformation?" And I said "You've got to leave. I don't know what else to tell you. You aren't going to have transformation from the bottom. You're not going to make the CEO have different values than a mid-level manager or a director." In general, if the institution doesn't have the values that you espouse, you need to get one that does. (Patty Gabow)

These leaders talk about the importance of passion, making a difference, loving your work, integrity, building relationships, courage, and willingness to walk away from a situation that does not support those attributes. *Do these attributes describe who you are as a leader? Are you satisfied that you are living these attributes? If not, are you changing the environment, or do you need to move on? Can you lead in health care if you do not aspire to these attributes?*

Career Planning

These leaders are proof that having a predetermined career path is not necessary to success and that not having a plan may allow you to discover unexpected and rewarding career directions. They have poured themselves into every role, embracing it and learning from each experience; as a result, they or others often recognized a new, expanded role that would capitalize even more on their talents.

Sometimes I think maybe my career would have progressed faster and I would have gotten to be a CEO sooner if I had had a plan like this one young lady I know. She had this plan, and it states where she is going to be at each stage of her career. What I told her was I think this is a great plan and I think it will actually work for you, but don't get wed to the plan, deciding it's going to take me two years in this role, it's going to take me three years in that role. You've got to realize there may be opportunities that present themselves before the two years are up. Or that it will take you somewhat longer. So be flexible in thinking about how you are going to get there, and it may not always be the straight shot. What you have to look for are, where are the opportunities that are going to help you get the experiences that you need and

*build the relationships that you're going to need to get to that
point that you've set as your goal, whether it is your next step
or your long-term goal? So I always tell them they have to be
flexible.*

*They will also ask me: How do I get noticed, or How do I
get to be a director? That's the big one. They have just finished
their fellowships and they all want to be directors in hospital
operations. I have told them as they go into their fellowship, one
of the beauties of the fellowship is you get to see many different
aspects of an organization, and it's not all just about hospital
operations, so be open-minded and look at some new potential
avenues like business development or physician liaison.*

*Your progression is not always the linear path that an orga-
nization chart would suggest. It's really getting the right opportunities, volunteering to do things that you may feel comfortable
doing or don't know anything about. That's good because it's
going to push you. Or ask your supervisor or mentor to push
you. I had one VP that I worked with who is phenomenal. But
she lacked confidence in her ability to present and explain things
to a larger audience like physicians or board members. She used
to say to me "Why do you always put me on to present at the
hospital oversight committee? You know how I hate to do it." I
told her "You do such a good job."* (Donna Sollenberger)

*Never take a job to get another job down the road. You might
not be happy if you take a job for the sake of another job. I
have never done it because you can do so much with a job.
The job you're given is the job you're given day one, and that's
it. I mean, day two, it's a whole new job if you want it to be.
You can create it; take it and do anything you want with it. So
you are never trapped. Or the next thing down the road might
be a bad job. Who knows? You've got another board, another
medical staff in another community, and gosh knows what that
situation is about.*

*So just take the job that you're given and lucky enough to
have and make it whatever you want to make it. And if it's
exciting and challenging, impactful and fun, it is a great place
to be. Don't worry about the other job that may never happen
or may look good from the outside; it may be miserable on the
inside.* (Phil Newbold)

I've never taken a job on the way to another job. When I went to Cook County Hospital somebody said "You're probably leaving because you want a bigger job at Rush and you plan to leave and come back." Truly, when I took the medical director job at County my thought at the time, and what I talked to my wife about, was: As far as I know this is the last job I'll have. I'll do infectious disease rounds plus I'll be medical director at County and that's that. There was no other agenda, no other plan, and I would never have done it nor would I ever advise somebody to take a job because it's on the way to another job. It's one thing to get experience that might be necessary to get to another job, but to do this because it might get me to that, I just don't think it's great advice.

People talk to me and say "Well, I don't have any desire to do this job over here, but I'm hoping I'll be seen by this guy or it'll look good on my resume." And I'm thinking, that's two or three years of your life, buddy. I mean, life is short. You should do something that you like to do or that you really feel is instructive. It's not just because you have a chance once a month to see this person that you're hoping you'll be noticed by. If you ask me, I would say there are plenty of other jobs out there. Do something you really like, and there will be a lot of ways to get that experience in a job you enjoy. And if this job you don't enjoy is not one of them, remember that this may be your last job. You will end up in a dead-end job that you're not so sure about. I have never been one to lay out my five- or ten-year career plan; I'm going to do this for two years and get that job after five years. I'd rather be doing a job at the time that I really like doing and find fulfilling. And if something else comes along, great. You take those opportunities and you give them a try.
(Larry Goodman)

A young woman asked me what she should do next. She asked "Should I look for a particular kind of job, seek one outside of my current zone of comfort, or look for a specific level?" I said "No; look for the leader who's going to trust you." She has been in an organization where the CEO has allowed her to do lots of things. In her very brief time there she has done many things that a person her age normally would not have done. I said if she were to try and get a higher-level job in a more traditional hierarchy, she will never find that nurturance and that degree of freedom.

> *Match the culture with your aspiration, and if you want to*
> *succeed, find a place where you like your co-workers and you*
> *can find joy in work every day. If you smile on the way to work,*
> *then you are going to do a better job. If you do a better job, you*
> *are going to open the doors. Match your style with a culture that*
> *has an appreciation for the gifts that young people bring and that*
> *values the differences in approach. If you go to a bureaucracy*
> *that says "You are not supposed to want to move yet; you have*
> *only been in this job for eight months," you may not thrive.*
> (Maureen Bisognano)

> *I never spend any time talking about career planning because*
> *in my experience, it doesn't work. And it's no better if you've*
> *planned a career. I have listened to a lot of people who say,*
> *I planned my career and I did this, this, and this, and I keep*
> *saying to myself: How might it have been better if you didn't*
> *plan it out?* (Tim Porter-O'Grady)

Nine of the ten leaders we interviewed never aspired to become
a CEO. *Have these pearls of wisdom changed how you see your*
own career path? Are you prepared for it to emerge rather than
have it be driven by a predetermined plan?

Be Effective in Your Job

Those highlighted in this work never skated in a job, wasted time
and energy wishing they had a better job, or schemed for another
role they really wanted. They were satisfied to give themselves
wholeheartedly to their work (even when it was not ideal) and
continued to learn, build on their strengths, and produce great
results. That is why they became candidates for larger roles. That
is why they found value in every part they have played.

> *I see people who spend so much time trying to be sure as they*
> *grow up in an organization that they are right and that they're in*
> *a position where they're supposed to be supervising someone, that*
> *they deliver on the budget or the metrics of their area because*
> *that's their job and that's how they're going to be measured.*
> *Well, it is partly their job, and it is partly how they're going to be*

measured, but I would give a great deal of credit to a supervisor who comes back and says at an appropriately early point "Look, I know we all agreed on this budget, but here's what's happening in my area, so I'm predicting an X budget variance. But if we do that, here's all the good stuff that'll happen, and if we don't do it, I really think I wouldn't be doing my job if I didn't come back and say we need to change the budget in midstream." That's usually something that I think takes a fair amount of confidence and maturity and won't always be met with the positive response at the senior end, but I do think it requires somebody thinking about what they're really trying to get done, rather than they're just driving towards a number. (Larry Goodman)

It is an absolute waste to spend a lot of your time or anyone else's time developing your weaknesses. We are never going to make our weaknesses something we excel at. Once you know what you excel at, the questions become: How are you going to compensate for those parts of leadership capacity that are necessary but that you don't excel at; who are you going to build relationships with, what structures or processes can you put in place, what other support will you tap? (Tim Porter-O'Grady)

The leaders in this book are financially responsible and expect that accountability from others, but they are not financially driven; they are mission driven. *How much of your work life is about the mission, and how much is about making your numbers? And what comes first?*

These leaders focus on strengths, their own and others', to nurture a successful organization and successful individuals and teams. *Do you spend a lot more time building on your strengths than on shoring up weaknesses—your own and others'?*

Know What Will Be Asked of Health Care Leaders in the Future

The viewpoints of our ten leaders are unique, but they reflect common themes for future leadership in health care. First, our leaders advise others to embrace a spirit of innovation, lead bold change, and find ways to learn from inside and outside of health care—not only techniques but also changes in mind-set. Second, our leaders would probably say: Learn to be prepared to lead an interdependent, agile organization with a nonhierarchical mentality that works as a team, with leaders defined by their actions, not by their title.

> *You have got to get out of the office and away from familiar surroundings and from your comfort zone. Realize that there is so much to learn and that you are going to have to unlearn the old to learn the new. Do everything with teams and other people to build collaborations and partnerships. You need to carve out the time to make these things happen.*
>
> *Innovation will need to be a core competence of leadership in health care. And innovation has more to do with thinking and imagining than any "10 steps to innovation" process. The longer I am in leadership, the larger role intuition plays—it helps me synthesize, get more perspective, imagine—if we can't imagine it, we cannot innovate. I believe it is very important as a leader to take some time out of busy days to be more present: to do some journaling about what is going on every day, to slow down by taking time in nature, for example, to get quiet so our intuition can be heard. From that place of reflection and intuition we can create the new. The job then is to take existing resources and work together to build a way to bring the new into reality.*
> (Phil Newbold)

> *Develop on a process level and on a cultural level. On the process level, organizations, in order to succeed in the future, need to be really good at three things. One is innovation. The current processes are just changing under our feet; even old, staid organizations need to be innovative with new processes, new ways of doing things. Second is improvement—getting better every day at the processes you do. Third is quality control, assuring that things are working safely, for patients and for the staff. That's the Juran trilogy: innovation, improvement, and control. Leaders need to get really good at all three. Right now some are wonderful at control, others are wonderful at*

incremental improvement, and others at innovation. It's going to be the marriage of the three that will give a leadership team success.

On the cultural side, with the new generations in the workforce, we're going to need to manage in very different ways. The old bureaucracy is not going to work, even in a bureaucracy. Working in multigenerational management with people whose approach to work is different and to get them engaged is a huge challenge: being able to engage everybody in the work. We're going to run into shortages, and trying to keep people engaged in the old bureaucracy and hierarchy isn't going to work. (Maureen Bisognano)

I believe there will be less on leadership as an individual quality and a lot more on development of team, on the plurality of it all, not the singularity of it all. I think that what you are writing about, which is whether it is attributes or issues with individuals who are in leadership positions, is in some way missing the more important point about leadership. Far too much credit is given to the person who happens to be the CEO at the time. I realize they are in a terrific position to screw things up, and if they have not done that, they deserve some modicum of credit. But so many people are involved in getting things to work that if there is an organization that has sustained something positive for more than three or four years, that is a big deal, and it means that both the atmosphere and a larger array of people have done something positive. The critical thing is the development, attraction, and retention of that team. (Larry Goodman)

One of the things that I have also come to believe is that the idea of leader should not be given only to people who have titles, that, in fact, we have leadership at every level of the organization. I've seen people in some of our entry-level positions who exhibit greater leadership than some of our titled people. So the idea of leader in the future is not the traditional one. When I see people who come up with some of these great ideas for patients, who come up with all kinds of safety ideas, who are willing to stand up and say what we are doing is not right and I will not move beyond that position until somebody does something about it— they are leaders. (Sister Mary Jean Ryan)

Future leaders need to be absolutely out-of-the-box thinkers.
They will need to shake up the status quo, big time. We need
to have leaders who are willing to take risks and try things
and be supported in that. Maybe they will try in a learning lab
situation, move on to the next model if it doesn't work, because
I don't know that anybody has all the answers. It's going to take
some innovation and courage. We need to raise those leaders up;
we can't hold them back. They are going to find an outlet for
their energy, and I am afraid they may not find it in the health
care industry. (Julie Schmidt)

The leaders profiled in this book led dramatic improvements
in their organizations. Innovation is in their blood, fueled by
their positive future orientation and their dissatisfaction with
the status quo. It gives them a hunger to learn from whomever
and wherever they can, including from people throughout their
organization. *Do you learn from inside and outside your orga-*
nization, including from outside of health care or outside of the
country you work in? Do you believe that your role as a leader is
to access wisdom that lies around you everywhere and not to be
the font of wisdom yourself?

A Personal Leadership Diagnostic Tool

Ask others who work with you to assist you in your learning
and development with the personal leadership diagnostic tool
in figure 12-1. Ask a wide range of people in the organization
to complete it. Include those whose perspectives you value, not
solely those who agree with you, to share their assessments as
well as suggestions for how to build on your strengths.

This tool can be included in an existing 360-degree feedback
process. But if this is the first time you have used a 360-degree
evaluation, you will need to ensure confidentiality. Some do this
by asking that the diagnostic be returned to a human resources
executive, who takes steps to de-identify the feedback. Be
explicit about why you are seeking input from others and how
you will use it. The diagnostic tool can then become a trust-
building aid.

Figure 12-1. Personal Leadership Diagnostic Tool

The Personal Leadership Diagnostic Tool identifies key elements for a 360-degree feedback assessment based on the themes in the book *The Heart of Leadership: Inspiration and Practical Guidance for Transforming Your Health Care Organization* (Chicago: Health Forum, Inc.), copyright © 2010 by M. Barbara Balik and Jack A. Gilbert. All rights reserved.

The elements of this tool are intended to be incorporated within a full 360-degree assessment. If a 360-degree tool is currently not used, the elements of this tool are intended as a brief assessment.

My relationship to this person is:
- ☐ Peer
- ☐ I report to them
- ☐ They report to me
- ☐ Other

Complete the following questionnaire by circling the appropriate response.

Passion for care is a personal value

I know that he/she is passionate about patient care.	Yes	Somewhat	No
He/she puts the quality of patient care above everything else.	Yes	Somewhat	No
He/she is happiest when our patients and their families are well cared for.	Yes	Somewhat	No
He/she is in health care because of his/her calling to patient care.	Yes	Somewhat	No

Intelligent; hungry for learning; reflective

He/she understands an issue quickly but does not make hasty decisions.	Yes	Somewhat	No
He/she looks to learn from people who do the work, those closest to care and service, to better understand issues and opportunities.	Yes	Somewhat	No
He/she looks to learn from outside our organization to better understand issues and opportunities.	Yes	Somewhat	No
He/she challenges us to aim high.	Yes	Somewhat	No

(Continued on next page)

Figure 12-1.   (Continued)

Genuinely care about and trust others

He/she genuinely cares about my well-being and that of my co-workers.	Yes	Somewhat	No
I know that he/she trusts my opinions and ideas.	Yes	Somewhat	No
He/she wants me to be successful and helps me get there.	Yes	Somewhat	No
He/she understands that our success is driven by teams, not individuals.	Yes	Somewhat	No

Words and actions match; authenticity and humility are demonstrated

His/her words and actions match.	Yes	Somewhat	No
I feel comfortable approaching him/her directly if I have a question or concern.	Yes	Somewhat	No
He/she shows humility in how he/she relates to us.	Yes	Somewhat	No
I am proud to have him/her as a leader.	Yes	Somewhat	No

Please provide any other observations, thoughts, or recommendations you think will contribute to this person's development.

Describe three stories or examples of this person's leadership and why they stand out for you.

You may choose to have informal conversations with others you trust to better understand the responses. The more clearly you understand the responses, the richer will be the information you gain for your growth and development. The worst reactions you can have to the feedback are to rationalize, justify, or explain away the responses, positive or negative, and thus not learn from them.

The final step is to publicly share what you heard from the feedback and your specific plans to act on it. Keep sharing what you learn as you act on your work plan. To the greatest extent possible, link the findings here with other organizational data that provide insight into how leaders (you and your colleagues) are viewed. Other data may include safety culture and staff-physician engagement surveys.

13

Guidance for Boards

We were interested to know how board members recruit and develop executives with similar characteristics to those leaders we interviewed. We asked colleagues with governance development expertise how they offer guidance to boards seeking executives who role model the personal and organizational characteristics we discovered and described earlier in the book. We were curious about what others had learned about looking deeper than the facade of the usual search and interview questions. The consistent response was "That's a very good question!"

We also asked in our interviews with the leaders and the board members working with them what they would advise other boards to do in searching for a similar leader. Several commented that "You know it when you see it." While intuition can play a part in selection, we strive to offer a variety of ways to gain insight into a candidate who may demonstrate these remarkable skills. To frame this guidance we include leader insights and recommendations as well as knowledge from our own experience with behavioral interviewing.

Our intent is to also help boards avoid the candidate who interviews well but fails to live up to the impressions, as illustrated by this story: A search advanced a candidate who was later found to have significant ethical breeches in past work. When that information surfaced, the board declined to eliminate the

The authors gratefully acknowledge the following individuals for their contributions to the content of this chapter: Jim Reinertsen, The Reinertsen Group; Dan Ford, Furst Group; Jim Conway, senior fellow, Institute for Healthcare Improvement; John Coombs, MD, Center for Healthcare Governance, American Hospital Association; and Rebecca Yanish, Keystone Research.

candidate because "we really like him." Seeing beyond the superficial is essential. The most skillful interviewee may not be able to demonstrate the personal characteristics necessary for the demands of transformational change.

As board members steadily learn more about their full responsibility for outstanding results in quality, safety, and financial management, the selection of and partnership with senior executives is one of their most critical roles. This guidance speaks to the board's crucial role of selecting executive leaders for health care organizations and essential questions the board answers in their search:

- How do boards seek a leader who is able to demonstrate the personal and organizational characteristics outlined in this book?
- What processes do boards use to understand the capacities of potential executives?
- How do they increase the potential for a positive, synergistic match between the organization's culture, mission, and needs with executive candidates?

A Brief Review

To answer those questions, we first offer a brief review of the personal and organizational characteristics introduced in chapter 1. (See especially figure 1-1 on page 2.)

Personal Characteristics

Four personal characteristics emerged in our inquiry about transformational leaders:

- Their words and actions match; they are authentic; they demonstrate humility.
- Their passion for patient care is a personal value.
- They are intelligent, hungry for learning, reflective.
- They genuinely care about and trust others.

The most important point we want to make about these personal characteristics is that they are not what these leaders *do* (a role they play); these attributes are *who they are*. These characteristics pervade their lives and their leadership. They are this person in every context, whomever they are speaking to—the board, a housekeeping aide, a physician, the community—and these characteristics are as natural to them as breathing.

Organizational Characteristics

Five organizational characteristics emerged from the interviews complemented by the personal characteristics:

- Patient care constancy of focus; disciplined action
- Positive future orientation; aim high; challenge the status quo
- Engage everyone
- Part of the team, part of the solution
- Grow others

Who these leaders are shapes how their organizations create exceptional results. If we examine an organization's structure, it will not look much different from any others. Each has leadership teams, chains of command, committees and meetings, and staff functions. But what their organizations emphasize and how their CEOs act are distinct and fuel their effectiveness and success.

Hiring Effective Leaders

Boards that find a leader who is the right match for the culture and aspirations of the organization are crystal clear on three key factors—they know themselves as a board and as an organization, they prefer to look inside the organization for leadership talent, and they know how to look deeper than the facade when spending time with candidates.

Board Members Know Themselves

I'd advise the board to think it through by themselves first. How much risk are we willing to take? How much trust are we willing to impart? Then look for the person who's going to match up with their expectations. (Maureen Bisognano)

Boards sometimes look for skills-based experience rather than values-based experience. (Carolyn Corvi, board chair, Virginia Mason Medical Center, and former senior executive, Boeing)

Succession planning and CEO selection need to be driven by strategic fit, not relational fit. The big question is: What is the goodness of fit between who the candidate is and who the organization needs to become? (Tim Porter-O'Grady)

First, the board members of exceptional organizations know themselves—as a board and as an organization. They use the personal and organizational characteristics for their own assessment. This self-knowledge is more than the traditional board self-assessment. They are clear on values, culture, aims, and needs—both current and future—to achieve the mission. They know what that looks like in concrete, real terms; they do not lean on vague abstractions.

Boards move beyond basic competencies in their expectations for executives. Competencies such as change leadership, strategic orientation, talent development, and financial management are traditionally listed. Boards move to deeper personal and leadership skills found in the personal and organizational characteristics when they seek a leader who is beyond the traditional.

Some behaviors of highly engaged boards consistent with the personal characteristics include the following:

- **Words and actions match; authenticity and humility are demonstrated**
  —Devote more than 25 percent of time to quality-of-care issues
  —Always strive to do better, seeking better outcomes

—Demonstrate an unwavering standard for respectful communication and productive teamwork

—Are intolerant of a belief in a cost-versus-quality trade-off

—Demonstrate a trusting partnership with the executive team

- **Passion for patient care is a personal value**

  —Have a passion for the mission and the time commitment to it

  —Show an abiding, unflagging commitment to the quality and safety of care

  —Aim for ideal or zero defects or 100 percent effectiveness; "We're better than average" is not accepted

- **Intelligent; hungry for learning; reflective**

  —See patients and families as essential partners and demonstrate that partnership—not just in one example but in many ways, such as hearing directly from patients and families about their care experiences, joining with senior executives in apologies to patients and families when things go wrong

  —Know current level of performance in all performance domains and the gap to ideal performance

  —Seek to learn from those who excel

  —Support risk taking in search of better ways to achieve the mission

- **Genuinely care about and trust others**

  —Hold a positive, long-term view of the engagement of staff and providers as vital to the mission, not as "nice to have"

  —Seek others' perspectives, including those who disagree, to aid in decision making

Boards that reflect on their personal characteristics can be better equipped to articulate what they need and want in an executive leader.

Boards Prefer to Look Inside for Potential Leaders

In this book, the majority of senior leaders came from within the organization. While not a requirement, promoting from within was seen as a benefit by the leaders and board chairs for three reasons. First, the candidates have a deep knowledge of and appreciation for the history and culture of the organization; second, long-standing relationships and trust with others are built; and third, an intimate relationship with the organization and its mission is generated.

Concerns about internal candidates sometimes noted are lack of new ideas, lack of ability to see beyond the perspective of the organizational culture, and unwillingness to change. The leaders profiled in this book consciously address those potential limitations through their hunger for learning with reflection on their practice and on the organization's performance. They count on others inside and outside the organization to assist them in thinking broadly and deeply about complex topics, to challenge them. Most importantly, their passion for the mission extinguishes complacency.

When boards prefer to look inside, their role in succession planning leads to conversations with the current senior executives about the depth of talent and skills within the organization. Some questions include the following:

- What is the strength of internally grown leaders relative to the personal and organizational characteristics?
- What systems are in place to develop the next generation of leaders?
- How effective is that system? How do you know?
- Are we tapping nontraditional and diverse backgrounds in our development?
- Are any individuals within the organization ready to be the next CEO?

Boards Know How to Look Deeper than the Facade

Finally, board members look beyond the usual, often superficial, résumé and interview content to find a leader of the caliber displayed in this book. The reason that offering such guidance garners the response "That's a good question" is that it is challenging work for boards and those who assist them.

In the remainder of this chapter, we provide suggestions in guiding searches and conducting interviews to aid in attracting the type of transformational leader represented here.

Personal Characteristics

The personal characteristics of our leadership model provide a template for boards as they examine applicants. The opportunity is to go beyond the exterior appearance and words of an applicant to the heart of their personal values.

Words and Actions Match; Authenticity and Humility Are Demonstrated

Talk to them about their lives, ask about behaviors, what do they value, ask them how and where they spend their time—look for integrity between what they say is important and what they do. (Sister Rose Dowling, past chair, SSM Health Care)

He is one of the most outstanding people I have ever known. (Dick Jaffee, chairman, board of trustees, Rush University Medical Center, about Larry Goodman)

He is not out for himself; [he] puts his own ego aside and truly looks to do what is best for the organization with no hidden agendas. (Dick Jaffee)

She is confident, hopeful—demonstrates a commitment to the duty, not to oneself. (Don Berwick, former president and chief executive officer of the Institute for Healthcare Improvement, now administrator of the Centers for Medicare & Medicaid Services, about Maureen Bisognano)

Why, and What to Listen For

These characteristics create a source of trust, an essential aspect of leadership. The trust comes from the leader's consistent match of words and actions, the authenticity of the person's intent, and his or her humility in recognizing his or her strengths and weaknesses as well as the vital contributions of others. Their employees talk about them as being "real," "genuine," "not arrogant," "easy to talk to." Simply put, what you see is what you get. And what you get is a focus on doing the right thing, communications you can count on being consistent with their actions, transparency, no hidden agendas, and natural ease in giving credit to others for success and in assuming responsibility themselves for failure.

What to Ask

- What is at the heart of your success?
- What would staff nurses, physicians, and managers in your organization say about you as person?
- How do you spend your time? What does your calendar show about your priorities?
- What is the drumbeat of your leadership? What do you talk about daily?
- What does "doing the right thing" mean to you? Tell us about a time when doing the right thing was very difficult.
- What are you known most for by:
  —the board?
  —physicians?
  —nurses?
  —your leadership team?
  —employees in general?

Passion for Patient Care Is a Personal Value

You look for someone who is passionate about the vision and can articulate it to others, someone who is able to translate vision

into action for the front line—not just theorize about it.
(Sister Rose Dowling)

A passion—even an obsession—for the mission; patient care is primary to him. (Dick Jaffee, about Larry Goodman)

Do they have alignment of personal and organizational values? (Carolyn Corvi)

Why, and What to Listen For

This personal characteristic is why people are in health care, the reason the organization exists; it is the North Star that guides decisions and actions every day. This characteristic is about an abiding commitment, not a particular style or personality. For these CEOs, a focus on patient safety, quality of care, and community health is not a strategy or an important organizational emphasis. It is why they are in health care, and it is what drives them every day, pure and simple, irrespective of whether they come from a clinical background.

Patient safety and high-quality patient care are so important to them that they do not delegate accountability for it. They also avoid the cost-quality trade-offs that sometimes dominate executive leaders' conversations. Their confidence in the focus on safety and quality is clear—always.

What to Ask

- Tell us about your pathway to health care.
- Tell us about your pathway to leadership.
- How does your personal background influence your leadership?
- What is a good day for you?
- What is a bad day for you?
- Tell us about a patient story that changed you and how you lead.
- How are patients and families involved in decision making?
- How do nurses, physicians, housekeepers, and others know you have a passion for patient care?

Intelligent; Hungry for Learning; Reflective

Listen for a commitment to learning. (Don Berwick)

Seek someone who has the essentials you must have in the role—not the usual position description. (Sister Rose Dowling)

Hire someone who comes with the core skills—don't train for essentials; know what you can teach and what you can't (Joan Grzywinski, board chair, HealthEast)

Look for someone who seeks the inclusion of others in decision making, the development of others, and the engagement of employees and other stakeholders. (Don Berwick)

They need the strength of character to make difficult decisions. (Bruce Alexander, board chair, Denver Health)

Why, and What to Listen For

Intelligence is not solely IQ but how it is used to make sense of complicated information so others understand and can use it. It is also real-world wisdom. The innate intelligence extraordinary leaders have is complemented by a hunger for learning and their ability to reflect on their leadership practice. It shows a never-ending quest to seek information from all sources to move themselves and others closer to the mission. They go outside the organization to learn; they listen to their leadership team, their employees, and other stakeholders and engage them in dialogue in order to learn. They match this intelligence and desire for learning with the ability to be reflective, to take the learning and consider how what they have learned can improve them, their colleagues, the life of patients, and the welfare of the communities they serve.

What to Ask

- Tell us about one or two people you could call today to help you with a complicated issue who would challenge your thinking or add new ways of seeing.
- Who or what do you learn most from on a daily basis?
- Where do you find new sources of information for your work?

- What education have you sought out in the past year?
- What's the most interesting lesson you learned in the past six months?
- What risk have you recently taken that you thought would result in better performance?
- Share a story of a painful organizational failure and what you learned from it.

Genuinely Care about and Trust Others

She is truly a servant leader—empowering others. (Bruce Alexander, about Patty Gabow)

He has a sense of humanness, a balance in life. (Carolyn Corvi, about Gary Kaplan)

They come into the room with positive energy—you want to see them again. (Don Berwick)

Why, and What to Listen For

The "how" matters as much as the "what." These leaders care deeply about others and what they have to say. More than caring, they trust others, believing people want to do the right thing and make a positive impact—and they are rarely disappointed. They are not naive; they know that not everyone will rise to the challenge or fit the organization. Nor are they cynical or negative. They call to the best of others.

What to Ask

- How have conversations with patients and families influenced you this year?
- When you spend time outside your office, what do you do?
- Share experiences in which you have engaged others in the mission.
- How do employees know you trust them to do the right thing?
- What specific processes or structures do you have in place that represent how you exhibit that trust?

Organizational Characteristics

These leaders' personal characteristics shape important organizational characteristics that lead to exceptional results. Boards need to learn how candidates will foster these organizational characteristics.

Patient Care Constancy of Focus; Disciplined Action

It is critical to engage everyone in the organization's vision with a passion. And you need to feel that passion yourself, and then it has to be communicated to the workforce. (Patty Gabow)

Why, and What to Listen For

These leaders' personal passion and commitment to patient care fuels and sustains their organizations' focus on the mission. They leave no doubt that patient care trumps everything else. They combine their focus on patient care with a disciplined, accountable, effective means of achieving outcomes. Expectations are clear.

What to Ask

- We have the expectation that the CEO is the person responsible for and has the greatest impact on the quality and safety of care. How would you act on that expectation? What would we see in your leadership?
- How do you know what is going on with patient care outcomes?
- How do you stay in touch with the mood of the organization?
- What do you do personally to achieve better patient outcomes?
- Physicians have long been treated as customers, and we want to change that to treating them as partners. It's been difficult to develop systems where they are accountable for standards in safety and teamwork behaviors. We

know that one of the reasons CEOs can get in trouble is that the doctors rebel when one of them is held to account and take a "no confidence" vote against the CEO. What is your approach to this difficult cultural change?

- What does the term *safety culture* mean to you?

Positive Future Orientation; Aim High; Challenge the Status Quo

He tries every day to transform health care in an impossible situation. (Stephen P. Cushman, chairman of the board, Sharp HealthCare, on Mike Murphy)

Why, and What to Listen For

These leaders live in the gap between a very clear view of current reality and the organization's vision. They routinely celebrate success and are always aware that more is left to be done. They are never satisfied, and this dissatisfaction energizes rather than distresses them; they convey a positive spirit to the organization; they are undaunted; and they look for zero defects or 100 percent effectiveness for their outcomes.

What to Ask

- What results are you most proud of?
- What do you see as the biggest gaps in outcomes? What are your aspirations for those outcomes?
- We are told by our attorneys to be very cautious about discussing serious patient events and apologizing to patients when facing an adverse event. And yet we read that other organizations openly display and talk about their performance and apologize to patients. Are we too cautious, or are those other organizations taking a big risk?
- Tell us about the most exciting personal and organizational goals you have on the horizon.
- Who do you look to as an outstanding example of health care outcomes?

- What would others say about what you expect of them?
- Research shows that it takes five to seven years for a major cultural change initiated at an organization to be self-sustainable. What have you done to ensure that major changes you have made will be sustained after you have gone?

Engage Everyone

The ingredient missing was not in the recipe but in the cook. (Dick Jaffee, using a quote for another leader to describe Larry Goodman's impact on Rush)

The board was impressed by her track record of transformational, sustained success over time by engaging a wide range of stakeholders. (David Callender, president, University of Texas Medical Branch, on Donna Sollenberger)

Why, and What to Listen For

Everyone has a significant role to play; everyone is a significant part of the whole. By engaging everyone, these leaders optimize organizational performance. They engage through their clarity about organizational priorities, and especially their passion for patient care, as opposed to other cases where the primacy of the bottom line dampens the passion for patient care. They engage by being transparent about the organization's condition, its goals, its successes, and its failures. They engage by expecting everyone to step up and embrace their own accountability by doing their part in realizing the vision and meeting goals. They have a broad definition of quality that encompasses everyone in the organization. An inclusive definition leads to measures of quality in safety for patients and all involved in care, clinical quality, patient/family engagement, staff and provider commitment, and financial vitality.

What to Ask

- We hear from human resources leadership that they would like to be more selective in those we hire, but with so many shortages of trained people, we sometimes have to compromise on some of our criteria. What is your position on this? When we hear that engaging employees and providers is essential to great patient experience and care, we are not sure what that means. What does it mean to you?

- What story best describes how you engage others in the vision, mission, and values of the organization?
- How do you describe the mission to housekeepers?

Part of the Team, Part of the Solution

He makes the board part of the solution by truly caring [about], seeking, and listening for our input. (Stephen P. Cushman, on Mike Murphy)

Why, and What to Listen For

These leaders do not see themselves as *the* decision maker, nor will they make a decision alone for the sake of appearing in charge or because they think it is their job as CEO. On the contrary, they see their job in decision making as enabling the best possible decision or solution. Even when they have a strong point of view they resist the temptation to decide, appreciating that a full discussion that entertains different points of view will validate their personal bias or yield a better solution.

Their use of teams is not situational but part of their philosophy of leadership. They look to teamwork throughout the organization as a fundamental vehicle to get work done well. And they see themselves as team members. They know they have a unique role, but not as the brains of the operation. The whole organization is the brain, and they are part of it.

What to Ask

- What do you think the role of patients and families should be in major organizational decision-making bodies, such as the board, board committees, or performance improvement teams?
- What is the toughest decision you've had to make in your work? How did you decide on the actions you took?

- How do you build accountability throughout the organization?
- Describe how you developed strategies and goals. How did you make sure employees knew their contribution?
- We are looking for someone who has an ability to see the whole, not just parts of the organization—how they all fit together and engage everyone in our mission. Share some ideas about how you do that.
- What do you look for in your leadership team, individually and collectively?
- What is at the heart of team success?

Grow Others

To quote a great leader I worked with: "You can't teach others people skills and shit detection"; you need to look for the skills they come with. (Joan Grzywinski)

Plant yourself where your skills are supported by the culture. (Sister Rose Dowling)

Why, and What to Listen For

These leaders make others better, and they do so in many ways: by having a strong presence in every employee orientation; by creating training and development structures that provide ways for employees to grow personally and professionally, beyond their job requirements; or by making unpredictable personnel choices that reflect the leader's identification of a potential hidden to others, including the candidate. They get deep satisfaction when people they develop succeed. And they are mindful that personal success will usually translate into greater organizational success.

What to Ask

- Tell us about your role as a mentor in the organization.
- Tell us about someone you mentored successfully.
- Tell us about someone you mentored unsuccessfully.

- How do people in your organization improve patient care?
- What investments have you made in improving the capacity of people to succeed in their work?
- Share your most gratifying story of developing others.

Further Guidance for Boards

As boards seek to fill leadership positions, they may wish to employ additional means for understanding candidates, such as the following:

- Posing scenarios based on current real-world problems and asking how the candidate would approach them. The more detailed the scenario, the richer will be the opportunity to learn about the individual.
- Asking for a recent 360-degree feedback evaluation. If none is available, ask why their organization does not have a 360-degree evaluation.

Conclusions and Additional Resources

The guidance in this chapter provides a starting point for deep conversations among the board, within the executive and leadership team, and with potential candidates. Boards that hold a transformational aspiration create the environment to attract those who share in that aspiration.

Selected Governance Resources

Center for Healthcare Governance, American Hospital Association. www.americangovernance.com.

Gilbert, J., "Ethics and the Board: Pathways to Leadership Excellence in Healthcare," White paper (San Diego: The Governance Institute).

Institute for Healthcare Improvement, "Get Boards on Board," how-to guide, Getting Started Kit, 5 Million Lives Campaign [www.ihi .org/IHI/Programs/Campaign/BoardsonBoard.htm] (Cambridge, MA: Institute for Healthcare Improvement, 2008). Accessed March 24, 2010.

Selected Readings

Berry, L., *Discovering the Soul of Service: Nine Drivers of Sustainable Business Success* (New York: The Free Press, 1999).

Cashman, K., *Leadership from the Inside Out: Becoming a Leader for Life* (San Francisco: Berrett-Koehler, 2008).

Collins, J., *How the Mighty Fall and Why Some Companies Never Give In* (New York: HaperCollins, 2009).

_____, *Good to Great and the Social Sectors: A Monograph to Accompany Good to Great* [www.jimcollins.com]. Accessed March 8, 2010.

_____, *Good to Great: Why Some Companies Make the Leap . . . and Others Don't* (New York: HarperCollins, 2001).

Corrigan, J., M. Donaldson, and L. Kohn, eds., *Crossing the Quality Chasm: A New Health System for the 21st Century* (Washington, DC: National Academies Press, 2001).

Gilbert, J., *Strengthening Ethical Wisdom: Tools for Transforming Your Health Care Organization* (Chicago: Health Forum, 2007).

Giono, J., M. McCurdy, N. Goodrich, and A. Lipkis, *The Man Who Planted Trees* (White River Junction, VT: Chelsea, 1985).

Gladwell, M., *The Tipping Point: How Little Things Can Make a Big Difference* (Boston: Little, Brown, 2002).

Goleman, D., *Emotional Intelligence* (New York: Bantam, 1995).

Heifetz, R., A. Grashow, and M. Linsky, *The Practice of Adaptive Leadership* (Boston: Harvard Business School Press, 2009).

Heifetz, R., and M. Linsky, *Leadership on the Line* (Boston: Harvard Business School Press, 2002).

Institute for Healthcare Improvement, "Get Boards on Board," how-to guide, Getting Started Kit, 5 Million Lives Campaign [www.ihi .org/IHI/Programs/Campaign/BoardsonBoard.html] (Cambridge, MA: Institute for Healthcare Improvement, 2008). Accessed March 24, 2010.

_____, "Improvement Map, Leadership and Management Processes" [www.ihi.org/imap/tool]. Accessed March 8, 2010.

Jacobson, R., *Leading for a Change: How to Master the Five Challenges Faced by Every Leader* (Woburn, MA: Butterworth-Heinnemann, 2000).

Keroack, M., B. Youngbird, J. Cerese, C. Krsek, L. Prellwitz, and E. Trevelyan, "Organizational Factors Associated with High Performance in Quality & Safety in Academic Medical Centers. *Academic Medicine* 82 (December 2007): 1178–1186.

Kotter, J., and D. Cohen, *The Heart of Change: Real Life Stories of How People Change Their Organizations* (Boston: Harvard Business School Press, 2002).

Kouzes, J., and B. Posner, *Encouraging the Heart: A Leader's Guide to Rewarding & Recognizing Others* (San Francisco: Jossey-Bass, 2003).

_____, *The Leadership Challenge* (San Francisco: Jossey-Bass, 2002).

Krause, T., "NASA after Columbia and Lessons for Healthcare." National Patient Safety Board of Governors presentation (June 2007).

Langley, G., K. Nolan, T. Nolan, C. Norman, and L. Provost. *The Improvement Guide: A Practical Guide to Enhancing Organizational Performance* (San Francisco: Jossey-Bass, 1996).

Liker, J., *The Toyota Way* (New York: McGraw-Hill, 2004).

Schein, E., *Organizational Culture and Leadership*, 3rd ed. (San Francisco: Jossey-Bass, 2004).

_____, *The Corporate Culture Survival Guide: Sense & Nonsense about Cultural Change* (San Francisco: Jossey-Bass, 1999).

Senge, P., A. Kleiner, C. Roberts, R. Ross, G. Roth, and B. Smith, *The Dance of Change: The Challenges of Sustaining Momentum in Learning Organizations* (New York: Doubleday, 1999).

Senge, P., C. Roberts, R. Ross, B. Smith, and A. Kleiner, *The Fifth Discipline Fieldbook* (New York: Doubleday, 1994).

Senge, P., C. Scharmer, J. Jaworski, and B. Flowers, *Presence: Human Purpose and the Field of the Future* (New York: Doubleday, 2004).

Spear, S., *Chasing the Rabbit* (New York: McGraw Hill, 2009).

Stoddard, N., and C. Wyckoff, *The Right Leader—Selecting Executives Who Fit* (Hoboken, NJ: John Wiley & Sons, 2009).

Studer, Q., *Straight A Leadership: Alignment, Action, Accountability* (Gulf Breeze, FL: Fire Starter Press, 2009).

Womack, J., and D. Jones, *Lean Thinking* (New York: Free Press, 2003).

Index